MUST CHRISTIANITY BE VIOLENT?

Reflections on History, Practice, and Theology

EDITED BY

KENNETH R. CHASE
& ALAN JACOBS

Brazos Press

A Division of Baker Book House Co
Grand Rapids, Michigan 49516

© 2003 by The Center for Applied Christian Ethics

Published by Brazos Press
a division of Baker Book House Company
P.O. Box 6287, Grand Rapids, MI 49516-6287
www.brazospress.com

Printed in the United States of America

Library of Congress Cataloging-in-Publication Data is on file at the Library of Congress, Washington, D. C.

ISBN 1587430649

Unless otherwise noted, Scripture is taken from the New Revised Standard Version of the Bible, copyright 1989 by the Division of Christian Education of the National Council of the Churches of Christ in the USA. Used by permission.

CONTENTS

Preface   7

Introduction: The Ethical Challenge   9
    Kenneth R. Chase

Section One: *Histories*   21

1. The First Crusade: Some Theological and Historical Context   23
    Joseph H. Lynch
2. Violence of the *Conquistadores* and Prophetic Indignation   37
    Luis N. Rivera-Pagán
3. Is God Violent? Theological Options in the Antislavery
Movement   50
    Dan McKanan
4. Christians as Rescuers during the Holocaust   69
    David P. Gushee
5. Have Christians Done More Harm than Good?   79
    Mark A. Noll

Section Two: *Practices*   95

6. Beyond Complicity: The Challenges for Christianity
after the Holocaust   97
    Victoria Barnett
7. How Should We Then Teach American History? A Perspective of
Constructive Nonviolence   107
    James C. Juhnke
8. Christian Discourse and the Humility of Peace   119
    Kenneth R. Chase
9. Jesus and Just Peacemaking Theory   135
    Glen Stassen

Section Three: *Theologies*   157

10. Violence and the Atonement   159
    Richard J. Mouw

11. Explaining Christian Nonviolence: Notes for a Conversation with
    John Milbank   172
        Stanley Hauerwas
12. Violence: Double Passivity   183
        Addendum   201
        Testing Pacifism: Questions for John Milbank
        John Milbank
13. Christian Peace: A Conversation between Stanley Hauerwas and
    John Milbank   207
        John Milbank and Stanley Hauerwas

    Afterword   224
        Alan Jacobs
    Contributors   236
    Notes   237

PREFACE

In some sectors of Western cultural discourse, any attempt to promote Christian ethics as a solution for the troubles besetting us runs headlong into a presumed cultural fact: Christianity's historic and continuing complicity with violence invalidates a Christian claim to moral goodness. For some skeptical observers, our culture has for many years now believed that Nietzsche got it right, and that Christianity's tragic legacy has been a reversal of values through which an ethic purportedly driven by love and service has been used as an opportunity for control and subjugation. In this view, Christian ethics is an oxymoron.

If Christian ethics is indeed a complex apparatus legitimizing social coercion, then those of us who espouse such teaching are woefully misguided at best or cruelly subversive at worst. Of course, we Christians deny the necessity to this genealogy of our morals. Yet our denial ought not simply be asserted. We must engage the charge with candor and intellectual rigor, and we ought not be surprised if our investigations uncover painful truths. We also ought not fear vigorous inquiry, for our desire to proclaim the divine peace, a peace that we have as a gift from Jesus and that we experience at the core of our being (John 14:27), mandates a rigorous critique of our history, our practice, and our theology.

To this end, the Center for Applied Christian Ethics (CACE), a faculty-run organizational unit within Wheaton College (Illinois), sponsored a conference on Wheaton's campus on March 15–17, 2000, in which a group of scholars presented early versions of the chapters in this volume. The timing was fortuitous, for on the Sunday preceding the conference, Pope John Paul II offered an historic public confession of the various sins committed against humanity, including those of violence and hatred, during the Church's two-thousand-year history. The conferees were primed, then, to move forward with an appropriate degree of solemnity and courage. We could not have known, though, that between the conference and the publication of this book we would experience the events of September 11, 2001, in which the cultural talk linking violence and religion reached a fever pitch. A few of our authors decided to reference 9/11 in their revised chapters, and Alan Jacobs's afterword tackles this post-9/11 context directly.

The conference was made possible by the generous donation of time and money by many friends. The CACE National Advisory Council, chaired by Dr. C. Everett Koop, led the fundraising efforts necessary for this conference and many other CACE-sponsored activities of recent years. The CACE Faculty Steering Committee, chaired by Dr. David Fletcher, provided the needed intellectual guidance for a conference of this magnitude to occur on Wheaton's campus. Stanton Jones, Wheaton's Provost, offered timely words of encouragement and other forms of administrative assistance enabling those involved with CACE to carry forth their vision. In addition to these efforts, the PEW Younger Scholars Society of Wheaton College, at that time under the direction of Dr. Ashley Woodiwiss, and Wheaton's Faculty Faith and Learning program, under Alan Jacobs's direction, provided supporting funds for the conference. Of course, the views presented by the authors in this volume do not necessarily represent the views of any of these funding sources, nor of Wheaton College.

Several students have participated in various stages of the project. At each turn, a student would jump in and do marvelous work, reminding us again that Wheaton students are, indeed, an extraordinary group. Christian Vercler laid an intellectual foundation for the conference through his research that led to the development of a preliminary bibliography. Amy Vercler managed the conference, handling correspondence and arrangements with a high degree of professionalism. Lina Ekholm began work on the book by transcribing, editing, and source-checking the manuscripts in their early stages. Will Reaves did additional source-checking in the late stages; he also proofread most of the manuscript, making valuable corrections and clarifications throughout.

We easily could add many additional names to the list of those who have provided assistance and support for this project, from individual faculty members to many friends of CACE, yet space permits acknowledgment of only a few who were indispensable to the completion of this book. Patricia Reichhold, the CACE secretary, worked tirelessly on all facets of the project, from the conference to this publication. Without Pat's faithful effort from start to finish, this project would not have happened. Meredith Cargill, a close friend and scholar, worked diligently to sharpen Ken Chase's essays and, in the process, strengthen his editorial judgment. Any remaining weaknesses may be blamed on Ken's unwillingness to take Meredith's advice. Our Brazos editors, Rodney Clapp and Rebecca Cooper, have been far more patient that we have a right to expect. We are grateful for their constructive assistance offered throughout the process. The Brazos mission has captured our imagination, and we express gratitude to our Lord for our fortunate involvement with a press that celebrates "the inviting embrace of God." We pray this volume contributes, in some small way, to the advance of Christian peace in a violent world.

INTRODUCTION

The Ethical Challenge

At its most elementary level, Christianity celebrates peace. Jesus promises to give peace, he advocates forgiveness and mercy, he instructs his followers to be peacemakers and to love enemies, and he died so that we might have peace with God. The New Testament advocates love of a self-giving kind, even toward those who are evil or hostile toward Christians. The record of early Christians shows no evidence of military action, hostile planning, coups, or rebellions. Indeed, Jesus denounces the one instance where a disciple wields a sword. A Christian ethic would then appear to involve, in a straightforward and practical way, a promotion of peace and goodwill.

Since recent years have given us no reason to believe humans will stop killing each other anytime soon, we might believe that an applied Christian ethic of peace is needed now more than ever. Does the world need the healing that comes from Jesus' gospel?

Unsurprisingly, not all would agree that Christian peace is the answer. Despite the clear call to peace in the New Testament, and the clear need for peace in the world, living an ethic of peace has been one of the great challenges for Christians. The historical record demonstrates that believers have acted violently, made unholy alliances, conquered enemies, discriminated against others, and vilified pagans and each other. The love and peace that God promises through Jesus has been, it appears, compromised through the lives and words of many believers.

Oftentimes, the violence perpetrated by Christians is easily attributed to simple disobedience—a failure of the will to live worthy of the calling. Yet, in many instances, believers claim their violent actions and attitudes result from faithful obedience to the call of God through scriptural or personal revelation. Some Christians, based on their reading of God's judgment, such as in the conquest of Canaan and in the last day, may work violently to accomplish what they believe to be a divine end. Others, based on their reading about Christ's sacrifice, may provoke suffering and death upon themselves, or they may tol-

9

erate it more easily among others. Upon reading of God's passion toward the lost, Christians may engage in proselytizing by means that violate another's integrity and conscience. Upon reading of Jesus' own denunciation of hypocrisy and his physical disruption of the temple market, Christians may see some sorts of violence as necessary acts of righteous indignation against a wayward culture. Is it any surprise, then, that when the world cries out for peace, many mock the Christian answer? The skepticism that greets the Christian apologist of goodwill makes the matter of peace and violence within the Christian life all the more important.

The essays in this volume take seriously the question of Christian complicity with violence. To better situate the essays within a broader apologetic context, I will outline briefly the range of accusations linking Christianity with violence. Following this, I will highlight some specific contributions of the essays to the work of Christian peace.

Apologetic Context

We might place the arguments mounted against a Christianity of peace into two broad categories: the pragmatic argument and the inherency argument.[1] The pragmatic argument links acts of violence with those who claim to be Christians. So, for instance, Christians marched against the Muslims in the Crusades, and have oppressed the Jews in Reformation Europe, and have supported slavery in nineteenth-century America, and currently provide ideological footing for the nationalisms leading to religious wars and ethnic cleansings of our contemporary era. Not all Christians are violent, so the argument goes, but given the right circumstances, they who espouse Christian peace will expose their claws and reveal their true nature. The simple facts of history lead to the conclusion that Christians cannot be trusted because of their all-too-often complicity with violence. In practice, therefore, Christians act violently.

The defining characteristic of the pragmatic argument is its illustrative power, but the kinds of violence described add considerable variation and complexity to what is fundamentally a simple accusation. So, varieties of domestic abuse might be included in this argument type, as well as state policies—such as the rejection of gun control, the support of more aggressive policing, and an insistence on the death penalty. Notice as well that the agents of violence can be expanded to those who do not confess Christ but have been influenced by Christians or have lived in a culture with Christian heritage. So, for instance, the pragmatic argument also encompasses the charge that a Christianized culture is marked by violence, even though individual Christians may not be directly or legally responsible for the violence. Recent disputes over hate crimes in this country illustrate such an expansion. For instance, Christian opposition to homosexual rights, so the argument goes, supports a climate in which non-Christians who hate gays find a measure of legitimation for their attacks on them; and Christian efforts to evangelize may cultivate a climate of intolerance in which the potential for hate crimes is fostered. Thus, the pragmatic argument balloons by detailing the intricate and complex ways in which Christians are thought to be either directly or indirectly supportive of violent acts.

François Houtart, a noted Belgian sociologist of religion, illustrates this pragmatic complexity when he identifies some possible mechanisms by which religious commitment can be translated into social violence.[2] For instance, religion may serve, obviously, as a factor in ethnic identity. Houtart reviews several current scenarios, including Ireland, the former Yugoslavia, and the Middle East, for telling examples of how religiously shaped ethnic identities contribute to violence. Thus, religious people act violently, and since their religious identity is a contributing factor, then we may have reason to be critical of religion's role in social life.

Some extend the pragmatic argument even further. By adding semantic breadth to the concept of violence, some accusers blame Christians for all manner of alterations within a person's mind or within a culture. Thus, the pragmatic argument also encompasses accusations against missionaries for destroying indigenous cultures or evangelists for seeking converts. Proselytes become labeled as such with the suggestion, carried by the label itself, that some act of violence has been perpetrated upon them, as if they have been wrenched from normal human existence into a peculiar (namely, Christian) state of mind.

Whereas the pragmatic argument provides a visceral and experiential platform for the critique of Christianity, the second type of argument, which may be labeled the inherency argument, examines the philosophical, theological, and doctrinal elements of Christianity that either support or are characteristic of violence. Rather than merely pointing out violent incidents or attitudes perpetrated by Christians, these arguments note inherent features of Christian doctrine that allegedly discredit its claims to peace. Thus, this argument goes, something about Christianity in its very constitution or essence is violent, thus undermining its appeal to the world as the bearer of genuine good news.

Houtart, again, is helpful in illustrating the argument type. Also, again, he works on the general level of religion, not limiting his analysis to Christianity. He claims religion has at its core three elements that "serve as vehicles for violent tendencies": the promotion of sacrifice, the insistence on a "struggle between good and evil," and the impulse to expand the religion to new populations.[3] Given that these components are inherent in the teachings of most religions, we ought not be surprised that religion repeatedly is a factor in wars and oppressions.

For my purposes, I collapse Houtart's three elements into two broad themes: the exclusion theme, which sees the Christian insistence on evangelism linked with a struggle between good and evil, and the sacrifice theme, which sees an undesirable dependence of the Christian faith on bloodletting, substitution, and suffering. The exclusion theme emphasizes that the Christian God limits fellowship between humanity and deity in one or more ways, such as by setting up criteria of acceptability; by favoring particular people, actions, or attitudes; by ordering social and ecclesial hierarchies; or by providing only one name through which salvation comes to people. These "restrictions" provide the motivation and the urgency for proselytizing, for spreading the gospel far and wide. In order to overcome evil in personal or collective lives, people need to accept specifically Christian truth. Of course, divine exclusion would not be so odious if it did not have a history of being used by states to legitimize forced conversions, war, and other types of violent action. Yet for many critics today, the mere fact of Christianity's exclusive claims is offensive enough. Edward Schillebeeckx notes that religious beliefs promoting a unique connection to transcendence may discourage the "cohabitation of different religions within the same state frontiers." He states, in addition, that for some observers the very thought of any special connection with the Absolute tends to "fundamentally disqualif[y]" religious belief in our era.[4]

Divine exclusion also might not be so offensive if it were not for the fact that divine pleasure is linked to reward and displeasure is linked to destruction. The concept of a God who punishes sinners, thus, is an integral component of the exclusion theme and may, in fact, lie at the very root of the overall critique that Christianity is complicit with violence. (I often wonder if those who reject Christianity for its link to violence actually may be dealing with a more personal issue, namely, that they reject the idea of God's judgment.)

In the sacrifice theme the emphasis is not so much on the exclusionary nature of salvation as on the means through which salvation is achieved. The Judeo-Christian logic requires that a living creature must lose its life for God's favor to be restored to a guilty human. The sacrificial economy of the Old Testament gives way to the even more objectionable sacrifice by the Father of his Son in the New Testament. Any suggestion within the New Testament and within church teaching that the Son's sacrifice is a ransom, or satisfaction, or a pleasing aroma to the Father compounds the offense. Furthermore, the traditional Christian teaching that sanctification requires the denial of one's desires and of one's body glorifies ongoing sacrifices of the self and, sometimes, the other, in pursuit of greater holiness. The inherency argument also reaches into the very construction of identity, objecting that the peculiar construction of human lives through Christian sacrificial themes is morally repulsive.

Typically, the pragmatic and the inherency arguments work in tandem, the inherency providing the grounding and the pragmatic invoking the consequences. One argument works at the level of a deep structure, the other at the historical and cultural surface. In the strongest challenges to a Christianity of peace, the causal link between these two is not left to suggestion, but analyzed and specified with rigor. In *The Curse of Cain,* for instance, Regina Schwartz not only identifies the work of exclusion and of violent identity formation within the Old Testament promotion of monotheism, but she links that teaching to the rise of nationalisms and, consequently, to the violence that constitutes and results from border disputes, ethnic cleansings, and imperialism.[5] The violent actions of nations, therefore, are conceptually linked to the violence-laden formations of Judeo-Christian belief.

I suspect there are several more variations of pragmatic and inherency arguments, and probably even other types of argument that fit in neither the pragmatic nor the inherency category. For instance, Alan Jacobs's afterword in this volume lists some recent arguments connecting Christianity and violence in the wake of September 11, 2001. He provides additional categorization and perspective that is most helpful along these lines.

At this point, though, the argument categories I outlined here are suitable for placing this volume in the context of a particular critique of Christianity. The essays herein provide specific answers to many of the arguments I have reviewed above, and some are explicitly apologetic. Most involved with this project, however, recognize that a knee-jerk defense of Christian innocence may do more harm than good, for such an apologetic may enact a type of violence on the accuser or on the historical record, reinforcing the very accusation it seeks to overturn. So, the overall tone of the collection is less apologetic than investigative and reflective. The authors in this volume wrestle candidly over the complicity of Christianity with violence, but they also accept the realities of violence linked to Christian confession and behavior. The essays, therefore, provide a general orientation to historical, practical, and theological reflection that provokes valuable reconsideration of our avowed commitment to peace.

Overview

The leading theological emphasis of the volume is evangelical, yet many of the authors would not place themselves within this particular brand of Protestantism. As editors, our intent has been less to uphold a distinctively evangelical stance on all issues than to include authors who write on specific topics with expertise, with insight, and from a range of Christian perspectives. We hope this collection represents the best impulses within evangelicalism to cast our intellectual nets wide enough to challenge and sharpen Christian faith without needing to secure every argument within a predetermined frame of acceptance.

Yet, we do have a frame of acceptance, of course. The outer border is that Christian belief has intellectual integrity and ought to be shaped by a careful understanding of history, a vigorous theological engagement with Scripture, and a daily practice that leans heavily on the ethical preference of peace over violence. As far as we know (although we have not asked), every author in this collection shares these parameters.

The three divisions of this volume—Histories, Practices, and Theologies—are not rigid categories. We have grouped the essays according to central tendencies, yet there is much overlap. For instance, Juhnke's recommendation that we reconsider how to teach American history is, obviously, about history, yet his focus is on changing current practice, so we have placed it in the Practices section. Similarly, we have placed Barnett's essay on the Holocaust in the Practices section, since her review of Christian complicity leads her to draw important practical insights.

The Histories section, then, is restricted to those essays that provide detailed case studies of particularly troublesome moments when Christians have practiced violence in the name of Christ: the Crusades, the conquest of the Americas, nineteenth-century U.S. slavery, and the Holocaust. In each instance, the essays helpfully expand our understanding of causes, motivations, and historical options for peace and violence. As we might expect, history resists oversimplification.

In "The First Crusade: Some Theological and Historical Context," Joseph H. Lynch burrows into a firsthand account of the First Crusade (1096) written by an anonymous knight who provides theological and scriptural reflection on his involvement. Lynch notices the influence of scriptural images and quotations in the knight's account, and Lynch uses this to speculate on the interpretive differences between the crusaders and the early church when handling Old Testament warfare passages and Pauline instructions about spiritual battle. Likewise, Luis N. Rivera-Pagán contrasts two widely divergent approaches, rooted in alternative emphases within Scripture, to the European conquest of the Americas. In "Violence of the *Conquistadores* and Prophetic Indignation," he locates an essential dimension of Latin American Christianity in the historical tension between "messianic providentialism," which guided the violent actions of the *conquistadores,* and "prophetic indignation," which rejected violence in the light of God's mercy and peace. He contrasts Herman Cortés with Bartolomé de las Casas to illustrate this tension and to display the conflicting theological motives animating the move of Christianity across the Atlantic.

Two other authors plunge into the mysterious movement of historical forces that limit options for subsequent action. How Christians respond to violence depends heavily on the often inexplicable twists of evil. In "Is God Violent? Theological Options in the Antislavery Movement," Dan McKanan summarizes the theological wrestling done by four central figures in the nineteenth-century U.S. antislavery movement: Frederick Douglass, William Lloyd Garrison, Harriet Beecher Stowe, and Abraham Lincoln. McKanan claims that Lincoln's assassination was the turning point at which Lincoln's public articulation of God's providence became widely accepted. Therefore, McKanan concludes, the assassination left the United States with a legacy of accepting God's hand in violence, consequently reducing the attractiveness of a theology of nonviolence. In "Christians as Rescuers during the Holocaust," David P. Gushee explores the motivations of those few Christians who rescued Jews from the Nazis. Gushee concludes that Christianity was neither necessary nor sufficient for their actions. In some cases, though, Christian conviction provided a distinctive motivation, although this was idiosyncratic and context-specific. Given the magnitude of this evil, Gushee appropriately ends with speculation about factors that may encourage Christians to live up to the best in their faith.

Mark A. Noll provides the capstone essay in this section. In "Has Christianity Done More Harm than Good?" Noll develops an assertive apologetic evaluating the ethical desirability of Christianity in history. Sifting through a wide range of historical incidents, Noll concludes that a fair assessment of causation demonstrates that Christians have acted, on balance, less violently than others; furthermore, without Christians the world would be in a much worse situation than it is now. In the process of reviewing these basic pragmatic arguments, Noll also provides important theological perspective on the sinfulness of human actors and the nature of Christianity's reception within culture. His historical analysis, therefore, provides a challenge for improving the quality of our present-day actions.

Both pragmatic and inherency arguments question the capacity of Christians to practice peace effectively in difficult historical circumstances. The Histories essays add complicating factors to several of the vilest of historical offenses. Christians of the past, even in the most difficult times, often struggled toward the way of peace amidst horrendous violence. Yet, we must continually reaffirm this commitment. The essays in the Practices section provide some specific recommendations for Christian nonviolent action. Victoria J. Barnett begins by taking us back, again, to the Nazi horror. In "Beyond Complicity: The Challenges for Christianity after the Holocaust," she surveys a range of Christian responses to the Holocaust, including those supportive of Nazism and those promoting resistance. She rejects the claim that Christians directly advocated murdering Jews, but she finds the range of responses indicative that Christians, like others, can be caught up in a whirlwind of violence. Based on her survey, she challenges the church to initiate an embrace of the other. Through this action, Christians will experience productive developments in theology and practice.

Whereas Barnett focuses on the lessons learned from one specific historical moment, James C. Juhnke moves up to a historical metalevel and notes a disturbing principle that shapes much historical analysis. In "How Should We Then Teach American History? A Perspective of Constructive Nonviolence," he locates and rejects the myth of redemptive violence as a metanarrative for teaching U.S. history. In its place, Juhnke suggests multiple strategies, supported by numerous examples, for Christians to promote constructive nonviolence in the study of history or, for that matter, any analysis of social life.

The final two essays in this section move away from specifically historical analyses and toward contemporary concerns. These essays also turn the corner into more explicit theological formulations. In my essay, "Christian Discourse and the Humility of Peace," I recommend specific theological principles to guide Christian discourse in a hostile world. Given today's emphasis on multi-religious dialogue as a means to reduce interreligious violence, I suggest that a full Christian commitment to God's work in human salvation and eternal judgment does not mar Christian discursive contributions to peace, but, on the contrary, enables them. Without these theological principles, I argue, the Christian engagement with peace risks veering off into idolatry or indifference.

In the section's last essay, "Jesus and Just Peacemaking Theory," Glen H. Stassen moves even more directly into specific recommendations for our current global situation. His work develops in the wake of the historic debate between supporters of pacifism and the just war doctrine. He rejects the forced choice between supporting a just war and withholding support from all wars. He recommends a third way, called "just peacemaking," that seeks to reduce the chances of war through strategic peace-based initiatives. In this essay, he demonstrates how just peacemaking provides new insights into biblical texts; thus, this essay simultaneously reinforces the specific strategies already attested to in his previous publications and promotes peacemaking as integral to a Christian's daily practice.

The final section turns fully to theological exposition and debate. The authors deal directly with several substantial arguments for Christian complicity with violence. In some instances, such as Richard J. Mouw's essay ("Violence and the Atonement"), the defense is straightforward. In other instances, the defense is diffused through discussions of additional matters, such as the proper basis for Christian pacifism (Stanley Hauerwas, "Explaining Christian Nonviolence: Notes for a Conversation with John Milbank"). At times, the defense turns into a striking cultural counteroffensive, such as in John Milbank's analysis of violence and spectatorship ("Violence: Double Passivity").

Notably, each of these authors in the final section constructs his theological argument through a commitment to Christian uniqueness and absoluteness. This is not an easy theological road to follow in today's debate about violence. Too often, theological responses to the charge of Christianity's complicity have granted too much to the accuser, and orthodox biblical teaching has been compromised. For instance, one line of defense in answering the general critique of Christianity's complicity with violence is to situate Christianity within a larger plurality of religious beliefs. Theological work has been done, then, to soften the exclusionist posture of the historic Christian faith. By recognizing that other religions may be just as right as we are, the reasoning goes, then we will be less likely to proselytize, to force conversions, to react defensively, to act ethnocentrically, to support a militant nationalism, and so forth. Or, another line of defense seeks to strip God of his role in judgment and sacrifice. Once we sanitize the Scriptures of God's role in Jesus' death, for instance, or once we historicize the scriptural celebration of God's apocalyptic fury, then we can elevate the God of love to the point where our judgmentalism and bigotry fade away. The authors of these theological essays do not make such concessions. They locate authentic peace *within* historic Christian commitments. Mouw, for instance, notes how a Reformed understanding of atonement provides the basis for peacemaking. It is a mistake, he argues, to think that a substitutionary view of Christ's death is a perverse celebration of blood sacrifice. Hauerwas, as is well known, doubts the wisdom of shaping the church's life by ideas and practices that enter from without. Indeed, in his essay, he playfully, yet with deep earnestness, chides Milbank for engaging in an ontological investigation of violence without sufficient attention to the lived story of Jesus. Christians know peace, Hauerwas believes, not because it is an alternative to violence, but because the church lives the fellowship of peace in Jesus' name.

Milbank, for his part, turns the moral tables on those who would challenge Christianity's record of violence. He describes contemporary secular life in the West as saturated with violence. Linking violence with the passive gaze of spectatorship, Milbank finds real violence when people view artistic portrayals of simulated violence. He also extends this analysis to include exclusions and eliminations of an information-driven economy. He further argues that gazing on violent acts in Christian history with an attitude of moral superiority is itself an act of violence. His real target here, though, is the naive form of pacifism that resists all violence without distinction.

Milbank's position provides a provocative basis to begin his dialogue with Hauerwas. Under Alan Jacobs's watchful eye (yet frequently moving beyond his control), these two provide a spirited discussion of several issues in church history, contemporary politics, and theological ethics. This conversation, as well as Hauerwas's paper, retains the oral style from its initial presentation at the Christianity and Violence conference held at Wheaton College in March 2000. Hauerwas and Milbank both have reviewed the transcript and made several corrections. Given the personalities involved, we see no reason to delete the marks of oral style from either Hauerwas's paper or the ensuing conversation.

Jacobs closes our volume by directly considering the recent arguments linking Christianity and violence in the wake of 9/11. By pulling together insightful observations on both pragmatic and inherency arguments, he effectively refutes the attacks against Christianity and raises crucial questions for the accusers. His fitting conclusion, then, challenges the validity and coherence of claims that the world would be a better place without religion.

A Personal Note

The accusations of Christian complicity with violence provide us with numerous lessons on how we can avoid the temptation to conform our Christian faith to the violent conventions of cultural practices, whether in politics, social life, the arts and media, or religious dialogue. By examining the theological bases of peace, and the location of violence properly understood within the work of God's judgment, we can discern more readily the reach of peace into our lives and the extent to which peace should guide our actions. We also will gain wisdom concerning if and when Christians can support violence in private and public spheres. Both the pragmatic and inherency arguments by our opponents, then, throw our faith into relief, and our instruction can move more accurately and more pointedly toward living a life worthy of our calling.

Yet, life is fraught with many traps. Our best intentions often are short-sighted, and we experience the bewildering swirl of unintended consequences. For instance, we have compiled this volume in the tranquil far-western suburbs of Chicago. From where I sit, I can heartily endorse peace and find ample resources within the Christian tradition to argue confidently on its behalf. Yet, when I reflect on my social and political position (and I imagine Alan would agree), I cannot presume that the way of Christian peace is always the best answer for every trouble spot in the world. Yes, concerned Christians everywhere insist that peace is the default mode of operation for the Christian life, and peace with God through Jesus Christ is paramount. These hopes are not a veil for sinister wishes. Our brothers and sisters from southern regions of the globe, though, remind us that sometimes an insistence on peace may be used to perpetuate oppression, not liberation. Roughly a half-dozen years before the collapse of apartheid in South Africa, a group of concerned theologians produced the provocative Kairos Document, detailing a theological and political critique of the oppressive regime. In this they challenged the moral and spiritual legitimacy of the ruling authorities. As Charles Villa-Vicencio explains, for millennia now the church within Christendom has approved of certain forms of violence by the state when state power is challenged. When some rebelled against that power, though, the church often has shifted its stance to an ethic of peace, insisting that the violence of rebellion is anti-Christian. According to some Kairos theologians, the situation in South Africa in 1985 was such that the time for peace may have ended. If a political authority rules without regard for justice, then must Christians continue to obey such authority? At what point does rebellion, even to the point of violence, become acceptable?[6] Bishop Desmund Tutu, who is strongly committed to nonviolence, wrote the following in 1987: "Should the West fail to impose economic sanctions it would, in my view, be justifiable for blacks to try to overthrow an unjust system violently. But I must continue to work to bring an end to the present tyranny by non-violent means."[7]

If nothing else, the essays herein remind us that we ultimately face our violent world with great uncertainty. Alan and I have confidence that Jesus provides the best hope for living in this ungainly mess, but how this confidence works itself out in any given historical situation cannot be predetermined by strength of human will or depth of human knowledge. May we have the grace to live God's peace evermore, and may we have God's wisdom to know when that peace is not ours to live.

Kenneth R. Chase
Wheaton, Illinois
July 19, 2002

SECTION ONE
HISTORIES

ONE

THE FIRST CRUSADE

Some Theological
and Historical Context[1]

JOSEPH H. LYNCH

Historians count nine crusades, but that is a conventional number. Between the late eleventh and the sixteenth centuries, Christian rulers, popes, and a wide segment of the population were drawn to the crusading idea. Until the late thirteenth century, groups of knights went to the Holy Land almost every year to fulfill their pilgrimage vows and to fight. For ten or twelve generations, ambitious crusading plans were formulated and crusades were summoned, some of which went to the Near East or North Africa, but others failed to get off the ground, usually for political reasons. Each of the nine traditional crusades has its own history. It would not be possible to treat all of them in this essay. Instead, I shall try to put the First Crusade, which was the model crusade, into important historical and theological contexts.[2]

Let me remind you briefly of the course of that crusade.[3] In 1071, the Seljuk Turks inflicted a serious military defeat on the Byzantine Empire at Manzikert (Malazgirt, Turkey) in western Asia Minor, amputating a great chunk of Byzantine territory. Constantinople, the heart of the Byzantine world, was in danger of capture. The Byzantine emperor Alexius I Comnenus (ruled 1081–1118) appealed for help to Pope Urban II (papacy 1088–1099), probably seeking mercenary troops. Even though a pope and patriarch had excommunicated one another in 1054, the breach did not seem permanent and Alexius couched his appeal at least in part on the grounds of their shared Christianity. On November 18, 1095, at a council that met at Clermont in south central France, Urban called for aid for the Christian churches in the East and the liberation of the holy places, especially Jerusalem, from the Muslims. The response was remarkable and has never been satisfactorily explained. Knights vowed on the spot to go to the Holy Sepulchre. To symbolize their vow, they tore pieces of cloth into crosses, which they sewed on the right shoulders of their cloaks—hence the name "crusaders," which derives from the Latin word for cross, *crux*.

The call to liberate the holy places also resonated with nonwarriors. A lower-class group under the charismatic leadership of Peter the Hermit and Walter the Penniless set out for Jerusalem in 1096 before the main armies. It made its violent, disorderly way on a land march through central Europe. Modern estimates are that the lower-class expedition had as many as 150,000 people, the vast majority poor, many elderly, ill, and women.[4] Several armies of knights also set out in 1096 by land and sea for a rendezvous at Constantinople. The crusaders probably had no maps, no idea what upcountry Anatolia was like, and no experience of fighting Seljuk Turks. The march by horse and foot, which was more than two thousand miles, was horrible, especially the crossing of Anatolia, modern Turkey. But remarkably—from the crusaders' point of view, miraculously—they reached the eastern shore of the Mediterranean, captured Antioch on the Orontes, Edessa, Tripoli, Tyre, Sidon, and on July 15, 1099, they took Jerusalem by storm. The crusaders carved out the Kingdom of Jerusalem and several principalities that gradually shrank under Muslim counterattacks until the last remnant, the city of Acre, fell in 1291.

The Anonymous Knight

The thoughts of the ordinary knights and apocalyptic peasants who set out for Jerusalem are difficult for us to grasp. But contemporaries were aware that the expedition was unprecedented. They viewed as a miracle the capture of Jerusalem, the only real success that the crusades ever had (of course, they could not know that was how things would eventually turn out). At least five eyewitnesses to the First Crusade wrote histories. Anna Comnena (1083–ca. 1148), daughter of the Byzantine emperor Alexius I, wrote *The Alexiad,* in which the First Crusade was a significant theme.[5] Three church leaders—Foucher (Fulcher) de Chartres (ca. 1059–ca. 1127), Raymond d'Aguilers, and Peter Tudebode—also wrote participant accounts.[6] An anonymous knight wrote the fifth account, called the *Gesta Francorum et aliorum Hierosolimitanorum* ("The Deeds of the Franks and of the Others Who Went to Jerusalem").[7] The anonymous knight, who was probably a Norman from southern Italy in the service of Bohemond I (ca. 1050 or 1058–1111), the Prince of Antioch, made a rare accomplishment: the work is that of a lay eyewitness, an actual combatant who gave a soldier's viewpoint, often critical of the leaders, and able to describe tactics as only a soldier can. We do not know where he got his literacy in Latin.

Perhaps he had been intended for a career in the church, but some change in circumstances brought him to a knight's career—that was not unusual, but in his case it is just a surmise. The anonymous knight wrote in a Latin that a contemporary called "rustic and unpolished."[8] He was not a man who ornamented his prose with words from Virgil or Cicero. He cited the New Testament, but apparently from memory. He rarely cited the Old Testament explicitly, although he knew the Psalms, which is to be expected. For centuries young people learned to read Latin from the Psalms, which were lodged deep in the memories of most literate people, providing them with images, prayers, a ready source of quotations, and many theological ideas.

The knight was no trained theologian, but he did have views that were theological. His very lack of theological sophistication makes him a valuable witness to the meaning or, more precisely, the meanings of the First Crusade for contemporaries (or some contemporaries).

Modern, popular ideas about the First Crusade, and crusades in general, are often anachronistic. The knight would not have known what we were talking about when we call him a crusader: he saw himself as a pilgrim (*peregrinus*) on the *via sancti sepulcri,* the "way of the Holy Sepulchre." His pilgrimage was conceptualized as a religious undertaking: he explicitly said that he was following Jesus' command to take up the cross—he did literally have a cross on his garments—and follow him (Matt. 10:38, "whoever does not take up the cross and follow me is not worthy of me"). He wrote that "we suffered for the Name of Christ"—and they suffered appallingly—"and to set free the road to the Holy Sepulchre," which was Christ's tomb.[9] He took seriously his vow to pray at Christ's burial place. When his feudal lord, Bohemond, decided not to proceed directly to Jerusalem, but turned aside to conquer Antioch, the knight joined another lord who was intent on fulfilling his vows at Jerusalem.

The knight tells us about many things, but this essay is about Christianity and violence. What did the knight think about the warfare that his pilgrimage involved? His words reflect a fairly coherent view, a sort of theology. The knight used a vocabulary, much of it drawn from the Latin Vulgate version of the Bible, that throws vivid light on his views. The great mass of pilgrims, unarmed and armed, were the *gens Christi* ("people of Christ") or the *populus Dei* ("people of God"). The knights on the expedition were the *milites Christi* ("soldiers of Christ"), who were engaged in the *militia Christi,* "military service of Christ."[10] He called Tancred, one of the leaders, a *miles Christi* ("soldier of Christ"), and he called his lord and patron Bohemond a *fortissimus Christi athleta* ("most valiant champion of Christ").[11] In one rich phrase he encapsulated his view: the knights were the *Christi milites peregrini,* "pilgrim soldiers of Christ."[12] He did not think that he was engaged in the kind of warfare that knights pursued back home, which he called *bellum carnale* ("carnal warfare"). The pilgrimage involved *bellum spirituale,* "spiritual warfare." During a Turkish attack, Bohemond rallied his knights: "Charge at top speed, like a brave man, and fight valiantly for

God and the Holy Sepulchre, for you know in truth that this is no war of the flesh, but of the spirit. So be very brave, as becomes a champion of Christ. Go in peace, and may the Lord be your protector."[13]

The knight had a theologically inspired vision of humanity, which also comes out in his language. As did the three sibling religions of Judaism, Islam, and Christianity, the knight divided the world into "us" and "them"—in his case, Christian and pagan.[14] He had a term for "us," *Christianitas,* and for "them," *paganismus.*[15] (Let me say parenthetically that he understood nothing about Muslim beliefs—he thought that they were polytheistic idol-worshipers.) He welcomed Eastern Christians on his side of the "us-them" divide. He criticized those crusaders who acted badly with fellow Christians and thought it was wrong to fight against other Christians.[16] That view was modified somewhat by experience of actual Byzantines, whom he, like many crusaders after him, thought deceitful and treacherous.

The knight framed the preparation for battle and battle itself in religious and liturgical terms, probably because that is what he actually saw his fellow crusaders doing. His description of the preparations to defend Antioch against a relieving army of Turks was typical:

> After three days spent in fasting and in processions from one church to another, our men confessed their sins and received absolution, and by faith they received the Body and Blood of Christ in communion, and they gave alms and arranged for masses to be celebrated.[17]

Although the clergy accompanying the armies did not (or at least should not) fight with material weapons, the knight was sure they fought nonetheless. He described their role in the effort to storm the walls of Antioch with siege machinery:

> Behind the siege-tower stood the priests and clerks, clad in their holy vestments, praying and beseeching God to defend his people, and to exalt Christendom (*Christianitas*) and to cast down idolatry (*paganismus*).[18]

A key element of his theology was his conviction that God fought on the side of the Christians, who were after all the *populus Dei,* the "people of God." He made up a speech that he put into the mouth of the mother of Kerboga, the Atabeg of Mosul, one of the main Muslim opponents of the crusaders. These are surely the knight's own theological views (there is much more to the speech, but this excerpt makes the point about his theology of God's protection):

> O sweetest son, the Christians cannot fight with you by themselves—indeed I know that they are unworthy to meet you in battle—but their god fights for them every day, and keeps them day and night under his protection, and watches

over them as a shepherd watches over his flock, and suffers no people to hurt or
vex them, and if anyone wishes to fight them, their god will smite them, as he
says by the mouth of David the prophet, "Scatter the people that delight in war"
(Psalm 67:31) and again "Pour out your anger upon the people that have not
known you, and upon the kingdoms that have not called upon your name"
(Psalm 78:6). Even before they are ready to join battle, their god, mighty and
powerful in battle, together with his saints, has already conquered their enemies.
. . . Beloved, know also the truth of this, that those Christians are called "sons
of Christ" and . . . "sons of adoption and promise" (Romans 9:8 and Galatians
4:5) and the Apostle says they are "heirs of Christ" (Romans 8:17), to whom
Christ has even now given the promised inheritance, saying by the prophets,
"From the rising of the sun to the going down thereof shall be your bounds and
no man shall stand against you."[19]

But the knight did not think that God's favor was automatic. A pilgrimage,
armed or not, was a holy undertaking, which required that pilgrims behave in
holy ways. The knight criticized some crusaders' laxity and sin.[20] He found in
God's punishment of such sins the explanation for the defeats, sufferings, and
deaths that accompanied the long march. In his theology, holiness led to military victory just as sin led to defeat.

The knight had another theological paradigm within which he made sense
of his experience. On the journey, tens of thousands died from disease, hunger,
thirst, and, of course, violence. He regarded those who died as martyrs:

We besieged this city for seven weeks and three days, and many of our men suffered martyrdom there and gave up their blessed souls to God with joy and glad-
ness and many of the poor starved to death for the Name of Christ. All these
entered heaven in triumph, wearing the robe of martyrdom which they have
received, saying with one voice, "Avenge, O Lord, our blood which was shed
for thee, for thou art blessed and worthy of praise for ever and ever" [a remi-
niscence of Revelation 6:10].[21]

Finally, the knight also expressed another—I think subordinate—rationale
for the warfare in which he was engaged. He thought that the expedition was
justified in taking back for Christians what had been wrongfully taken by Muslims (which was true in the sense that North Africa and the Near East had been
the very heartland of Christianity until the seventh century and Anatolia had
been part of the Christian Byzantine Empire a mere twenty-five years earlier—
think of the long memories in modern times about what belongs or used to
belong to whom). For instance, when Antioch was captured, the knight wrote
that it was restored to the holy faith, and, in another passage, he said that the
city was recalled to the faith of Christ and to St. Peter, a reference to the belief
that Peter had been bishop at Antioch before he went to Rome. At other points
he wrote that the entire land rightfully belonged to the Christians.[22] Lying
behind such statements was some version of Augustine's theory of the just war,

which allowed warfare under restricted conditions, one of which was to get back something that had been stolen. I doubt that the anonymous knight had direct contact with Augustine's writing. Perhaps he heard a version of the just war theory from preachers who encouraged the crusade in Europe or those who accompanied the crusade.

I do not want to sanitize the knight's account. He regarded the warfare as "spiritual" in its aim, which was the liberation of the holy places, but in its methods it was as brutal as carnal warfare. Battle and its aftermath were by our standards cruel. Like so many ordinary soldiers in history, now and then the knight expressed admiration for the bravery and skill of his adversaries. But he recorded without negative comment brutal events perpetrated *by* his enemies and *on* his enemies.[23]

The Lord God of Hosts

As I described briefly the anonymous knight's theology of armed pilgrimage, I am sure that many readers were reminded of Old Testament parallels. The crusades, especially the First Crusade, are not comprehensible without factoring in the Old Testament, which permeated not just the language but the self-view and behavior of the warriors. A full analysis would take too long, but let me recall some points of comparison. The knight's view of God is that of the Lord God of Hosts, who leads and protects his people in battle. At crucial moments the crusaders acted out Old Testament scenes: Just as the ark of the covenant had been carried into battle (see Josh. 6, where the ark was carried around the walls of Jericho), so the Holy Lance, discovered at Antioch and purportedly the very lance with which the centurion pierced Christ's side, was carried into battle.[24] The Christian priests prayed during battle just as Moses held up his staff while Joshua fought Amalek (Exod. 17:10–11). The crusaders often slaughtered their enemies just as the Israelites destroyed everything in Canaanite cities and the Amalekites.[25] At many points in his narrative, the knight drew from the Old Testament quotations that he thought apt or even prophetic. At a deeper level, the knight's understanding of the interplay of the crusaders' victories and defeats was shaped by the Old Testament's recurring theme of Israel's keeping and breaking its covenant with Yahweh, which had real-world consequences.

An excursus will help to clarify the significance of the knight's seeing his experience through the lens of the Old Testament. It is safe to say that on the issues of violence and warfare, the New Testament and the Old Testament differ. Even in modern times, arguments among Christians, particularly about social issues such as capital punishment, often pit New Testament texts against Old Testament texts.

The New Testament opposes violence *by Christians,* who should be meek, nonresistant, and humble. But the New Testament does not, I think, explicitly forbid war, particularly when carried out by the pagan Roman state. Furthermore, how could wars be categorically rejected if God brought them about and used them to achieve his ends? For example, in Moses' song (Exod. 15:1–18), Yahweh himself is described as a warrior in verse 3. In Revelation 19:11–16, Christ will wage a war, but with the aid of his angels; his earthly followers will have no need to participate.

When some early Christian writers tried to describe the behavior proper to Christians, they found military imagery attractive. In the Roman world, where Christianity developed, the army was an admired model of social organization. Paul in particular liked military images and actually used the phrases "good soldier of Christ Jesus" (2 Tim. 2:3: *Labora sicut bonus miles Christi Jesu*), "Archippus our fellow soldier" (Philem. 1:2: *archippo commilitoni nostro*), and "serving in the army" (2 Tim. 2:4: *militans Deo*: The word *Deo* is only in the Latin Vulgate). He also used other words and images that had a military origin, for instance Romans 6:13–14 and 13:12; 2 Corinthians 6:7; Ephesians 6:10–17; and 1 Thessalonians 5:8.[26] There was a long tradition among later Christian writers to describe church discipline and the individual Christian's moral struggles in military words. The intertwined images of military service, military discipline, and battle were persistent themes in Christian literature for centuries—in fact in some traditions until the present: Think of the nineteenth-century hymn "Onward Christian Soldiers." But it is important to note that usually the military images were not *really* military or violent—they were understood as metaphors or similes. For instance, Paul's "soldier of Christ" (*miles Christi*) was apparently a missionary like himself.[27]

The third-century Alexandrian theologian Origen (ca. 185–ca. 254) set the interpretation of New Testament military words on an important path when he argued that the true soldier of Christ was the ascetic, who fought sin and demons with the weapons of prayer, fasting, meditation, good works, justice, piety, meekness, chastity, and abstinence.[28] The point I want to stress is that for centuries, exegetes did not interpret New Testament, particularly Pauline, military words as referring to real-world violence. Actual soldiers were in ill repute among many religious thinkers until the eleventh century. The anonymous knight was echoing relatively new ideas when he applied the Pauline designation "soldier of Christ" to himself and his companions—real soldiers, who fought, killed, and died.

The Hebrew Bible, the Christian's Old Testament, is a complex anthology of such genres as poetry, narrative, wisdom literature, and prophecy. A major portion of it is given over to telling of the Hebrews' warfare to conquer the land of Canaan and to defend it against attackers. In contrast to the New Testament, the Old Testament is not negative or even ambivalent about war and violence. We are so used to viewing the Old and New Testaments as constituting one book, the Bible, that we might forget how controversial the Old Testament was within the complex early Christian movement. Some important second- and third-century theological debates turned on the assessment of the Old Testament and its God. Gnostic Christians, in particular, were hard on the God of the Jews and his book. Marcion of Sinope (died ca. 160) provoked a crisis when he systematically contrasted the Old Testament God, whom he regarded as wrathful and cruel, with Jesus' loving Father. One point of contrast—not the only one or even the main one—was precisely the warlike ways of Yahweh. Marcion's critique struck a nerve among contemporary Catholic Christians, one indicator of which is that so many orthodox authors wrote against him.[29]

Catholic Christians, who venerated the Old Testament as Scripture, had to defend the God of the Old Testament and to affirm his book, which presented them with challenges. Origen also showed the way to a defense of the Old Testament when he thoroughly allegorized its wars: for him, they were really battles against sin and the powers of darkness. In a homily on Joshua, a book full of war and violence, he wrote:

> If the horrible wars related in the Old Testament were not to be interpreted in a spiritual sense, the apostles would never have transmitted the Jewish books for reading in the church to the disciples of Christ, who came to teach peace.[30]

Origen thus pointed the way to a learned solution for dealing with the difficulties of the Old Testament, including warfare and violence. For centuries exegetes and preachers allegorized the violence of the Old Testament narratives, making them refer to the moral struggles of the church against evil or of the individual soul against sin.

But the exegetes did not always have their way. As a pedagogical technique, I ask my students to think of the Scriptures as page after page of black ink on white paper. In different cultural contexts, some words, some phrases, some sentences, and some pages "glow," that is, those particular biblical words move their readers or hearers in a special way. This doesn't mean that, if asked, people would not have said they believed the entire Bible, but it is obvious that some parts spoke to them more directly than others. For instance, between the eleventh and the fifteenth centuries, tens of thousands of people acted on Jesus' advice to the rich young man: "If you wish to be perfect, go, sell your possessions, and give the money to the poor, and you will have treasure in heaven; then come, follow me" (Matt. 19:21; cf. Mark 10:21; Luke 18:22). Since the sixteenth century, millions of people have been moved and are still moved by Paul's declaration that "The one who is righteous will live by faith" (Rom. 1:17). Between the fifteenth and seventeenth centuries, thousands of people were moved to violent action against as many as 100,000 suspected witches by Exodus 22:18 ("You shall not permit a female sorcerer to live"). I would venture to say that in our times, the scriptural texts on love "glow" for many people.

In spite of the traditional scholarly allegorization of the violent stories of the Old Testament, those very stories were meaningful—they "glowed"—to the Roman, Germanic, and Celtic Christian peoples of the early medieval West, who identified themselves readily with the children of Israel fighting under the protection of their God. Some Franks actually saw themselves the new people of Israel.[31] When the monastic founder Benedict wrote his famous *Rule,* which by the way described the monastic life as a sort of warfare, he wanted his monks to have pious readings before going to bed:

> When there are two meals, all the monks will sit together. Immediately after ris-
> ing from supper, someone should read from the *Conferences* [of John Cassian]
> or the *Lives of the Fathers* or at any rate something else that will benefit the hear-
> ers, but not the Heptateuch or the Book of Kings, because it will not be good
> for those of weak understanding to hear those writings at that hour: they should
> be read at other times.[32]

Benedict feared bad dreams, I think, from the more violent books of the Old Testament. He was explicit that those without a firm grasp on the allegorical method (he calls them "those of weak understanding") were especially fascinated by the literal meaning of the Old Testament stories of war. Neither the tendency to allegorize biblical violence nor the tendency to understand it literally was triumphant in the early Middle Ages: this was contested ground.

Let me be clear. The Old Testament did not "cause" the First Crusade or its violence: eleventh-century European society was violent. But the Old Testament narratives framed the anonymous knight's understanding of the crusade, and gave him and other contemporary historians (and maybe the participants) a way to talk about and to justify war. The anonymous knight (and the other contemporary historians of the First Crusade) downplayed or set aside allegorization. They crossed over the long-standing barrier that stood between Christians and a literal understanding of the violent aspects of the Old Testament and Paul's soldier language. The knight probably spoke for many when he saw himself reenacting the Old Testament narratives of fighting and when he described his personal experiences in the Pauline terms, as a "soldier of Christ" (2 Tim. 2:3).

The Christian Knight

The anonymous author and his fellow warriors were, for want of a better phrase, Old Testament people, but they were not only that. They were also eleventh-century knights, and therein lies another approach to understanding crusading warfare. In the eleventh century, the military profession, traditionally regarded by church leaders as utterly sinful and secular, was reconceptualized, indeed "Christianized," that is, integrated into a Christian ethical structure and given a morally positive purpose.[33]

To understand that change, we have to begin long before the eleventh century. Pre-Constantinian Christianity was hostile to war, which was carried out by a secular state in an atmosphere of paganism. Such a stance was possible in the second and third centuries in good part because Christians were a relatively small minority in an empire that fought with professional armies. As a consequence, few Christians were forced into military service, though there were Christian soldiers who faced a moral dilemma.[34] When in the fourth century the Roman Empire legalized and then favored the Christian church, Christian numbers grew rapidly. When Christian rulers were in charge of the empire, Christians became in a sense responsible for its safety. The older tradition of hostility to military service did not entirely disappear, but Christian thinkers had to work out new views of war.

In the West, the most influential thinker on war, as on so many things, was Augustine of Hippo (354–430).[35] When Augustine formulated his theory of a just war, the situation he faced was that of a Roman emperor who was a military dictator with sole responsibility for peace and war. Augustine declared all war sinful, but sometimes necessary. There could be a "just war" (but never a "good" war) if it was waged in self-defense or to regain stolen property. Within the political structure of the late Roman Empire, ordinary soldiers were not required to make a personal moral judgment whether a war was just. The ruler was bound by the strictures of just war theory, but not ordinary soldiers, who had to obey their superiors.[36]

In a slow transformation that lasted for centuries, the Roman Empire gave way to quite different social, political, and religious structures in both East and West. In the eastern Mediterranean, the Roman Empire survived in shrunken but recognizable form as the Byzantine Empire. The western half of the Roman Empire had a different fate: it was divided up among Germanic invaders. The Carolingian kings of the Franks give much of western Europe a century of stability (approximately 750–850). But between the ninth and eleventh centuries, effective royal power in the West shrank or collapsed, especially in France and the Rhineland, which were to become the heartland of crusading. Political and military power fell into the hands of nobles and knights who were, in the last analysis, private citizens. Unlike kings, these holders of power, often crude, brutal, and illiterate men, had no explicit biblical stamp of approval, and no religious ceremony of induction into office.

The Germanic societies that divided up the western portion of the Roman Empire embraced a powerful warrior ethic that placed a high value on fidelity, bravery, and willingness to die for one's lord and companions. Even though the Germanic kingdoms were legally Christian and men of military standing ruled them, there was no Christian value attributed to the warrior ethic. The clergy, especially the monks whose ideas dominated these "Benedictine cen-

turies," regarded the *militia secularis,* "secular military service," as far from God
and full of moral dangers. It is symptomatic that the clergy were forbidden
even to carry weapons. It is remarkable that until the tenth or eleventh century, the church had no pastoral strategy for dealing with the ordinary knights
who were increasingly the real rulers of a localized society. Church leaders occa-
sionally gave advice to rulers, sometimes in books called "Mirrors of Princes,"
but even then there was no approval of warfare. Christian life in its fullest sense
was thought possible only for the clergy and ascetics, in particular monks and
nuns. Church leaders regarded lay people, and especially soldiers, as pitiable,
because they were enmeshed inextricably in sin: killing in battle was a defile-
ment for which stern penance must be done. Soldiers were regarded as almost
unavoidably sinners, to whom church leaders gave not much more advice than
the negative warnings that John the Baptist gave to the soldiers who came to
hear him: "Do not extort money from anyone by threats or false accusation"
(Luke 3:14). If in the ninth or tenth century a soldier became seriously concerned about his salvation, as many did, clergy told him to abandon the soldier's life to become a monk. In such a context, it is understandable that Christianity's rich heritage of military terms, similes, and metaphors was applied to
monks: they were the "real" soldiers of Christ, engaged in the "real" warfare of
Christ against "real" enemies, Satan and sin, and with the "real" weapons of
prayer and mortification.[37]

The ninth and tenth centuries were among the most disrupted and violent
in the history of the West (at least before the twentieth century). Viking, Muslim, and Magyar invaders threatened the very survival of Western societies and
their religion. In such circumstances, not only were warriors crucial but defensive warfare was sanctioned. Church leaders found in the books of Maccabees,
which told of the struggle of pious Jews against the encroachments of the Hel-
lenistic king Antiochus IV Epiphanes (ca. 216–164 B.C.), a model for contemporary Christian kings, dukes, counts, and knights, who defended the
church and its lands from marauders.[38] However, offensive warfare was still
morally suspect.

In the later tenth and eleventh centuries, some church leaders tried tenta-
tively to give knights a positive role in Christian society. This was a remarkable development, since it challenged the prevailing pessimism about the possibility of sanctifying ordinary secular life and especially the sinful profession
of soldiering. The movement for imposing the Peace of God and the Truce of
God on unruly knights, who were the main perpetrators of disorder, found
great popular support in the eleventh century.[39] Church leaders still deplored
the ordinary warfare of knights—what the anonymous knight called "carnal
warfare" (*bellum carnale*). But they asked knights to use their military skills for
ends regarded as good, for the "spiritual warfare" (*bellum spirituale*) to which
the anonymous knight alluded. War gradually came to be distinguished not
by its methods but by its purposes.

In the tenth and eleventh centuries, church leaders also began to apply to knights ethical norms, including just war theories, that had formerly been expected only of kings. War for territory or in feuds, which was endemic, was evil. But war on behalf of the weak, who were defined as churches, unarmed clergy, peasants, and the poor, was urged on knights as a holy act, in fact as their religious duty and their path to salvation. Aside from kings and emperors, who, because they were often anointed, were not regarded as mere laymen, the knights were the first laymen in the Middle Ages to be encouraged to accept an active, positive, nonclerical religious role.

Because liturgy was central to Christian life in the tenth and eleventh centuries, liturgical creativity was admired and cultivated. The new view of a knighthood with Christian duties and Christian dignity was expressed earlier in liturgical forms than in treatises and sermons. As is often true of profound social change, intellectuals wrote about the theory of Christian knighthood only after it existed as a fact. In liturgical texts, warfare and warriors began to be sanctioned in sacred words and actions. For instance, swords and military banners were blessed. Masses and prayers for warriors and armies were composed:

> Grant O Lord to our forces the help of Your compassion, and as You protected Israel when they departed from Egypt, so now send to Your people who go into battle an angel of light, who will defend them day and night from all misfortune. Let their march be effortless, their path without fear, their courage unwavering, upright their will to war; and after they have been victorious by the leadership of Your angel, let them not honor their own power, but give thanks for the triumph to the victorious Christ, Who triumphed on the Cross by humility.[40]

A tenth-century prayer shows a stage in the Christianization of the knightly calling:

> God, fountain of eternity, Lord of all good, and conqueror of all enemies, bless these Your servants, and pour out Your constant grace upon them. In the knighthood in which they have been tried, maintain them in health and prosperity, and whenever they call upon Your aid, be there at once, protect and defend them.[41]

This prayer would have been unusual, perhaps unimaginable, two centuries earlier. It is a signpost in the slow and imperfect process by which the military profession was Christianized. As Carl Erdmann noted:

> Around the turn of the millennium, the attitude of the church toward the military class underwent a significant change. The contrast between the *militia Christi* and *militia secularis* was overcome, and just as rulership earlier had been Christianized, so now was the military profession; it acquired a direct ecclesiastical purpose, for war in the service of the church or of the weak came to be

regarded as holy and was declared to be a religious duty not only for the king but also for every individual knight.[42]

In the eleventh century, the ancient secular rituals for making a young man into a knight were complemented by ceremonies full of Christian prayers and symbolic acts. The Christianization of knighthood was imperfect, and knights remained for centuries unruly, violent men. But the new religiously inspired views of knighthood did have influence.[43]

Thus, when Urban II preached at Clermont in 1095, many of the knights in his audience had probably internalized a self-view with explicitly Christian elements. They believed that if their warlike actions were devoted to the proper end, such as the liberation of the holy places, they were acting as Christ's disciples. The anonymous knight, who was not at Clermont and probably composed his narrative on the basis of others' reports, began his book thus:

> When that time had already come, of which the Lord Jesus warns his faithful people every day, especially in the Gospel where he says, "If any man will come after me, let him deny himself, and take up his cross, and follow me" [Matthew 16:24], there was a great stirring of heart throughout all the Frankish lands, so that if any man, with all his heart and all his mind, really wanted to follow God and faithfully to bear the cross after him, he could make no delay in taking the road to the Holy Sepulchre as quickly as possible. For even the pope set out across the Alps as soon as he could, with his archbishops, bishops, abbots and priests, and he began to deliver eloquent sermons and to preach, saying, "If any man wants to save his soul, let him have no hesitation in taking the way of the Lord in humility, and if he lacks money, the divine mercy will give him enough." The lord pope said also, "Brothers, you must suffer for the name of Christ many things, wretchedness, poverty, nakedness, persecution, need, sickness, hunger, thirst and other such troubles, for the Lord says to his disciples, 'You must suffer many things for my name' [Acts 9:16], and 'Be not ashamed to speak before men, for I will give you what you shall say' [Luke 21:15 and 2 Timothy 1:8] and afterwards 'Great will be your reward'" [Matthew 5:12]. And when these words had begun to be rumoured abroad through all the duchies and counties of the Frankish lands, the Franks, hearing them, straightway began to sew the cross on the right shoulders of their garments, saying that they would all with one accord follow in the footsteps of Christ, by whom they had been redeemed from the power of hell. So they set out at once from their homes in the lands of the Franks.[44]

Conclusion

Scholars still dispute about the ideological—let's call them theological—origins of the First Crusade. I do not claim that I have resolved the dispute in this modest essay. Although I have treated them only cursorily in this essay, the vigorous tradition of pilgrimage to the holy places[45] and the contemporary

plight of eastern Christians after the Seljuk Turks' victories were certainly pre-
conditions for the crusade. But I have argued that the First Crusade sprang in
part out of long-term theological and religious developments that changed the
way Christians viewed war and warriors. The emergence of holy war was facilitated by a change in exegesis, the deallegorization—if I may be permitted to
coin such a barbarous word—of the Old Testament war narratives. The crusaders saw themselves as the new Israel, fighting for territory under the leadership of God, just as the old Israel had. The crusade is also unimaginable without the transformation of knighthood into a religious calling, which could
fulfill its duties in carrying out spiritual warfare. It oversimplifies surely, but I
leave you with the image of the self-consciously Christian knights, the *Christi
milites peregrini* ("pilgrim soldiers of Christ"), who gazed without allegory (or
at least much allegory) into some parts of the Old Testament and saw themselves and who saw in Paul's military references to the Christian life their own
justification.

TWO

Violence of the Conquistadores and Prophetic Indignation

Luis N. Rivera-Pagán

To offer a sacrifice from the possessions of the poor is like killing a son before his father's eyes. Bread is life to the destitute, and to deprive them of it is murder.

—Sirach/Ecclesiasticus 34:24–25 REB (20–21 in some versions)

The Spanish Crown and the Evangelization of the Americas

In the spring of 1493, Christian Europe received amazing news. An Italian sailor, traveling under Spanish orders, had discovered strange lands and peoples, after an unheard-of navigation through the uncharted waters of the Ocean Sea, the dreaded *mare tenebrosum,* the Sea of Darkness. The first news of the event that would change the prevailing cosmological views and the destiny of human civilization was drafted by the pen of that mariner himself, Christopher Columbus. A letter written on February 15, 1493, aboard the caravel nicknamed *Niña,* begins with a succinct summary of the astounding event. "I arrived to the Indies with the armada that the most illustrious King and Queen, Our Lords, had given me, where I found many islands populated with num-

37

berless people, and of *all of them I have taken possession* on behalf of Your High-nesses with proclamation and extended royal banner."[1]

Columbus describes to the astonished Christian Europeans the fantastic islands encountered and their inhabitants who, according to the sailor sud-denly transformed into amateur anthropologist, "all go naked, men and women, as their mothers bore them," "have no iron or steel or weapons, nor are they fitted to use them," are "the most timorous people in the world," and, finally, "do not hold any creed nor are they idolaters," but will readily accept the Chris-tian faith, "towards which they are very inclined."[2] The letter closes with an expression of liturgical praise to the Holy Trinity, and with a hymn of triumph on behalf of Christendom, whose universal expansion has begun. "Thus the eternal God, Our Lord, gives to all those who walk in His way triumph over things which appear to be impossible, and this was notably one. . . . Chris-tendom ought to feel delight and make great feasts and give solemn thanks to the Holy Trinity, with many solemn prayers for the great exaltation which they shall have in the turning of so many peoples to our holy faith." Columbus, cer-tainly, does not forget another important potential consequence of the "great triumph" allowed to him by God, and hastens to add gratitude "for the tem-poral benefits" to be reaped in the discovered lands.[3]

Ferdinand and Isabella, Catholic Monarchs of Spain, gave Columbus, in 1493, the following instructions, when the now Viceroy of the Indies and Admiral of the Ocean Sea was to initiate the colonization of the lands. "Wish-ing that our holy Catholic faith be increased and augmented, we order and charge the said admiral . . . that by every means and ways possible he should try to persuade the inhabitants of said islands and mainlands to be converted to our Catholic faith."[4] To that end, the monarchs sent a group of religious and friars to evangelize the natives, thus laying the foundations for the world expansion of the Christian faith as the religious counterpart of European colo-nial outreach.[5] The missionaries, however, were too few and were not able to escape the tensions and hostilities that besieged the Columbus administration of the Antilles between 1494 and 1500.

The first shattering of illusions occurred at the arrival in Hispaniola, when all thirty-nine men left behind by Columbus in January 1493 were found killed, a clear sign that the paradise described by the admiral in his earlier reports existed only in his mind.[6] The natives were not as timorous as he had asserted; they were willing and daring to defend their patrimony, culture, and freedom. Nor did the islands seem to be Ophir, the region where King Solomon had obtained the gold to build the temple of Jerusalem. Neither was the conver-sion of the native communities a simple matter to be entrusted to a small band of unprepared friars. The natives also attested to many abuses on the part of the Spanish garrison, an ominous anticipation of the predatory conduct of the first generation of colonists, almost unrestrained by juridical norms. Those norms would begin to be established, at least in the lawgivers' books, in 1512 and 1513, two decades after the colonizing process had begun, a lawless period that proved to be lethal for the Caribbean indigenous communities.[7]

The colonization of the Americas proceeded at a very slow pace. Its Christianization was even slower. In spite of the many pious expressions of the *Christum ferens* (Christ-bearer), as Columbus was called, evangelizing the Native Americans was never in the forefront of Columbus's colonial projects. During those difficult six years, his main objective was not to proselytize the native communities, but to provide political stability and economic prosperity to the colony, aims that eluded him totally. When he failed to create even the appearance of civic control, he was unceremoniously chained and expelled from the lands he had found and inscribed in the history of Western civilization.[8]

In 1504, in the codicil to her will and testament, the dying Queen Isabella included the following clause, a forceful reminder to her husband, Ferdinand, her daughter, Juana, and her son-in-law, Philip, of the unfulfilled goal to Christianize the New World as the main purpose of the Spanish arrogation of sovereignty:

> From the time when the Holy Apostolic See granted us the isles and mainlands of the Ocean Sea which have been or will be discovered, our principal intention . . . was to try to lead and bring the peoples of the said areas and convert them to our Holy Catholic faith. . . . Therefore, I beg the King, my Lord . . . and I charge and command the Princess, my daughter, and the Prince, her husband, to carry out and fulfill this charge and that this be their principal aim . . . for this is what is enjoined on us by the Apostolic letter of the aforementioned grant.[9]

King Ferdinand, for his part, commanded Diego Columbus, son of the admiral and new Viceroy of the Indies, to make certain that the natives be instructed "in our Catholic faith, for this is the principal foundation upon which we base the conquest of these regions."[10] This kind of ordinance proliferates under the dynasty of Charles V and Philip II. The former "Ordinances about the good treatment of the Indians,"[11] decreed in 1526, and the latter "Ordinances regarding new discoveries,"[12] enacted in 1573, stress the conversion of the Native Americans as the main objective of the conquest and colonization of the Americas. The 1573 ordinances insist that "The zeal and wish that we have is that all that is yet to be discovered be discovered, so that our holy Gospel be made public and the natives come to the knowledge of our holy Catholic faith."[13]

In summary, despite the many changes in political strategies of conquest and colonization, in the century that goes from Isabella and Ferdinand to Philip II, the evangelization of the natives and their conversion to the Christian faith was continually made explicit as the transcendental goal of Spain's political, economic, and cultural dominion over America. It was explicitly and self-consciously an imperial expansion understood as a missionary enterprise.[14] It failed totally in the Antilles, but was able to produce the Franciscan missions to Mexico and the

Jesuit Reductions in different parts of South America, two of the most exceptional and exciting chapters in the history of the expansion of Christianity.[15]

Despite several attempts to conceive the colonization of America in the Old Testament pattern of the extermination of the infidels whose presence defiles the promised land and who thus deserve annihilation, the official model was always primarily missionary, whereby the military actions were perceived as paradoxical ways of fulfilling Christ's last commandment: "Go to all nations and make them my disciples." When references are made to Juan Ginés de Sepúlveda and his book on the justice of the wars against the Indians,[16] a work in which Aristotle's concept of the barbarians who are slaves by nature seems to converge with the Old Testament vision of the God-commanded destruction of the peoples of Canaan, we should not forget that this work was explicitly repudiated by a good number of Spanish theologians and was not printed in the sixteenth century for lack of official authorization.[17]

Genocide, which undeniably occurred in many parts of Spanish America, was never official policy. When and where it tragically happened, as quite different sixteenth-century Spanish historians like the Dominican Bartolomé de Las Casas[18] and the Franciscan Gerónimo de Mendieta stressed, it went against the explicit policy of the crown to preserve and evangelize the natives. This policy, adopted for religious and humanitarian reasons, or for the obvious inconvenience that the death of servile workers would represent, means that it is incorrect to ascribe to the Spanish conquest the Old Testament model of annihilating the Canaanite infidels.[19]

This is not to say that evangelization was devoid of military coercion. As the Jesuit José de Acosta states in the prologue to his 1589 missionary treatise *De procuranda indorum salute,* military coercion and religious conversion went as a general rule hand by hand.[20] The insistence of Las Casas in his own missionary work, *De unico vocationis modo omnium gentium ad veram religionem,* that the use of military force and compulsion should be a priori excluded from the process of evangelization, although it was the basis for some isolated experiments, was usually unheeded.[21]

Conquest and Christianization

Even the ambitious and bellicose Hernán Cortés insists on the Christianization of the American lands and peoples as the principal purpose of his military endeavors. He conquers the native communities, in his words, "to attract them so that they would come to the knowledge of our holy Catholic faith."[22] Cortés launches the attack against Tenochtitlán, probably the most violent military confrontation in the whole epic conquest of America, only after publicly, officially, and formally declaring his war a crusade, a religious and missionary enterprise. His Tlaxcala military ordinances constitute probably the most forceful statement of the prevailing paradoxical identification between conquest and christianization.

> In as much as . . . the natives of these regions have a culture and veneration of idols, which is a great disservice to God Our Lord, and the devil blinds and deceives them . . . I propose to bring them to the knowledge of our Holy Catholic faith. . . . Let us go to uproot the natives of these regions from those idolatries . . . so that they will come to the knowledge of God and of His Holy Catholic faith . . . because if war were carried out with any other intention it would be unjust. . . . And therefore . . . I affirm that my principal motive in undertaking this war . . . is to bring the natives to the knowledge of our Holy Catholic faith.[23]

Certainly, he is not slow to add that if his army were devoid of such a "right intention," then the acquisition of wealth and properties according to the ancient military tradition of the booty would be unjust and subject to restitution. Cortés is following the tradition of the Spanish *Reconquista,* whereby the lands and goods of the conquered infidels, the Moors, were considered rightly distributed between the triumphant troops, as long as the conflict is perceived as a holy war, a religious confrontation. Only post facto, after the Nahuatl society had been destroyed, would critics like Bartolomé de las Casas call attention to the obvious difference between the *Reconquista* model and the invasion of other peoples' lands and societies.[24]

God and gold are inextricably linked. Columbus wants the gold of America to finance a new and last crusade, to recover the Holy Land and the Lord's sepulchre.[25] Cortés perceives the preaching of the one and only God and the acquisition of gold (as well as glory) as distinct but inseparable goals of one and the same historical process of conquest.

The unity of God and gold, religiosity and avarice, is perhaps nowhere more strikingly expressed than in the May 1512 Capitulations of Burgos. It is the first formal agreement between the Spanish crown and the initial bishops of America.[26] The capitulations oblige the future bishops of America to care for the conversion of the natives. They are also charged, however, with the peculiar episcopal duty of persuading the Indians to work harder in the gold mines, suggesting to the reluctant miners that the product of their work will be used to wage war against infidels (the Muslim Ottomans) and to provide for their spiritual benefit.

The conquest of America takes place after the *Reconquista,* the long military struggle between the Iberian Christians and the Iberian Muslims.[27] I say Iberian Muslims because the great majority of the defeated followers of Allah were born and raised, as were their parents, the parents of their parents, and the parents of the parents of their parents, in Iberian lands. It is no mere coincidence that Cortés refers to the Aztecs' temples as "mosques," evoking in his army traditional holy war against the Muslims, "enemies of the Cross." The battle against Tenochtitlán becomes an ideological crusade, a holy war; a theomachy in which the most powerful God defeats lesser deities.[28] The conquest of America also took place after the expulsion of the Iberian Jews, followers of the Law of Moses who for generations and generations had considered as their home the same land and nation that now the Christians claimed to be only theirs.

The names of the Muslim Averroës (Ibn Rushd, 1126–1198) and the Jew Maimonides (Moses ben Maimon, 1135–1204), both of whom were born in the same city, Córdoba, Spain, also the birthplace of the Latin Seneca, and of many Christian writers, artists, and thinkers, constitute eloquent evidence of the common Spanish ancestry of the followers of the three great universal monotheistic religions, as the Spanish scholar Américo Castro insisted upon several years ago.[29] Christian *Hispania,* Muslim *al-Andalus,* and Jewish *Sepharad* for a time at least were able to forge a community of multicultural *convivencia.* It was fragile and vulnerable, but it was a historical reality. The *Reyes Católicos* (Catholic Monarchs), guided by their religious zeal, put an end to it. The Cross crushed the Crescent and expelled the Star of David. Messianic providentialism triumphed over religious tolerance. Religious dogmatic orthodoxy fed Christian Spanish national identity and propelled it into an imperial crusade.[30]

This peculiar Spanish history gives birth to an exceptional identification between confession and nationality, religion and nation. This is the hermeneutical key to understanding the paradoxical mentality of conquerors like Cortés, who commands that the first thing to happen every morning in the camp of his invading army is a Mass; who has no scruples in accepting women as gifts of subordination by the Mexican *caciques* (chieftains) and using them carnally, but only after baptizing them; who has no qualms in torturing and executing Cuauhtémoc, but humbles himself in front of the Franciscan friars arriving in New Spain to start the Christianization of the conquered people.[31]

It is symbolically significant that Cortés had a cross in his military banner accompanied by a Latin inscription that declares, *"Amici, sequamur crucem, et si nos fidem habemus, vere in hoc signo vincemus"* ("Friends, let us follow the cross, and if we have faith, truly in the name of this symbol we will conquer"). The presentation of a cross was, as noted by some scholars, one of the symbolic paraphernalia of a crusade, as required by medieval canon law.[32]

When Cortés began his final assault on Tenochtitlán (1521), Western Christianity was undergoing the first agonizing signs of the process of division and antagonism that soon would fragment it and transform the *communio sanctorum* into a field of warring armies, in which Protestants and Catholics would violently face each other with opposing dogmas and weapons. The Spanish crown and church decided to "protect" America from the contamination of the European heresies, giving birth to a history of ecclesiastical repression still waiting to be narrated in its totality.

The Jesuit historian Pedro de Leturia has written: "The crusade of Granada continues in the Indies."[33] We might add that in the Indies also continues the expulsion of the Jews and the persecution of those who defy ecclesiastical dogmas. The medieval dictum—*extra ecclesiam nulla salus*—that was meant as a theological judgment becomes a political condemnation of all kinds of heterodoxies, and also of the native creeds and religions. Historians and scholars differ pointedly in their evaluations of whether it was fundamentally a case of an ecclesiastical state, or of a state church. The difference might be significant, but not for the victims of the repressive violence that usually accompanies such an intimate conjunction of material and spiritual institutions.[34]

Providential Messianism

Gerónimo de Mendieta, the Franciscan scholar who at the end of the sixteenth century wrote a history of the conquest and Christianization of Mexico, *Historia Eclesiástica Indiana,* a work similar in scope to the patristic *Ecclesiastical History* of Eusebius, asserts that Hernán Cortés was born the same year as Martin Luther, emissary of the devil, and the same year that the Aztec Templo Mayor was consecrated with the human sacrifice of more than 80,000 persons (truly a hyperbolic figure). The birth of Cortés becomes thus a providential event, an extremely significant element in the cosmic struggle between Christ and Satan, manifest in the attempt to counter the Protestant heresy and to eradicate the Native American idolatries. Mendieta praises the Spanish crown for being the only European state that has firmly stood up against "Muslim falseness," "Judaic perfidy," the "household malice of heretics," and "idolatrous blindness." He goes one step forward in the discernment of God's providence, as he boldly asserts that the discovery and conquest of America is a particular divine reward for the strict manner Spain has kept the faith uncontaminated.[35] The notion of the elected nation, to which God has conceded a providential and transcendent mission, becomes the hermeneutical key to understand the conquest of America.

It is an idea previously put forward by Fray Toribio de Benavente (Motolinia), one of the twelve Franciscan missionaries who beginning in 1524 forged the monumental Christianization of the vast Mexican territory. Motolinia perceives the conquest and evangelization of New Spain as an apocalyptic divine intervention expressing both God's wrath against the many devilish traditions of the natives and God's merciful redemption of the peoples blinded by Satan.[36]

It was ideologically impossible for the Spanish crown to conceive the conquest and colonization of America in terms other than missionary evangelization. It could not articulate the legitimacy of its colonial dominion exclusively from a political or economic perspective. What for other modern empires might be possible, namely, to control the instruments of political and economic power while allowing the dominated peoples spiritual solace for their troubled subjectivity in their native religiosity, was absolutely out of the question for sixteenth-century Spain. The spiritual conquest, as Robert Ricard has called it, and the "extirpation of idolatry," according to Pierre Duviols, were essential elements of the Spanish conquest and colonization of the Americas. They constituted their ideological matrix and symbolic configuration.[37]

The conquest of the Americas was guided by a strong Spanish mentality of providential messianism that perceived historical events in the context of a cosmic and universal confrontation between true faith and infidelity. This providentialism can be perceived very early, in the writings of Columbus himself. In one instance he writes: "It was Our Lord who clearly opened my understanding . . . and who opened my will. . . . Who shall doubt that this light was from the Holy Spirit?"[38] This messianic providentialism is even more intense in Cortés. His many expressions attributing his war victories to divine guidance and protection are not mere literary rhetoric. An example: "As we carried the banner of the cross, and were fighting for the faith . . . God gave us so great a victory that we killed many of them without our people suffering any harm."[39] Pope Clement VII, who granted Cortés, in 1529, a plenary bull of indulgence forgiving all guilt and penalties of his sins, because, according to the Holy Father, Cortés had exposed his life to every danger "for the yoke of Christ and obedience to the Holy Roman Church," recognized such messianic devotion.[40]

In this context, it is important to note something usually disregarded. It is Hernán Cortés himself who pioneers the concept of the new church as an essential element of the New World. Even before the arrival of the Franciscan missionaries, the conqueror of Mexico conceives the linkage of the two eschatological notions: *novus mundus—nova ecclesia*. Shortly after defeating Tenochtitlán, he asks the Emperor Charles V to send as missionaries friars from the mendicant orders, renowned for their fidelity to the most stringent vows of poverty. The missionaries shall devote themselves solely to the spiritual well-being and redemption of the peoples of the conquered territory.[41]

Cortés rejects a former suggestion that the evangelization of Mexico be given to the secular clergy and diocesan hierarchies. The repudiation of the secular church and clergy reveals a common judgment about the moral decadence of the Renaissance church. "Having bishops and other prelates they would follow the customs which they have acquired . . . of disposing of the goods of the Church by wasting them on luxuries and other vices," Cortés fears that if the natives were exposed to the worldliness of the secular clergy and ecclesiastical hierarchy it might prove extremely difficult to demonstrate the spiritual superiority of the Christian gospel. For, as he writes to Charles V, "If they were to see the things of the Church in the hands of the clergy and other ecclesiastical authorities, and were to see them in the profanities and vices in which they indulge in Europe, they would have our faith as worthless. . . . Your Majesty should supplicate the Pope to have as His delegates in this region two religious persons, one from the order of Saint Francis and the other from the order of Santo Domingo."[42]

Only if these precautions are taken, Cortés writes, could in the New World be established a new church, in which God, more than in any other place, would be exalted and glorified. "It could be with certainty asserted that in a very brief period of time, it will be raised in these lands a new church, in which God will be more praised than in any other in the whole world."[43]

The bellicose, ambitious, and lascivious conqueror metamorphoses into an apostle of the American infidels. But beware: immediately after writing this paean to the new church to be developed in the New World, Cortés recommends that the natives of Michoacán, who refuse to submit to the Spanish conquerors, be enslaved. "We should make them war and take them as slaves. . . . Bringing these savages as slaves, to work in the gold mines, would produce to your Majesty and the Spanish people benefits, and it might even happen that thanks to such a familiarity with us some might even be redeemed."[44]

The new apostle to the natives is also their enslaver. Cortés's messianic providentialism does not bear to tolerate any insurmountable obstacle, especially if it comes from the infidels.

Prophetic Voice and Indignation

Cortés's messianic and militaristic providentialism does not represent the sole attitude of the Spanish protagonists of the conquest of America. Indeed, the sixteenth century abounds with different and contradictory voices and perspectives. It truly constitutes a polyphony, one not always harmonious. The basic failure of the perennial followers of the black legend is their inability to perceive the critical and important participation of the prophetic voice, of the prophetic church, in the conquest of America. Sixteenth-century Spain vibrates intensively with disputes and debates about the legitimacy and justice of the conquest. No official colonial axiom was left unquestioned.

It is hard to pinpoint when the debates begin. Maybe the disgust of father Bernard Boyl, who accompanied Columbus in the second journey and left the expedition in discomfiture, was a reaction to the attempt of the admiral to initiate a trans-Atlantic Indian slave trade. It is also possible that the sharp repudiation given in 1500 by Queen Isabella to such slave trade was not an impromptu solitary reaction of an ethically sensitive woman. She probably had received some unknown theological advice adverse to Columbus's slave initiatives. The record is not altogether clear. Some feet-upon-earth historians interpret Isabella's outburst—"Who does the Admiral think he is to dare distribute my vassals?"—as rather a clever political maneuver to inhibit the development in America of a powerful feudal class with extensive private holdings of lands and slaves.[45] That might be, but I doubt it was the only reason. Qualms about the theological legitimacy of enslaving infidels who had not injured in any way Christian nations might have weighed in the mind of the queen.[46] For the

Catholic Monarchs of fifteenth- and sixteenth-century Spain theological arguments did count,[47] even when, as always, kings and queens had a proclivity to
harmonize their theological views with their material and political interests.

Certainly, the critiques of the second decade of the sixteenth century were
consequences of serious and profound soul struggle.[48] That is clear at least with
respect to Bartolomé de las Casas. What Felipe Fernández-Armesto calls the
"sudden revelation"[49] of Las Casas was not so sudden. His *Historia de las Indias*
gives us a portrait of a man of faith, conscience, and courage, who, between
1502 and 1514, underwent a slow but inexorable spiritual transformation from
being another wealthy *encomendero,* a Spaniard who ruled Indians but also
sought to civilize and Christianize them, into the irate prophet that would
denounce to the church, the state, the whole world, and God, the sinful oppression of, ironically, the godless infidels by the God-fearing Christians.

It is las Casas who preserves in his *Historia* the first clear, unequivocal, and
loud voice of Christian prophetic protest.[50] By the end of 1511, the Dominican monks of Hispaniola were disgusted with the abuses received by the Native
Americans. They became convinced that such a mistreatment constituted a
violation of the so-called "donation bulls" decreed by Pope Alexander VI in
1493. The bulls had recognized Castilian sovereignty over the lands discovered
in order that the native communities be converted to the Christian faith,[51] and
the Dominican friars were not fool enough to confuse evangelization with slavery and demographic collapse. They also came to the conclusion that the European Christians in America were, according to the ecclesiastical norms, in mor-
tal sin, on the basis of their cruel conduct. The destiny of the Indians' bodies
and of the Europeans' souls weighed heavily in the minds of the friars, and
thus, they concluded, they could not keep silence anymore. They felt impelled
to protest by their religious vows. It is a religious imperative, not any alternative political or social conception, that promotes the first strong prophetic challenge of the conquest.

Las Casas's narration acquires dramatic overtones.[52] On the fourth Sunday
of Advent the prominent members of the colonial establishment received the
moral shock of their lives. After reading the biblical passage of John the Baptist (Matt. 3:3), "ego vox clamantis in deserto," the Dominican friar Antonio
de Montesinos, selected by his brethren for his homiletical abilities, pierced
the ears and minds of the respected white European and Christian hearers with
the following burning words:

> You are in mortal sin . . . for the cruelty and tyranny you use in dealing with
> these innocent people. Tell me, by what right or justice do you keep these Indi-
> ans in such a cruel and horrible servitude? On what authority have you waged
> a detestable war against these people, who dwelt quietly and peaceably on their
> own land? . . . [Y]ou kill them with your desire to extract and acquire gold every
> day. . . . Are not these people also human beings? Have they not rational souls?

Be certain that in such a state as this you can no more be saved than a Moor or a Turk.[53]

The commotion produced by the homily was such that the principal authorities of the Dominican order in Spain and King Ferdinand himself intervened with threatening admonitions. The royal order was categorical: "They [the Dominican friars] should never speak about this subject; neither in public, nor in private, neither directly, nor indirectly shall they ever refer to it."[54] The Dominican prior in Spain commanded silence to the rebel brethren: "*Sumittere intellectum vestrum*" ("Submit your intellect").[55] But it would not be so. The first prophetic voice had been uttered, in the unquenchable style of John the Baptist. From then on, the prophetic voice would never cease to claim for justice and mercy.[56]

The authority of the irate prophetic voice should not be underestimated. It was the guiding force behind the 1537 bull *Sublimis Deus* of Pope Paul III. After receiving a letter sent by several bishops of New Spain and Guatemala denouncing the exploitation suffered by the Native Americans, Paul III called for the recognition and respect of the humanity and freedom of the autochthonous communities:

> The enemy of the human race [Satan] . . . inspired his satellites who, to please him, have not hesitated to publish abroad that the Indians . . . should be treated as dumb brutes created for our service. . . . We . . . consider, however, that the Indians are truly men. . . . We define and declare . . . that . . . the said Indians and all other people who may later be discovered by Christians, are by no means to be deprived of their liberty or the possession of their property, even though they be outside the faith of Jesus Christ; and that they may and should, freely and legitimately, enjoy their liberty and the possession of their property; nor should they be in any way enslaved.[57]

The main exponent of the prophetic tradition was doubtless Bartolomé de las Casas.[58] The history of the conquest of the Americas cannot be narrated without constant reference to him. He was responsible for the preservation and transmission of the diary of Columbus's first journey.[59] His *Historia de las Indias* is one of the best sources for the first three decades of colonization and Christianization.[60] And during more than five decades, between 1514 and 1566, he filled the air with his strong comminations and the printing press with his burning treatises.

Las Casas never mellowed. His last letter to the Council of Indies summarizes and culminates his denunciations of five decades. It is brief, but its sharp, condemning prophetic tone can hardly be matched:

> 1. All conquests are unjust and tyrannical; 2. we have illegally usurped the kingdoms of the Indies; 3. all *encomiendas* are bad per se; 4. those who possess them and those who distribute them are in mortal sin; 5. the king has no more right

to justify the conquests and *encomiendas* than the Ottoman Turk to make war against Christians; 6. all fortunes made in the Indies are iniquitous; 7. if the guilty do not make restitution, they will not be saved; 8. the Indian nations have the right, which will be theirs till doomsday, to make us just war and erase us from the face of the earth.[61]

That strong statement was followed by an epistle to Pope Pius V.[62] Las Casas requests from the *Vicarius Christi* the promulgation of a decree that would: (a) anathematize all those who justify military conquest on the basis of the infidelity of the natives or their alleged rational inferiority; (b) order all bishops and ecclesiastical authorities to defend the powerless natives from the aggression and oppression of the powerful invaders, even, if necessary, to sacrifice their lives in their protection; and (c) make restitution of the wealth already accumulated by the young American church, thus cutting short its participation in the economic exploitation of the native peoples.

This denunciatory type of writing made las Casas, up to this day, an extremely controversial figure, the most polemical antagonist of the conquest of America. He was harshly censored by the Franciscan Motolinia and eulogized by the also Franciscan Mendieta. Oviedo and López de Gomara, the two great chroniclers, were his personal adversaries, but Herrera y Tordesillas as well as numberless other historians were indebted to his research. Cortés considered him his enemy, but Charles V respected him so much that he wanted to make him bishop of Cuzco, probably the wealthiest American diocese of the time (las Casas finally accepted the bishopric of Chiapas, a poor region between Guatemala and Mexico).[63]

He has been extolled by people like the Cuban patriot José Martí, who in his *Edad de oro* considered him a paradigmatic figure, at the same level with the Latin American liberators Miguel Hidalgo, José Francisco de San Martín, and Simón Bolívar.[64] Bolívar, on his part, once suggested that a new capital city, named Las Casas, be built for his dreamed-of unified great Colombia.[65] Spanish scholars and patricians have either anathematized or canonized him. The eminent historian Manuel Giménez Fernández dedicated many years of scholarly efforts to his unfinished monumental biography of las Casas,[66] whereas the great literary critic Ramón Menéndez Pidal wrote a stinging book to lambaste las Casas.[67]

Many of these opposite evaluations, be they positive or negative, miss the essential mystery of this man. *Las Casas was a man educated in the spirit and style of the biblical prophets.* His conversion to the freedom of the American communities was intimately linked, as in Saint Augustine's case, to a biblical text. In the case of las Casas the text was Sirach/Ecclesiasticus 34:24–25 (20–21 in some versions):

> To offer a sacrifice from the
> possessions of the poor
> is like killing a son

before his father's eyes.
Bread is life to the destitute,
and to deprive them of it is murder.[68]

The Latin text used by las Casas is even stronger. "To offer a sacrifice from the possessions of the poor is like killing a son before his father's eyes" is rendered: *"Qui offert sacrificium ex substantia pauperum, quasi qui victimat filium in conspectu patris sui."*[69] The expression *"ex substantia pauperum,"* "from the substance of the poor," implies that what is taken from the dispossessed is decisive for their existence. The crux of the matter is indeed the life or death of the Native American peoples.

The old discussion about las Casas and Spanish national identity can be settled only from the perspective of the prophetic understanding of the relationship between nation and mission. The prophets of the Old Testament have a peculiar love for Israel, their nation. It is a scorching and ethically demanding love. It is a love that requires justice and righteousness. This is the school of mercy and justice in which las Casas learned his particular historical role. To consider las Casas anti-Spanish, as some have suggested, would be like accusing Jeremiah, Isaiah, or Amos of anti-Semitism.

Las Casas, like Columbus or Cortés, developed a messianic providential concept of himself, but with a strong prophetic character and content. His messianic consciousness compelled him to consider himself as the chosen prophet who would chastise his nation in the name of the God of justice and mercy.[70] His patriotism reveals itself not in chauvinistic eulogies to the fatherland, but in the courage to speak the word of God against those who dared to destroy the poor and powerless, forgetting that they might be, in their destitution and poverty, the predilect creatures of God.[71]

Edwin Sylvest has argued that the Bible was the main source of authority and inspiration for the mendicant orders during the period previous to Trent and the Counter-Reformation.[72] In las Casas's case, at least, the biblical prophets and the Jesus of the Gospels, not an abstract concept of human rights, provided the paradigmatic model for his providential self-understanding. The hermeneutical circle between the Bible and the lived experience of cruelty led him into the tragic but splendid dilemma of prophetism and patriotism.

Latin American Christianity—as well as Latin American cultural identity and national consciousness—was born in the midst of the encounter and clash between two paradigmatic and paradoxical sources—the messianic providentialism guiding the violence of the *conquistadores* and the prophetic indignation reacting in the name of the biblical God of mercy and justice. We cannot escape that history. It is an essential dimension of our cultural and religious memory.

THREE

Is God Violent?

Theological Options in the Antislavery Movement

Dan McKanan

It is no accident that this volume on Christianity and violence is associated with Wheaton College's Center for Applied Christian Ethics. We naturally think of violence as a topic for Christian ethics—it has to do with what Christian people should or should not do. But Christian ethics is necessarily rooted in Christian theology. Our views of what people should do are shaped by our understanding of what God does and who God is. If we begin by asking, "May Christians use violence?" we will eventually come round to asking, also, "Is God violent?" That is, is God ultimately responsible for the violence that exists in nature and society? Can violent experiences ever disclose God's presence in the world?

To be sure, the questions of human violence and divine violence are logically separable. Some Christians, in fact, have taught that God claims violence as a divine prerogative while forbidding it to human beings. Some might even argue the reverse: that God is nonviolent but sanctions human violence in some circumstances. But human violence and divine violence are hard to separate at the emotional level. Christians who embrace even the most cautious version of the just war theory often come round to seeing God's hand vividly present in their every military adventure. Similarly, Christian pacifists are most likely to take risks for peace if they believe that the ultimate power in the universe is also nonviolent.

In this essay, I shall look closely at four nineteenth-century Americans who struggled to make sense of the connection between human violence and divine violence, and between human nonviolence and divine nonviolence. These four—Frederick Douglass, William Lloyd Garrison, Harriet Beecher Stowe, and Abraham Lincoln—had much in common. All were influenced by both orthodox and liberal strands of Protestantism, and yet none was able to embrace the Protestant theological system without reservation. All were fiercely opposed to slavery; indeed, in some way each gave his or her life to the struggle against slavery. And yet none was able to give a theologically consistent account of either the violence intrinsic to slavery or the revolutionary violence to which opponents of slavery sometimes resorted. Their staunch ethical commitments were grounded in theological ambivalence—an ambivalence that continues to haunt contemporary Christians who are opposed to violence.

The basic problem was one of theodicy. Was God responsible for the violence of slavery? If so, why should the Christian expect God to support the nonviolent struggle against slavery? Perhaps God had some mysterious purpose for slavery, and would end it only when that purpose had been fulfilled. But if God was not responsible for the violence of slavery, why should the Christian believe that God had the power to end it at all? Perhaps God's power was effective only in places far distant from slavery—in heaven, in Canada, or within the psyche of the rebellious slave.

As nineteenth-century Christians sought an alternative to these two unsatisfactory positions, they returned again and again to the two central ideas of providence and the *imago dei*. The doctrine of providence holds that God is present throughout history, and that even the most troubling or violent incidents have a place in God's mysterious plan. The doctrine of the *imago dei* holds that God is uniquely present in the human conscience, which is created in the image of God, and thus that God's will can best be seen in the conscientious effort to transform the world. The two claims are not inconsistent, but in nineteenth-century America they marked a major dividing line in Protestant theology. Orthodox Protestants, following John Calvin, placed central emphasis on providence. For them, the world was a "theater of God's glory," and they accepted violent events as "chastisements" intended to prod them to a deeper respect for that glory. Liberal Protestants, by contrast, complained that the orthodox understanding of original sin obscured God's image in the individual human being. For them, the Christian's task was, in William Ellery Channing's words, to seek "that perfection of the soul, which constitutes it a bright image of God."[1]

A position of ethical nonviolence could be articulated in terms of either theology. Orthodox pacifists, like David Low Dodge, held that Christians were bound by divine decree to renounce violence, but that war, slavery, and even murder nevertheless served the mysterious purposes of providence.[2] Such pacifists could hold little faith that human effort would bring an end to earthly

violence; at best, they hoped for providential intervention or even an apocalyptic war to end violence. Liberal pacifists, like Henry Clarke Wright,
responded by placing all their faith in human effort, insisting that the only true
theology was an "anthropology" emphasizing the human capacity for love and
sympathy.[3] These pacifists, however, could hardly show that love and sympathy really had the power to overcome entrenched systems of violence.

Given these difficulties, opponents of slavery like Douglass, Garrison, Stowe,
and Lincoln could not rest comfortably in either theology. Instead, they vac-
illated inconsistently, sometimes placing their faith in the nonviolent *imago
dei* and at other times anticipating an apocalyptic intervention of Providence.
At times, also, they sought to bridge the gap by seeing themselves, or other
activists, as both conscientious imitators of God *and* passive instruments of
providence. This move had the effect of diluting their commitment to nonviolence, for the most "providentially" successful activists were not always the
most "conscientiously" committed to nonviolence. By 1865 all four individuals had to confront the puzzle that slavery had been destroyed by neither apocalyptic intervention nor conscientious activism, but by the military might of
the Union Army. This, I contend, marked the end of an era in American theology—but let us turn first to the individual stories.

Frederick Douglass's story begins in 1824, on the plantation of Colonel
Edward Lloyd, a prominent politician and one of the most prosperous slave
owners in Maryland. Or, perhaps, it begins in 1855, for I shall describe events
as they appear in Frederick Douglass's second autobiography, written thirty
years after the fact. Douglass came to the plantation as a seven-year-old boy,
the slave not of Colonel Lloyd but of Lloyd's employee Captain Aaron Anthony.
Previously he had lived with his brothers and sisters at his grandparents' secluded
cabin; now he came face-to-face with the habitual cruelty of plantation slavery. He soon heard rumors that his master was also his father, and he also realized that his aunt Esther was now the object of their master's unwelcome sexual attention. Esther, for her part, was in love with another slave, and this
provoked Captain Anthony's fierce jealousy. One morning, young Frederick
woke to the sounds of Esther's "shrieks and piteous cries." Looking out of the
kitchen closet where he slept, he saw that Captain Anthony had tied Esther's
wrists and hung her from a ceiling beam, and was whipping her with a cow
skin. Watching the blood stream down Esther's back, Frederick was not sure
whether to pity or identify with his aunt: "From my heart I pitied her, and—
child though I was—the outrage kindled in me a feeling far from peaceful; but
I was hushed, terrified, stunned, and could do nothing, and the fate of Esther
might be mine next."[4]

This traumatic experience forced young Frederick to ask the fundamental
questions of slave theodicy: "Why am I a slave? Why are some people slaves,
and others masters? Was there ever a time when this was not so? How did the

relation commence?" When he asked these questions of his fellow slaves, they gave him a stock providential answer: God, for his own mysterious purposes, had made white people to be masters and blacks to be slaves, and this system was "best for everybody." But Douglass resisted this explanation, for it "came, point blank, against all my notions of goodness." It was also inconsistent, insofar as it presupposed a perfect correlation between race and social status. "I knew of blacks who were not slaves; I knew of whites who were not slave-holders; and I knew of persons who were nearly white, who were slaves." Eventually, Douglass concluded that the true root of slavery was human violence. People born in West Africa became slaves through the violence of slave traders; their children born in America became slaves only through the whippings inflicted by their so-called masters. "It was not color, but crime," Douglass concluded, "not God, but man, that afforded the true explanation of the existence of slavery."[5]

This conclusion had profound theological implications. By ascribing an entire social institution to human and *not* divine agency, Douglass implicitly denied the traditional doctrine of providence, according to which *everything* ultimately has some place in God's plan. This was a new departure in anti-slavery thought. Most earlier activists, including the ex-slave Olaudah Equiano, had accepted the popular notion that God had willed the enslavement of Africans as a means to the eventual Christianization of Africa. Often, they squared this notion with their own opposition to slavery by drawing a distinction (implicit or explicit) between God's providential government and God's moral government. According to this distinction, God governs in two ways: providentially, by determining everything that happens, and morally, by setting up a system of ethical rules. Disobedient humans may violate God's moral government, but no one can escape the rule of providence. Instead, providence "overrules" moral violations, turning them to its own mysterious purposes. This distinction led the Christian pacifist David Low Dodge to affirm both "that war is a judgment of God's providence" *and* that it is "a sin of the highest magnitude," and even to claim that the assassin's weapon is "under [God's] control."[6]

Douglass exploded the distinction between moral and providential government, and thus placed the issue of slavery in a theological rather than a narrowly ethical context. For him, the realm of slavery—whether the individual plantation, the slaveholding South, or the entire United States—had a special theological status. It existed outside the rule of Providence. An event like Esther's whipping was "the blood-stained gate, the entrance to the hell of slavery," and within that "hell" prayers and tears could not ward off the "fiendish barbarity" of the slave-masters. Subject to the "dehumanizing character" and "soul-killing effects of slavery," the slaves had no access to genuine religion but only to "the corrupt, slaveholding, women-whipping, cradle-plundering, partial and hypocritical Christianity of this land." At the nadir of Douglass's own life as a slave, this "sham religion . . . cast in my mind a doubt upon all religion, and led me to the conviction that prayers were unavailing and delusive."[7]

Paradoxically, Douglass's recognition of the godforsaken character of the slave world gave him a profound hope. Immediately after his discovery that man, not God, had created slavery, he realized a corollary: "What man can make, man can unmake." This was "knowledge quite worth possessing," for it filled him with a fierce determination to break free of his shackles. By becoming an atheist to the religion of slavery, Douglass recognized his own human capacity to resist slavery, and thus began to imagine the possibility of a different sort of world and a different sort of religion. Even though he knew nothing of the free states or the world beyond slavery, he was "most strongly impressed with the idea of being a freeman some day." The road to the free world began in Douglass's own soul; it was "an inborn dream of my human nature—a constant menace to slavery—and one which all the powers of slavery were unable to silence or extinguish."[8]

Because Douglass vested his hopes in "human nature" rather than in a providential governance of the world, some orthodox critics concluded that he had secularized the problem of slavery, taking it out of a theological context altogether. Even Harriet Beecher Stowe scolded Douglass for his attacks on the church and reminded him that "Every thing is against you—but *Jesus Christ* is for you."[9] Stowe failed to recognize that Douglass's position was deeply rooted in the theology of the *imago dei*. Even as Douglass downplayed God's power over society, he emphasized God's power and presence in his own soul. By appealing to the "inborn dream of my human nature," Douglass echoed the Jeffersonian theology of the Declaration of Independence. His fellow fugitive Henry Bibb made the same point even more vividly when he wrote that his first encounter with slavery's violence "kindled a fire of liberty within my breast which has never yet been quenched. This seemed to me to be a part of my nature; it was first revealed to me by the inevitable laws of nature's God."[10]

This Jeffersonian theology runs throughout Douglass's autobiography, though at times he expresses it in the language of providential doctrine. He makes much, for example, of the fact that as a boy he was sent to the port city of Baltimore, where he gained many of the skills that would ultimately help him escape. At the time, and for much of his life, he viewed "this event as a special interposition of Divine Providence in my favor"—but in autobiographical retrospect he concedes that such a view may have been "superstitious and egotistical." Nevertheless, he insists that he must be "true to myself" by acknowledging the power of his early faith in providence: "In the darkest hours of my career in slavery, this living word of faith and spirit of hope departed not from me, but remained like ministering angels to cheer me through the gloom." Douglass is liberated not by an actual providence operating in the world, but by the *belief* in providence acting in his own soul.[11]

Because Douglass's providence is inside himself, he can portray his struggle with the forces of slavery not as part of the providential plan but as a struggle between providence and human evil. The outcome of this struggle is not fore-ordained, for Douglass is surrounded by powers inimical to his own providential faith. Indeed, at the nadir of Douglass's life—six months into his stay with a professional "slavebreaker," Covey—his providential spark is actually snuffed out by Covey's violence. Even when alone in the woods, he cannot pray, for "the sham religion which everywhere prevailed" has convinced him "that prayers were unavailing and delusive." This dark night of the soul, Douglass makes clear, is not providentially ordained as a chastisement or preparation for grace. Instead, it is a genuine death of the soul: "Mr. Covey succeeded in breaking me. . . . [T]he cheerful spark that lingered about my eye died; the dark night of slavery closed in upon me, and behold a man transformed into a brute!" Douglass's defiance of Covey is thus nothing less than a resurrection: "It was a glorious resurrection, from the tomb of slavery, to the heaven of freedom. . . . However long I might remain a slave in form, the day had passed forever when I could be a slave in fact."[12]

A number of scholars have noted that Douglass's account of his escape both runs parallel to and diverges from the classic conversion paradigm. It has the emotional intensity and life-changing effects of a conversion, and yet Douglass makes very clear that it is not sinful to be a slave, that the fall into slavery was not ordained by God, and that he does not need to acquire a new self.[13] What Douglass does, I would suggest, is offer a conversion that is a resurrection rather than a rebirth. It does not involve replacing an originally corrupt self with a new and purer self, but rather restoring the life of an originally pure self that has been killed by violent institutions.

The power that effects this resurrection inheres in the self's divinity rather than in the prevenient grace of an external God. Unlike orthodox conversion, it is not guaranteed in advance by the atoning sacrifice of Jesus Christ. On the contrary, the self and God could, for Douglass, be vindicated only in the concrete event of liberation. Up to the eve of his escape, Douglass admitted, he continued to ask fundamental questions of theodicy: "May not this, after all, be God's work? May He not, for wise ends, have doomed me to this lot?" Such questions simply could not be answered *theoretically*, but they were *practically* dissolved by the escape itself: "The contest was now ended; the chain was severed; God and right stood vindicated. I WAS A FREEMAN, and the voice of peace and joy thrilled my heart."[14]

This contingent, internalized view of God's providential power led Douglass to a rather nuanced understanding of violence. Though he absolved God of any responsibility for the violence of slavery, he simultaneously gave God credit, implicitly, for the much milder violence he used to bring about his own escape. Though Douglass's actual escape did not involve violence, the event that triggered his resurrection experience was his forceful refusal to be whipped by Covey. Douglass's account of this is oddly ambivalent: in places he revels in the "fighting madness [that] had come upon me," while in other places he stresses the defensive character of his action. He also offers two competing explanations of why his resistance was so important. First, he claims that "a man, without force, is without the essential dignity of humanity," but a few sentences later he reflects that "I had reached the point at which I was *not afraid to die*. This spirit made me a freeman in *fact*, while I remained a slave in *form*."[15] The tension between these two claims runs parallel to that between the providential and *imago dei* theologies. Was Douglass freed by his use of physical violence in the world, or simply by the courage present in his own heart? He could not resolve the puzzle—but simply by raising it, he provoked the wrath of his more ardently nonviolent mentor, William Lloyd Garrison.

Fifteen years before the publication of *My Bondage and My Freedom,* Douglass's career as an antislavery lecturer began when he encountered Garrison, then the most prominent of white abolitionists. In August 1841 Douglass made his way from New Bedford, Massachusetts, where he worked in the shipyards, to the island of Nantucket, in order to attend an antislavery convention. Despite his newness to the movement, Douglass was allowed to make a speech at the convention, and his performance made a big impression on Garrison, whose recollection of the moment is worth quoting at length:

> I shall never forget his first speech at the convention. . . . I think I never hated slavery so intensely as at that moment; certainly, my perception of the enormous outrage which is inflicted by it, on the godlike nature of its victims, was rendered far more clear than ever. There stood one, in physical proportion and stature commanding and exact—in intellect richly endowed—in natural eloquence a prodigy—in soul manifestly "created but a little lower than the angels"—yet a slave, ay, a fugitive slave,—trembling for his safety, hardly daring to believe that on the American soil, a single white person could be found who would befriend him at all hazards, for the love of God and humanity![16]

The key to this passage is the little phrase "the godlike nature of its victims." In Douglass, Garrison saw a slave and a victim, but he also saw a human being and, most importantly, an image of God. The doctrine of the *imago dei* was thus the key to his theological interpretation of slavery and violence.

Just who was Garrison, and why was he so preoccupied with the *imago dei*? It may be best to characterize him using some of the phrases that were current in the 1840s. In the language of that decade, he was an "ultra" reformer, indeed, the most "ultra" of the "ultraists"; he was a "non-resistant"; and he was a "come-outer." As an "ultraist," Garrison believed in taking principles to their logical conclusions. If slavery was bad because it compromised individual freedom, then so was the inequality of the sexes, the imposition of mandatory Sabbath observance, and even tariffs and other barriers to free trade. If war was bad because it destroyed the divine image in the human body, then so was the use of coercive police powers, and so was voting for a government that might sponsor an army or a police force. This particular sort of ultraism is what made Garrison a "non-resistant." He believed that Christians should never resist evil with evil, and that "under the new covenant, the forgiveness, instead of the punishment of enemies, has been enjoined upon all [Christ's] disciples, in all cases whatsoever."[17] This nonresistance was quite different from passivity. Garrison sought to "assail iniquity" with his words, and even to overthrow governments through the "spiritual regeneration of their subjects." He also encouraged his supporters to resist evil by "coming out": physically separating oneself from any church and any government that supported or tolerated violence. Garrison's commitment to ultraism, nonresistance, and come-outerism set him apart from the majority of white abolitionists, and yet it also made him the personification of the abolitionist movement in the eyes of both friend and foe. Depending on one's perspective, Garrison represented either the fervent idealism of abolition or else its inevitable dangers.

Garrison's "come-outerism" led many contemporaries to brand him as an infidel, and some twentieth-century historians to characterize him as a sectarian pacifist who wished to create a pure church separate from the corruptions of the larger world. In fact, he was neither an atheist nor an Anabaptist, but rather a committed Christian liberal. Though his views were extreme, they were rooted in the consensus values of the larger society. The two documents on which Garrison based most of his rhetoric were the New Testament, especially the Sermon on the Mount, and the Declaration of Independence. For Garrison, these two bore witness to a common truth: that human beings are created in God's image and thus have a right to absolute freedom, especially freedom from all coercion and violence. Garrison made no distinction between the authority of the New Testament and that of the Declaration; both, ultimately, were authoritative only because they corresponded to the witness of the individual conscience. Thus, Garrison could call the Declaration "a revelation adapted to the common sense of mankind," and could insist further that the ultimate authority was "the law written by the finger of God upon the heart of man."

This latter phrase was a liberal commonplace, and its roots go back at least to the Scottish common sense philosophical school of the late eighteenth century. Scottish thinkers including Francis Hutcheson, Thomas Reid, Dugald Stewart, and Lord Kames all reacted against John Locke's view of the human mind as a "blank slate," insisting instead that we are born with a "moral sense" in addition to the five physical senses. This inborn capacity to tell right from wrong gave each person a bias toward virtue—in sharp contrast to the bias toward depravity postulated by orthodox Protestants.[18] In North America, this view was picked up by Thomas Jefferson. "The moral sense," he wrote to John

Adams late in life, "is as much a part of our constitution as that of feeling, seeing, or hearing; as a wise creator must have seen to be necessary in an animal destined to live in society; that every human mind feels pleasure in doing good to another."[19] Jefferson enshrined his understanding of the content of the moral sense in the Declaration of Independence, where he claimed that human equality and liberty were both given by God and "self evident" to humanity. Moral sense theory also had a big influence on Protestant liberals like the Unitarian preacher William Channing, who recognized its intimate connection with the ancient Christian doctrine of the *imago dei*. Garrison was not a Unitarian, but many of his closest associates were members of Channing's congregation and he himself was intimately familiar with Channing's theology.

Garrison, then, stood consciously in a long liberal theological tradition. He differed from the majority of liberals only in his "ultraism"—in his willingness to destroy even liberal institutions if they compromised, even slightly, the liberal principle of absolute individual freedom. The United States Constitution, for example, was unacceptable because it allowed the government to execute criminals and declare wars, and it recognized slavery by means of the notorious provision that slaves would be counted as only three-fifths of a person in determining legislative districts. Thus, while the Declaration was "a revelation adapted to the common sense of mankind," the Constitution was an "infamous bargain" by which the founding fathers "virtually dethroned the Most High God, and trampled beneath their feet their own solemn and heaven-attested Declaration."[20]

This passage suggests the theological ambivalence underlying Garrison's ethical convictions. Was it really possible for the founding fathers to "dethrone the Most High God"? Or was their violation of the moral law only a "virtual" dethroning that left God's providential government firmly in place? Similarly, what did Garrison mean when he wrote, in the Non-Resistance Society's founding declaration, that "the dogma, that all the governments of the world are approvingly ordained of God . . . is not less absurd than impious"? Was he rejecting the providential theology of Romans 13, in which Paul claims that all governments are ordained by God? Or did he insert the word "approvingly" to clarify that God's providential "ordaining" of governments did not imply a moral "approval" of them?[21]

Garrison avoided giving clear answers to these questions, I suspect, because such answers would have distracted attention from his main point: God is present first and foremost in the acts of the nonviolent Christian. Christ's kingdom, he predicted, "is destined to break in pieces and consume all other kingdoms," but it will do so entirely through the efforts of subjects who "are forbidden to fight." Indeed, he wrote, "we expect to prevail through the foolishness of preaching." The power of preaching, and of moral persuasion more generally, was divine but not supernatural. That is, it relied on the divine image that was naturally present in the human heart. Conscience was the foundation of Garrison's revolution, and he believed that he had history as well as God on his side. "The history of mankind," he wrote rather optimistically, "is crowded with evidences, proving that physical coercion is not adapted to moral regeneration; that the sinful disposition of man can be subdued only by love; that evil can be exterminated from the earth only by goodness."[22]

Garrison's nonresistant friend, Henry Clarke Wright, buttressed this claim with dozens of saccharine stories about malicious little boys who do not hurt rabbits because they don't fight back, but Garrison's own optimism was tempered by his keen awareness of the intractability of slavery. Many slaves refused to "return evil for evil," and yet they remained slaves. In light of this fact, Garrison was willing to recognize a certain divine inspiration in men, like Nat Turner or John Brown, who instigated slave rebellions. God was not responsible for their use of violence, but God did inspire their love of freedom. The fact that people would use violence on behalf of liberty, when it had so often been used on behalf of oppression, was a sign that God was active in the world: "It is an indication of progress, and a positive moral growth; it is one way to get up to the sublime platform of non-resistance." Garrison was less charitable to men like Douglass who embraced and then renounced nonresistant principles, but he reserved his deepest scorn for those whites who endorsed the American Revolution but rejected slave rebellions. "It is not for the American people, as a nation," he wrote, "to denounce slave rebellion as bloody or monstrous. . . . Every sentence that they write . . . against foreign oppression, is a call upon their slaves to destroy them."[23]

Garrison's qualified admiration for Nat Turner and John Brown also reflected his underlying penchant for the apocalyptic. In the very first issue of the *Liberator* he fantasized that both the tyrannies of Europe and the American slavocracy might soon "feel the upheavings of the earthquake which is to overthrow its strong towers, and the heat of a fire which is to melt every chain." "Have we no reason," he concluded, "to fear the judgments of Heaven upon our guilty land?"[24] It was typical of Garrison that he framed this as a question rather than a statement of dogma. His consistent strategy was to hint at apocalypse, to pose it as a possibility that might yet be averted through spiritual regeneration, and to leave ambiguous the question of whether it would be a divine intervention or simply the consequence of natural laws. The rhetorical effect of this ambiguity is obvious: it allowed Garrison to appeal to two factions within his readership: to Northern white liberals who optimistically assumed that they could change the world through sheer moral effort, and to free blacks and fugitive slaves who knew too well that pious nonresistance alone was not likely to change many slave owners. However effective rhetorically, it is not very satisfying theologically. And yet perhaps Garrison's point, like that of Frederick Douglass, was that in a violent world theology must be ambiguous. The true character of God's power will be revealed only in the moment when all people are free from violence.

Garrison held no patent on ambiguous apocalypticism. Like him, Harriet Beecher Stowe *hoped* that slavery could end through the moral efforts of non-violent Christians, but *feared* it would end in an apocalyptic conflagration. In the conclusion to *Uncle Tom's Cabin,* she made a classically sentimental appeal to moral feeling: "There is one thing that every individual can do,—they can see to it that *they feel right.* An atmosphere of sympathetic influence encircles every human being; and the man or woman who *feels* strongly, healthily and justly, on the great interests of humanity, is a constant benefactor to the human race." But she then added an apocalyptic threat. An "earthquake" was coming, she predicted, a *"day of vengeance"* in which Christ "shall break in pieces the oppressor." It could be avoided only if both North and South took advantage of the "day of grace" by committing to "repentance, justice and mercy."[25]

Despite this fundamental agreement on the theology of violence, Stowe saw herself as a fierce theological opponent of Garrison. When he invited her to participate in a twentieth anniversary celebration for the *Liberator,* she replied that she was a faithful reader and that "to *me* the paper is decidedly valuable." But, she added pointedly, "What I fear is that it will take from poor Uncle Tom his bible & give him nothing in its place."[26]

At first glance, Stowe's criticism seems like a straightforward defense of biblical literalism against the attacks of Garrison and other liberals. This would not be surprising, given Stowe's family background: her father, Lyman Beecher, was the scourge of Unitarian liberals, a fierce defender of traditional views of biblical authority and divine sovereignty. And yet Stowe was hardly a consistent adherent of her father's theology. The orthodox doctrines of predestination and original sin offended her much as they did Garrison. For her, orthodox views of divine sovereignty were relics from the age of human monarchies, and she described the Hopkinsian view that Christians ought to be willing to be damned for the greater glory of God as a "refined poetry of torture."[27] Her novels are filled with villains who have fully internalized the doctrine of innate depravity, and who corrupt their children by expecting them to be equally depraved. Many of her heroes and heroines, by contrast, seem quite Garrisonian in their willingness to trust their own natural affections and sympathies.

More to the point, Stowe's understanding of biblical authority was far from orthodox. She recognized that both the Old and New Testament take slavery for granted as an inherent aspect of human society, but she did not let this fact impede her abolitionist commitments. In *Uncle Tom's Cabin* she presents several exegetical debates on slavery, and, at a strictly logical level, the proslavery characters usually win these debates. The antislavery characters do not attempt to refute biblical arguments, but appeal silently to feeling: one "smoke[s] on like a volcano" after having his say; another sits silently; still another "whistle[s] a tune." This strategy has its intended effect on at least one half-hearted defender of slavery, who has "the sense in which some logicians on this particular subject do not excel,—that of saying nothing, where nothing could be said."[28] Stowe clearly believed that liberal appeals to conscience could override literal appeals to the Bible.

In her second antislavery novel, *Dred,* Stowe went a step further, acknowledging that the Bible could mean virtually anything to anybody. Yet, paradoxically, she saw this as an argument in favor of biblical authority. The Bible's malleability was the source of its power. In revelation, as in nature, "there is something . . . for every phase of man's nature; and hence its endless and stimulating force."[29] The same principle was implicit, earlier, in Stowe's depiction of Uncle Tom's Bible-reading habits. Though only marginally literate, Tom reads regularly, recruits his friends to read with him, and marks the passages he finds most inspiring. When he falls into the hands of the brutal Simon Legree, the Bible becomes his lifeline, keeping his spirit alive in a place where the other slaves have been brutalized by toil. Yet this life-giving power seems to depend on Tom's uneducated simplicity: he is not troubled by "a thousand questions of authenticity, and correctness of translation." Unhindered by questions, Tom can reflect that the Bible "must be true; for, if not true, how could he live?"[30]

This passage suggests Stowe's real objection to Garrison. Her complaint was not that he denied the literal authority of the Bible, but that he failed to see that it had a life-giving power that transcended its literal meaning. It didn't matter whether the Bible was literally opposed to slavery, or whether Tom possessed the scholarly tools to make a judgment on that question; what mattered was that the Bible had a supernatural power that allowed Tom to stand courageously in the face of horrific violence. More broadly, Stowe objected to the naturalism that pervaded Garrison's theology. Garrison believed that all humans are naturally capable of exercising perfect nonviolence, and that the doctrines of supernatural religion only distracted people from the gospel's ethical demands. Stowe shared his enthusiasm for nonviolence but regarded it as a supernatural gift, imparted by the Bible and by the indwelling of Christ. She could thus join Garrison in his critique of violent providentialism, and go even further in depicting God as nonviolent.

Stowe's great exemplars of Christian nonviolence were Uncle Tom and Little Eva—an elderly Methodist slave and the frail white girl who befriends him. Little Eva dies early in the novel, of tuberculosis; Tom dies later at the hands of his demonic master, Simon Legree. Both deaths obviously echo the death of Christ, and both have immediate, supernatural effects. Eva's death is "the victory without the battle,—the crown without the conflict." It enables her to distribute curls of her hair to the community, one of which will eventually have a talismanic power over Simon Legree, and helps her extract from her father a promise to emancipate his slaves. Tom's death guarantees the escape of his friends Cassy and Emmeline and instantly converts Sambo and Quimbo, Legree's brutal accomplices in his murder.[31] Given the significance Stowe ascribes to these two deaths (and to the deaths of heroines in most of her subsequent novels), there is justice in Leslie Fiedler's comment that "not love but death is Mrs. Stowe's true Muse."[32]

Stowe's two dying saints, Tom and Eva, are for her at once models of human action and of divine action. Again and again, Stowe attributes to God both the absolute sympathy and the apparent powerlessness of Tom and Eva. Effectively eliminating divine omnipotence in order to affirm divine omnipresence in a violent world, she describes a God who is present at every calamity, who listens to every prayer, but who rarely responds. This first becomes clear when Tom is en route from Kentucky to Louisiana on an Ohio River ferryboat filled with other bereaved slaves. Tom overhears a slave woman bidding her husband a final farewell, and the narrator comments that the story "of heartstrings rent and broken . . . needs not to be told;—every day is telling it,—telling it, too, in the ear of One who is not deaf, though he be long silent."[33] Tom then befriends a woman who has just lost her child; he tells of Jesus' love and the promise of heaven, but she is too grief-stricken to hear. Stowe's poignant, oddly pacific narration of her suicide echoes Frederick Douglass's depiction of the slave South as a godforsaken universe:

> Night came on,—night calm, unmoved, and glorious, shining down with her innumerable and solemn angel eyes, twinkling, beautiful, but silent. There was no speech nor language, no pitying voice or helping hand, from that distant sky. One after another, the voices of business or pleasure died away; all on the boat were sleeping, and the ripples at the prow were plainly heard. Tom stretched himself out on a box, and there, as he lay, he heard, ever and anon, a smothered sob or cry from the prostate creature,—"O! what shall I do? O Lord! O good Lord, do help me!" and so, ever and anon, until the murmur died away in silence.[34]

Godforsakenness resurfaces in a powerful way three hundred pages later, when Tom arrives at the Legree plantation in the Red River Valley. Here Tom is introduced to Legree's spurned mistress Cassy, a proud and brilliant woman who has suffered the worst of all slavery's evils. "The Lord never visits these parts," she assures Tom at their first meeting. Later, when she has told him of her many tribulations and he continues to suggest that she look to Jesus for living water, she elaborates, "I used to see the picture of him, over the altar, when I was a girl . . . but *he isn't here!* There's nothing here, but sin and long, long despair! O!" Gradually, Tom comes to see her point. As the workload increases at the height of the cotton-picking season, as weeks pass without any word from his Kentucky friends (who Tom hopes will come to redeem him), and as Tom becomes increasingly aware of slavery's degrading effects on all those around him, he slips into a dark night of the soul. Physically and spiritually exhausted, he stops reading the Bible and must even "crush back to his soul bitter thoughts,—that it was vain to serve God, that God had forgotten him." Noticing Tom's despair, Legree is exultant and invites Tom to discard his

Bible and "join my church!" The best response Tom can muster is that whether or not the Lord helps him he will continue to believe.[35]

For Stowe, paradoxically, such scenes of earthly godforsakenness are the places where God, in Christ, is most fully present. Thus Tom's dark night ends with a mystic vision of the crucified Christ:

> The atheistic taunts of his cruel master sunk his before dejected soul to the lowest ebb; and, though the hand of faith still held to the eternal rock, it was a numb, despairing grasp. Tom sat, like one stunned, at the fire. Suddenly everything around him seemed to fade, and a vision rose before him of one crowned with thorns, buffeted and bleeding. Tom gazed, in awe and wonder, at the majestic patience of the face; the deep, pathetic eyes thrilled him to his inmost heart; his soul woke, as, with floods of emotion, he stretched out his hands and fell upon his knees,—when, gradually, the vision changed: the sharp thorns became rays of glory; and, in splendor inconceivable, he saw that same face bending compassionately towards him, and a voice said, "He that overcometh shall sit down with me on my throne, even as I also overcome, and am set down with my Father on his throne."[36]

This vision both anticipates Tom's death and infuses him with the power to defy Legree to the end. He experiences "an inviolable sphere of peace" that places him beyond "the bleeding of earthly regrets"; indeed, his will is "now entirely merged in the divine."[37]

Tom's vision changes the entire theological calculus of the novel. The power that was at first dispersed in all the natural affections of this earth—in a slave mother's love for her children, a slave man's passion to be free, and a Quaker matron's sympathy for the oppressed—is now concentrated in a Christic power that is *always* suffering on earth, yet always triumphant in heaven. This theology had already been suggested when, a few chapters earlier, Tom tells Cassy, "Ye said the Lord took sides against us, because he lets us be 'bused and knocked round; but ye see what comes on his own Son,—the blessed Lord of Glory,—wasn't he allays poor? and have we, any on us, yet come so low as he come?" It is reiterated in Stowe's later novels: in *Dred,* the pious slave Milly has a vision of Jesus "suffering, bearing with us, year in and year out—bearing—bearing—bearing so patient! 'Peared like, it wa'n't just on de cross; but, bearing always, everywhar!"[38] And *The Minister's Wooing,* Stowe's most theological novel, contains an elaborate apotheosis that simply identifies Christ with sorrow:

> Sorrow is divine. Sorrow is reigning on the throne of the universe, and the crown of all crowns has been one of thorns. There have been many books that treat of the mystery of sorrow, but only one that bids us glory in tribulation, and count it all joy when we fall into divers afflictions, that so we may be associated with that great fellowship of suffering of which the Incarnate God is the head, and through which He is carrying a redemptive conflict to a glorious victory over evil. If we suffer with Him, we shall also reign with Him.[39]

Here the distance between Stowe and Garrison becomes crystal clear. For Garrisonian liberals, a notion of God as pure love, mirrored in the sentimental identifications of ordinary people, served as a bulwark against the despair they associated with both orthodoxy and infidelity. Stowe, by contrast, embraces the despair, labels it Christ, and asserts that it is the mark of heavenly triumph. To be sure, she does not endorse the orthodox view of Christ's death as a sacrifice needed to satisfy God's violent demand for justice: she never attributes Tom's or anyone else's death to God's providential plan. Stowe's plot resonates more closely with the ransom theory of the atonement, in that the devilish Simon Legree is responsible for Tom's death and Tom's defiance ensures the escape of Cassy and Emmeline. But Tom is not exactly a "Christus victor." Though Cassy and Emmeline escape, and though George Shelby arrives to collect Tom's body and knock Simon Legree down, Legree remains in full control of his hellish plantation: when other slaves ask young George to purchase them he replies dejectedly that "it's impossible!" What Stowe offers is really a new theory of the atonement in which the earthly effects of the passion are irrelevant: the suffering itself is all in all.

The point can perhaps be clarified through a comparison of Tom's dark night with the experiences of Frederick Douglass just before his decisive fight with Covey. For both slaves, a period of atheistic despair gives way suddenly to a new faith, which enables them to confront a diabolically violent white power. But the *goal* of Douglass's confrontation is to live and escape, while Tom's goal (and *not* merely the undesirable consequence of his defiance) is to die. Thus Tom confronts Legree not by saying that he *will* be free, dead or alive, but that he wants to die: "I'd as soon die as not. Ye may whip me, starve me, burn me,—it'll only send me sooner where I want to go."[40] Heaven, it seems, is the only goal that counts. Stowe could affirm divine nonviolence only by taking God out of this world altogether.

And yet Stowe's book made quite a splash, and not only in heaven. "So you're the little woman who wrote the book that started this great war!" said Abraham Lincoln when he welcomed her to the White House in 1862.[41] The quote is telling, for Lincoln spent his entire presidency trying to figure out just who had caused the Civil War. Had abolitionists like Stowe provoked it through their relentless, injudicious hostility to the South? Was it the fault of the Southern zealots who attacked Fort Sumter in 1861? Had Lincoln himself caused the war when he called out federal troops to restore the Union he treasured so deeply? Or was the war best explained as part of God's hidden plan, a mysterious way of ending slavery and punishing the nation for its accumulated sins?

Ultimately, Lincoln opted for the last alternative, which he expressed most cogently in his second inaugural address: "If we shall suppose that American slavery is one of those offences which, in the providence of God, must needs come, but which, having continued through His appointed time, He now wills to remove, and that He gives to both North and South, this terrible war, as the woe due to those by whom the offence came, shall we discern therein any departure from those divine attributes which the believers in a Living God always ascribe to him?" With these words, Lincoln articulated a providentialist view of both slavery and war. He was ambivalent about the liberal theory of the *imago dei,* believing that individuals should try to discern God's will for their lives but doubting they could fully succeed. But he had no doubt that God's will *would* be done, despite the absence of human understanding or obedience. The divine will was both inscrutable and inevitable, and it was as manifest in the bloody tactics of Sherman and Grant as in the earnest reforms of Garrison and Stowe.

Lincoln was a surprising champion of orthodox providentialism. The only president who was never a member of a church, he had spent much of his young adulthood reading the works of Tom Paine and other freethinkers. As a fervent patriot, he took for granted much of the liberal theology implicit in the Declaration of Independence, and once told a crowd gathered at Independence Hall, "I have never had a feeling politically that did not spring from the sentiments embodied in the Declaration of Independence."[42] The liberal teaching of the founding fathers reinforced his lifelong aversion to slavery, and in another speech he endorsed the fathers' view that "nothing stamped with the Divine image and likeness was sent into the world to be trodden on, and degraded, and imbruted by its fellows."[43]

Yet Lincoln's liberal idealism was overshadowed by his conviction that ideas could not survive unless they were embodied in solid institutions. He admired Jefferson's audacious use of a mere "proposition" as the basis of a nation, but he could not stomach Jefferson's confidence that the proposition could do its work alone. Thus, while Jefferson had hoped for a new revolution in every generation, Lincoln fought a war to preserve not the Declaration of Independence but the Constitution—a document that even he admitted fell far short of the egalitarian ideals of the Declaration. In this regard, he was a disciple not of Jefferson but of Henry Clay, a man whose "deep devotion to the cause of human liberty" had led him to make compromise after compromise with slaveholders, all for the sake of preserving the Union. According to Lincoln, Clay stood as a bulwark against the disunionism of abolitionists and apologists for slavery, rejecting both "those who would shiver into fragments the Union of these States; tear to tatters its now venerated constitution; and even burn the last copy of the Bible, rather than slavery should continue a single hour," and those "who, for the sake of perpetuating slavery, are beginning to assail and to ridicule the white-man's charter of freedom—the declaration that 'all men are created free and equal.'"[44]

Lincoln's refusal to put liberal ideals ahead of liberal institutions has earned him the admiration of countless political realists, from Lincoln's own contemporaries to Reinhold Niebuhr and Jean Bethke Elshtain in the twentieth century. But it raises difficult questions. Lincoln affirmed that liberal ideals must sometimes be sacrificed for the sake of institutions that might eventually become means to the realization of those ideals. But if this is *sometimes* the case, why not always? What is to prevent the entire liberal vision from being sold out to the god of institutional prerogatives? Lincoln's answer was that the sovereign God rules over all human individuals and institutions, directing them toward ends that conform to liberal ideals but yet transcend precise human imaginings.

This confidence in divine sovereignty, a staple of his parents' Baptist theology, is the thread that holds together the many phases of Lincoln's religious life. In his freethinking youth, he espoused the "Doctrine of Necessity"—a belief "that the human mind is impelled to action, or held in rest by some power, over which the mind itself has no control." Lincoln noted, in his political handbill, "I have always understood this same opinion to be held by several of the Christian denominations," and his own perspective gradually fused with more conventional Christian providentialism. At times this took rather complacent forms. Lincoln refused to allow immediate abolition to disrupt the Union because he was confident that slavery, though evil in itself, could be part of God's plan for the "ultimate redemption of the African race and African continent." At other times, however, Lincoln suggested that although God's plan will necessarily prevail, humans must nevertheless strive to conform their own lives to it. This was the theme of Lincoln's preinaugural speech in Trenton, New Jersey. Lincoln posited a vital connection between God's will and the "something more than common" for which the Revolutionary fathers had struggled. He pledged to continue their work: "I shall be most happy indeed if I shall be an humble instrument in the hands of the Almighty, and of this, his almost chosen people, for perpetrating the object of that great struggle."[45]

Lincoln's felicitous insertion of the word "almost" suggests the most characteristic theme of his theology, a theme which was not fully articulated until the final months of his life. Lincoln believed that individuals and nations should seek to conform themselves to God's will, but he also believed that discerning God's will was ultimately a matter of guesswork. No one could know it perfectly or adhere to it exactly; no nation or community could claim definitively to be "chosen." The tragic prolongation of the Civil War seems to have driven this point home for Lincoln. He began the war fairly confident that the Northern cause of union and the ultimate extinction of slavery conformed more closely to God's will than the Southern cause, but it soon became clear that divine providence had not provided for a speedy Northern victory. By September 1862 Lincoln wrote, in a private reflection, that "In the present civil war it is quite possible that God's purpose is something different from the purpose of either party—and yet the human instrumentalities, working just as they do, are of the best adaptation to effect His purpose. I am almost ready to say this is probably true—that God wills this contest, and wills that it shall not end yet." Two years later he reiterated this unsettling thought in a letter to his Quaker friend Eliza P. Gurney, and then incorporated it into his powerful Second Inaugural Address.[46] Both sides in the war, he noted then,

> read the same Bible, and pray to the same God; and each invokes His aid against the other. It may seem strange that any men should dare to ask a just God's assistance in wringing their bread from the sweat of other men's faces; but let us judge not that we be not judged. The prayers of both could not be answered; that of neither has been answered fully. The Almighty has His own purposes.[47]

Lincoln has been almost universally lauded for the sentiment expressed in this passage. It has been rightly seen as a warning against the ideology of Manifest Destiny, against the constant temptation to domesticate providence by identifying God's purposes with those of one's own community. It has been praised for its sense of "mystery" and its "subtlety and humility." "Lincoln makes no claim to know God's purposes," Glen Thurow notes, "but claims only to see that they are different from the purposes of men."[48] What may be lost in this chorus of praise is the fact that Lincoln's theology, precisely because it is so open-ended, seems to provide no guidance in resolving the tensions between justice and order, the Declaration and the Constitution, which vexed Lincoln's career. If God's will is unknowable, who can say whether God prefers to see the Union dissolved for the sake of abolition or slavery perpetuated for the sake of the Union?

Yet this reading is not quite right either. Lincoln's theology implicitly points to a resolution of the dilemma of order and justice by introducing a conservative bias in favor of actuality rather than ideality, providence rather than the *imago dei,* what *has* happened in the past rather than what *might* happen in the future. Lincoln comes off as uncertain and humble, and in a sense he is, but he is serenely confident of two things: that human purposes for the future, however noble, do not conform perfectly to God's will, and that historical events of the past, however violent and troubling, *do.* As a postinaugural note to Thurlow Weed makes clear, Lincoln simply could not imagine a theology without these two propositions. "Men are not flattered by being shown that there has been a difference of purpose between the Almighty and them. To deny it, however, in this case, is to deny that there is a God governing the world."[49] Because he was unsure of God's purposes but certain of God's governance, Lincoln's spirituality was Puritan rather than liberal. He discerned God's hand not in his own aspirations and agency, but in the things that happened to himself and his community.

Lincoln, in short, resolved the ambiguities of Douglass, Garrison, and Stowe by opting for a providential theology of divine violence. And, through his armies, he imposed this new theology on the entire nation. As Sherman and Grant marched through the South, nearly everyone—at least in the North—

could affirm that "mine eyes have seen the glory of the coming of the Lord." The war was so big and so inescapable that it simply *had* to be a manifestation of God's will. The feeble efforts of nonresistant agitators paled by comparison to this awe-inspiring revelation, and the Emancipation Proclamation led even Garrison to "feel . . . in a thoroughly methodistical state of mind, disposed at the top of my voice, and to the utmost stretch of my lungs, to shout 'Glory!' 'Alleluia!' 'Amen and amen!'"[50] To be sure, a few Confederates could see the loopholes in Lincoln's doctrine. One general, Edward Porter Alexander, commented that "It is customary to say that 'Providence did not intend that we should win.' But Providence did not care a row of pins about it. If it did, it was a very unintelligent Providence not to bring the business to a close—the close it wanted—in less than four years of most terrible and bloody war."[51] But it was easy to dismiss this objection as the carping of a loser.

Ultimately, Lincoln sealed the new theology with his blood. When an assassin's bullet felled the sixteenth president on Good Friday 1865, no one stepped forward to echo Douglass's early belief that "man, not God" was responsible for earthly violence. Instead, preachers of all theological stripes offered providential explanations of his death. Perhaps Lincoln had been killed to expose the depths of slaveholding violence, to prevent the idolization of Lincoln, to punish the sins of the North, to make way for a sterner leader for Reconstruction, to ensure a broader diffusion of Lincoln's ideas, or simply to unify the sympathies of the North. Amid this diversity, almost everyone anticipated that Lincoln's death would lead to the new national birth that he had prophesied at Gettysburg. "Even here, in the cause of Liberty," said George Dana Boardman, "as in the cause of the Church, it shall be found that the blood of the martyrs is the seed of the Republic."[52]

Lincoln's sacrificial death, in short, saved the nation from the ambiguities of liberal theology. But it also destroyed the dream of a genuinely nonviolent theology. God was no longer to be seen in the earnest sympathies or heroic convictions of individual reformers, but rather in the military, governmental, financial, and industrial institutions that seemed to have been the instruments of God's victory. The legacy of the Civil War was neither an end to racism nor a renewed dream of peace, but a permanent standing army, the expansion of the central government, an industrial boom in the North, and the lasting impoverishment of the South. This outcome troubled few Northerners. Lincoln's violent death had saved the nation, just as Jesus' death had saved the world, and there was no longer a need to heed his quiet words, echoing the Sermon on the Mount: "Let us strive on to finish the work we are in; to bind up the nation's wounds; to care for him who shall have borne the battle, and for his widow, and his orphan—to do all which may achieve and cherish a just, and a lasting peace, among ourselves, and with all nations."[53]

FOUR

CHRISTIANS AS RESCUERS DURING THE HOLOCAUST

DAVID P. GUSHEE

Introduction

In recent years withering criticisms rightly have been directed at those who casually stomp around in, and make a comfortable living off of, the field now called Holocaust studies. Holocaust scholars, researchers, and various aficionados are charged, by some, with desecrating the dead and trivializing their suffering. By now I have been writing and speaking about the Holocaust for about twelve years. In those years I have sought earnestly to avoid any kind of trivialization of the Jewish people's shattered civilization and murdered millions. But it is true that continual revisiting of the Holocaust tests the heart's endurance. Those engaged in such study are tempted to go a bit numb, if only to preserve their sanity.

So it is good to be brought up short from time to time by a fresh stab of horror about the events now firmly implanted in Western consciousness under the name "the Holocaust." That happened to me recently in reading a memoir by American Jewish leader Arthur Hertzberg. Hertzberg recounts this story:

> The conversation about the Holocaust that lives with me—and haunts me—is one that never took place. Rabbi Aaron Rokeach, the rebbe of Belz in south-eastern Poland, lost his entire family—his wife and all his children and all their children—in the *Shoah*. He never again mentioned them or even said prayers in any visible ritual in their memory. I was in his presence in Tel Aviv in the summer of 1949. I tried to get the rebbe to talk to me about my grandfather and my uncles, who had been his disciples and friends, but he simply did not respond, not even with a gesture. The dead were too holy, so his closest associates explained, to need words.[1]

"The dead were too holy" to talk about. The rabbi's grief was too deep for words. This need for silence rather than speech as a response to the Holocaust was at one time a major theme of Holocaust literature; it certainly characterized the initial Jewish response to those horrible events. That theme has receded now, and words about the Holocaust are everywhere, but the point is still very well taken. And so I enter into this discussion today with trepidation. We are treading on ground that is desperately, simultaneously, holy and unholy.

My topic is "Christians as Rescuers of Jews during the Holocaust." This topic is being considered here against the backdrop of a conference devoted to the theme of Christianity and violence. In that context it seems appropriate to begin with some general reflections arising at the intersection of Christianity, violence, and the Holocaust.

What we now call the Holocaust was, depending on when one wants to begin the chronology, a twelve-, six-, or four-year campaign of governmental violence by the Nazi regime, and its collaborators, against those defined as Jewish. Germany's Jews experienced the lash of that regime beginning in January 1933; the onset of World War II in September 1939 introduced many millions more Jews to Hitlerian evil; and the effort to annihilate all Jews within reach began in the summer of 1941. By May 1945, barely four years after full-scale genocide was launched, approximately six million Jews had been murdered in ghettos, concentration and death camps, and mass shootings. Another five to six million other noncombatants, including Gypsies, Poles, Soviet prisoners of war, and others, were also murdered by the Nazi regime during those few terrible years.

Christianity and the Holocaust: Continuity and Discontinuity

What Christianity has to do with any of this is a hotly debated question. Steven Haynes of Rhodes College helpfully writes of the *continuity fallacy*, on the one hand, and the *discontinuity fallacy*, on the other. The continuity fallacy is seen when, as Haynes puts it, "it is implied that Christianity is *the* reason for the Holocaust."[2] Some have implied or directly charged that Christianity bears full responsibility for the Holocaust. On this view the Holocaust was a direct result of historic Christian anti-Semitism, or at least the inevitable culmination of that anti-Semitic heritage. Sometimes the Holocaust is treated as something akin to a Christian crusade, a church-sponsored *jihad* with Hitler at the head of the crusading army.

Such claims are neither accurate nor justified. However, Christians need to avoid the discontinuity fallacy as well, which, quoting Haynes again, "eschews Christian responsibility for the Holocaust."[3] Here the Christian apologist seeks to distance Christianity from the Holocaust, to reject any charge that Christianity had anything to do with the Holocaust at all. If tempted to that position, as evangelical Christians tend to be, we ought to consider the following five points:

- *Context:* The Holocaust was launched from and largely occurred in the heart of historically Christian Europe.
- *Killers:* Both the planners of annihilation and its executioners were, overwhelmingly, baptized Christians, and not all of them were conscripted German soldiers—some were happy local volunteers in various lands in which these mass murders took place.
- *Bystanders:* The great majority of the 300 million or so bystanders among whom the victims were taken and murdered were baptized Christians, a significant percentage of them committed ones.[4]
- *Targets:* The Nazis did not conjure up the Jews as their premier victims out of nowhere; historic Christian anti-Semitism provided the target and a rancid storehouse of anti-Semitic images, symbols, and policies.
- *Testimony:* Postwar testimony from Jews and non-Jews clearly reveals the impact of Christian hatred of Jews on the sometimes murderous and often indifferent attitude of Christians toward Jews during the Holocaust.

The Nazis were racist pagans who hated both Christianity and Judaism. But it was Jews who were targeted for total annihilation, not Christians. And it was Christian people—by the definition of Christianity used in most of the churches of the region at the time—who murdered them, stood by watching, or tried very hard to look away.

Christians as Rescuers during the Holocaust

But not all Christians murdered Jews or stood by. Some risked their lives to help Jews survive. These good folks are called "the Righteous Gentiles of the Holocaust" or simply "Christian rescuers."

Much of what we know about the rescuers is due to the work of the Department for the Righteous at Yad Vashem, the Israeli Holocaust museum and research center. The 1953 law that established Yad Vashem required efforts to identify, honor, and study the "high-minded righteous who risked their lives to save Jews."[5] Just as Jews were murdered one by one, so rescuers are identified one by one by a grateful Jewish nation. At last count, some 14,000 rescuers had thus been named and honored by the state of Israel. No one knows the exact number of non-Jews who rescued Jews, but the director of the Righteous Gentiles office indicated to me that there may have been as many as 250,000 who would meet Yad Vashem's criteria for rescuer status. Interestingly, he estimated that they helped to save as many as 250,000 Jewish lives. One

rescuer/one survivor—an apt empirical confirmation of the truth of this reading from the Talmud inscribed on the medallion given to each rescuer: "Whoso-
ever saves a single life, saves the entire universe."

Most rescuers were at least nominally Christian, which is to be expected
given the geography of the Holocaust. But several different studies of verified
rescuers have shown that only a relatively small percentage of rescuers acted on
explicitly religious grounds—between 12 and 27 percent.[6] These percentages
are derived from rescuer self-reports through interviews. While there may be
grounds for questioning this method of ascertaining motivation, it does seem
clear that those Christians who rescued Jews for explicitly religious reasons—
as an expression of their Christian faith—constituted a minority within the
already tiny minority of non-Jews who rescued Jews.

Yet the way in which this minority of a minority described the impact of
their faith on their behavior during the Holocaust is extremely important. Here
we have Christian people who reported that their faith made the difference in
motivating them to risk their lives to help a hunted and hated people. Some
said that their faith was the only motivation; others that it was one motivating factor among several. But in both cases, consider the context: Jews were
being destroyed all over Europe and almost all of those Christians who were
not helping destroy them were doing nothing to prevent it. How can we account
for the difference between murderous Christians and bystanding Christians on
the one hand, and rescuing Christians on the other? What makes Christianity
a force for compassion and courage in a context in which hard-heartedness and
fear are the norm? If we can gain insight on these two questions perhaps we can
learn something about what Christianity should look like in our context or, for
that matter, in any context.

Patterns of Motivation for Christian Rescuers

In my book *The Righteous Gentiles of the Holocaust,* I devote a full chapter to
exploring patterns of motivation that can be discerned in religiously motivated
Christian rescuers.[7] Here I will briefly summarize the contents of that chapter.

Sense of Special Religious Kinship with Jews

Perhaps the religious motivation most remarked upon in rescuer literature is
a strong sense of religious kinship with Jews as a people. Evidence of this sense
of kinship crops up both in anecdotal material and in research studies of rescuers.

This sense of kinship with Jews can be further broken down into two categories. *The first category is the philo-Semitic individual reared in a generally anti-
Semitic environment.* Both the Catholic and the Lutheran traditions, for example, were at this time profoundly anti-Semitic. Leaders of both traditions have,

since the Holocaust, confessed and repudiated this anti-Semitism. But it clearly left its mark on men and women steeped in these (and other) anti-Semitic Christian traditions. Rescuers emerging from those contexts normally had to *overcome* that aspect of their faith in order to rescue, rather than *drawing on* their faith at that point as a resource for rescue. Yet the evidence reveals that there was a handful of Christian rescuers from such traditions who managed to arrive at a way of understanding the Christian faith that created a highly motivating sense of kinship with Jews.

The second strand of philo-Semitic rescuer emerges from Christian traditions that can be described, arguably at least, as philo-Semitic *as traditions*. The most prominent of these groups in the literature of rescue is the Reformed tradition, both in the Netherlands and in France. Rescuers from these confessions regularly and unblinkingly attributed their rescue efforts to the special place of the Jewish people in God's economy. Dutch Reformed rescuers, for example, surprising their secular researchers quite a bit, said things like this:

> When it came to the Jewish people, we were brought up in a tradition in which we had learned that the Jewish people were the people of the Lord. The main reason [for rescue] is because we know that they are the chosen people of God. We had to save them.
> My background is Christian Reformed; Israel has a special meaning for me.[8]

Other groups in which philo-Semitic rescuers were reported include Ukrainian Baptists, Hungarian Methodists, German Plymouth Brethren, and French fundamentalists. What these disparate groups all had in common was an emphasis on the reading of the entire scriptural canon, in which the Jews, of course, play such a prominent part. Their special concern for the Jewish people is akin to the way some contemporary conservative evangelicals—especially dispensationalists—display a theologically driven interest in the Jewish people and a strong commitment to the state of Israel. Jews today, like those Jews fortunate enough to encounter such people during the Holocaust, don't share the theology but are certainly glad for the help that the theology engenders.

The Remembered Experience of Religious Persecution

Researchers on the rescue efforts of the French village of Le Chambon-sur-Lignon[9] and other nearby largely Protestant communities have drawn attention to the historic Huguenot experience of religious persecution and the way in which its memory proved fruitful as a resource for rescue. Likewise, the distinguished Holocaust scholar Yehuda Bauer claimed that the small Baptist minority in Lithuania and western Ukraine stood out in the extent of their rescue activities, and that their experience of persecution was a factor in their actions.[10]

I have argued in my analysis of the evidence emerging from Le Chambon that at least three particular strands of thought proving useful for rescue were directly traceable to their carefully cultivated memory of former persecutions in Catholic France. *The first was a sense of identification with all suffering people.* Identification of the people of God with the victimized is one of the Bible's central moral commands, and yet all too rare is that Christian congregation or tradition characterized by that commitment. Yet the Chambonnais, as they are called, both thought that way and acted on it, and had done so for several centuries.

Second, the Chambonnais felt *a sense of identity with the Jewish people in particular* as a suffering religious minority. Many considered what was happening to the Jews during the war a direct parallel to the suffering of their own ancestors. They saw the Nazi project against the Jews as religious persecution akin to the Catholic project against their ancestors three centuries before. While this was not strictly the case at an empirical level, it certainly proved a powerful motivation to provide hospitable shelter not just to Jews but to the practice of Judaism.

A third resource enjoyed by the Chambonnais was *an appropriately critical eye toward government and a quite constructive ethic of resistance.* Unlike so many Christians in Europe, the Protestants of Le Chambon understood Romans 13 and other texts to enjoin subjection to the legitimate, and only the legitimate, demands of government. When the Nazi government, like previous regimes in Huguenot memory, transgressed the appropriate boundaries of government authority, these Christians believed that they were not just *permitted* but *required* to resist—using, as their courageous pastor André Trocmé liked to say, the "weapons of the Spirit." This the Chambonnais did, saving at least 5,000 Jews during the war.

The Incompatibility of Nazism with Christian Faith

In 1955, in one of the earliest essays written about the Holocaust, historian Philip Friedman wrote:

> For the first time in the history of humanity, mass murder, with millions of victims, was carried out, by the Nazis, in a methodical, efficient, cold-blooded manner . . . [and] all previous ideas of law, justice, and morality were abolished. It is understandable that this policy had to be opposed by all organizations, especially the Church, whose basic [worldview] was threatened by that legal and moral revolution. The Church had to oppose the Nazi ideology, not so much for the "love of Mordecai" as for their "hatred of Haman."[11]

This striking comment gets at a third religious motivation for rescue: *the conviction that Nazism and Christianity were fundamentally incompatible.* As an ideology, Nazism was a heresy; as a set of practices and policies, Nazism posed a fundamental threat to Christian values. This theme appears most frequently in the documents of the German religious resistance, but can be found elsewhere as well. In this case, Jews were not rescued because of any kind of particularistic philo-Semitism (love of Mordecai) but instead because of a revulsion toward Nazism (hatred of Haman).

There were many elements that, woven together, constituted this religious indictment of Nazism. Nazism was viewed as an alien idolatry, and thus a violation of the first commandment. The deification of Aryan "blood and soil," development of a Führer-cult with strong religious overtones, infringement on ecclesial freedom, imposition of racist laws, encroachment of totalitarian social control, and unleashing of wanton and gangsterlike violence as state policy, among other things, marked Nazism as a desperate threat to Christian convictions and values. Sometimes, though far too infrequently, Nazi anti-Semitism—as ideology and as policy—was also viewed as fundamentally alien and incompatible with Christian faith.

One of the best treatments of these themes was found in the work of the Dutch clergyman K. H. Miskotte, who offered penetrating analyses of Nazi neopaganism and that regime's effort to annihilate not only the Jewish people but, in his view, the God of the Jews.[12] While this kind of reasoning sometimes motivated Christian resistance that did not include help for the Jews, it also played a role in undergirding rescue efforts among some Christians. Again, what is striking—and disastrous—is how many Christians living in the very same contexts, including some learned theologians, did not at all interpret Nazism in this way but in fact saw it as harmonious with national and Christian values.

The Dignity of Human Life

Some Christians rescued Jews because of their commitment to the dignity, equality, and preciousness of human life. This conviction could be found both at very high levels of church life, in official documents and statements, and in the comments of unschooled Christian laypeople. Theologically, this perspective was most commonly rooted in the doctrine of creation—all human beings having been made in the image of God and precious in God's sight. Others focused on doctrines of the cross or the church—"there is no longer Jew nor Greek . . . in Christ Jesus" (Gal. 3:28)—while still others spoke the language of human rights and expressed their visceral outrage at the violations of the rights of innocent Jewish men, women, and children by the Nazis.

The dignity, or sacredness, of life is something that could be apprehended with both head and heart, both cool reason and churning emotion. One of my favorite rescuer accounts reflects the latter phenomenon. The words are those of Jan Sagan, a Polish farmer who, after some hesitation, decided to rescue an eighteen-year-old Jewish boy named Morris Krantz, whose entire family had been massacred. In a postwar letter to Krantz, Sagan recalled the moment when the desperate young man approached him for help:

> That morning will not leave me as long as I live. I was startled by the sight of you—overgrown hair, face swollen from the cold, all in rags—a ghost, a wild

man, a barely human creature. When I [at first] asked you to leave, I was reacting to my first impulse, to shock. I was in turmoil over it for two days. I considered it the biggest crisis of my life, to jeopardize my family by allowing you
to stay, or to turn you out to certain death. . . . You made me aware of what a
precious gift life is and of the God-given power in it. When I considered your
presence on the farm and its effect on me, I suddenly realized that whatever I
had done for you had resulted in as much good for me—more. I had never felt
so good, so alive.[13]

Karen Lebacqz has written that a passion for justice often emerges out of the
experience of injustice.[14] It is as if we know what justice really means only as
we experience—or witness—its negation. As the Nazi regime cruelly splattered
Europe with the blood of millions of innocents, some who witnessed the car-
nage were prompted to a profound reapprehension of the sacredness of human
life, and to a sense of obligation to preserve it where they could.

Resources of Christian Piety

I have found a final pattern of motivation rather difficult to name—
"resources of Christian piety" is the phrase used in this paper. By this I mean
to point to the evidence of lived Christian spirituality as a critical resource for
rescue, at least among the devout. In accounts stretching from one end of
Europe to the other, one sees a snapshot of aspects of Christian piety at work
empowering that tiny minority of Christians who saved lives during the Holocaust. It began with a certain way of viewing life. Many rescuer accounts reveal
men and women who saw their purpose in life as the quest to know and to do
God's will. Thus, when an awareness arose of Jews, or a particular Jew, in need
of help, such Christians thought first about what this need and opportunity
to help meant in terms of God's will. The Jew at the door, then, was not primarily a stranger, or a threat to my well-being, but instead a signal from God
as to his will for the Christian's life at that time.

If, as these rescuers came to believe, God had sent Jews their way, there could
be no question of turning them away. To do so would be to disobey God directly,
to violate Christian duty, to court divine displeasure. This intuitive conviction
was then reinforced by a reading of Scripture. Rescuers—unlike, apparently,
nonrescuers—understood Scripture to *command* them to rescue. Rescuers have
cited passages such as the story of the Good Samaritan, the Golden Rule, the
royal law of love, and dozens of others as mandating their rescue activities.
Here is biblical authority doing its proper work.

Devout Christian rescuers, according to their testimonies as well as those
they rescued, spent a lot of time in prayer. They prayed about whether to rescue, how to manage rescue, and next steps to take in rescue activity; for strength
to endure the strains of rescue; for protection from the enemy; and for the

safety of their charges and their own families. Rescuers prayed according to the traditions of their own particular Christian denominations—on their knees or standing, in Jesus' name or in adoration of the Virgin Mary, in ancient Christian formulas or extemporaneous groanings. However they did it, prayer strengthened and sustained ordinary men and women undertaking an extraordinary challenge.

Conclusion: Christianities and a "Certain Kind of Christianity"

Formally, the Christian faith was neither necessary nor sufficient for motivating Christians to rescue Jews during the Holocaust. Not *necessary*—because there were non-Christian rescuers, and Christians who rescued without reference to their faith. Not *sufficient*—because there were millions of nonrescuer Christians, many devout, with some Christians happily aiding in the destruction of the Jews.

Yet Christian faith clearly and indisputably motivated a minority of rescuers. The Christian faith was for some *the* factor responsible for saving Jewish lives.

Is there a way to resolve this riddle of a faith that motivates some to life-risking behavior but motivates others to busily murder the same people their brothers and sisters are trying to save?

Maybe the answer is this: at least in the realm of actual moral practice (as opposed to ideal theoretical forms) there is no such thing as "Christianity," or "the Christian faith." Instead, what really exist are *Christianities* and Christian *faiths.*

Let's trace out this claim a bit further. These Christian faith*s* we are speaking of, these Christianit*ies,* would emerge from the interaction of believers with at least the following:

- The content of Christian faith as communicated by family/local/denominational tradition and interpreted by leaders, teachers, parents, ministers, and so on
- The practice of Christian faith as modeled by paragons of the tradition as well as by leaders, teachers, parents, ministers, etc.
- The believers' own level of seriousness about Christian belief and practice, itself deeply affected by the teaching and modeling of mentors in the faith
- The character and temperament of the faith's recipients in all their individuality
- The social context of the faith's transmission and reception
- The historical circumstances in which that faith's application is tested

On this view, what Christian faith will come to look like, and how it will come to be lived, is hugely idiosyncratic and context-specific. It comes to believers not in any pristine state but as a *traditioned* body of beliefs and practices with which individuals then interact in their own unique ways.

Further, in broader context that faith is always a *contested* matter. Sometimes the contest is quite visible and public, as when various local Christian authorities clash over an item of doctrine or practice; other times it goes on outside of public view, as believers are confronted with a quiet but real diversity of Christian vision just in the process of going to church, or reading books, or watching family members with various lived renderings of the meaning of Christian existence.

If I am correct, the role of Christian leaders, teachers, parents, and others with responsibility for construing and transmitting the Christian faith becomes all the more important. Despite a settled biblical canon, and despite the illuminating role of the Holy Spirit promised in the Scripture, history seems to show that it is always possible for more or less aberrant versions of Christianity to be developed. What is understood as "Christianity" in any context will be that version of it that tradition-transmitters teach to tradition-recipients. If the transmitters' Christianity is, say, nativistic, anti-Semitic, racist, and hateful, then that is the "Christianity" that the recipients are most likely to learn. The normative question then becomes whether what we leaders and teachers say "Christianity" is bears any resemblance to a *sound* understanding of the teachings and example of the one whose name we bear.

The Jewish sociologist Nechama Tec survived the Holocaust with Christians in Poland. At a conference I attended she was posed this question: Did Christianity motivate rescuers? Her response, after some reflection, was the following: "Yes, but not any kind of Christianity did it—only *a certain kind of Christianity.*" She said that she could not define that "certain kind of Christianity." But she knew it when she saw it. The task of the church's leaders in every generation is to figure out what that "certain kind of Christianity" looks like and to see that it prevails.

FIVE

HAVE CHRISTIANS DONE MORE HARM THAN GOOD?

MARK A. NOLL

This is a most serious question, which, for several reasons, Christian believ- ers should take even more seriously than those who are not believers. Although this is not by any means a new question, it arises sharply in our era because of increased sensitivity, especially in the university world, to the abuses of power, in particular to the self-deceiving employment of idealistic language to justify the oppression of the culturally marginalized by the culturally hege- monic. Theories about the ways in which discourses, supposedly humanitar- ian or religious, actually mask an exploitative loathing for the Other abound. The greatest difficulty posed to Christian believers comes from the fact that it seems very easy for the promoters of such theories to find evidence in the his- tory of Christianity to support the proposition that Christians, whatever we believers may say, have acted persistently to violate the health, well-being, and even lives of our fellow human beings. It is important to review the historical indictments that have been made and to indicate the kind of historical evi- dence that supports such indictments before turning to what a Christian his- torian might say in response. That response will suggest several mitigations against the charge that Christianity has been, on balance, a malignant force in human history, but it will also concede that there is enough substance in the charge to force careful thought about the nature of the Christian faith itself.

The heart of the indictment against Christianity is the assertion that, despite their language of goodwill, mercy, and love, Christians have historically transformed doctrines about their own salvation into instruments of oppression directed at those whom they consider not to be saved. Believers have, that is, translated what we say is good news for all—Jesus Christ redeems sinners—into bad news for anyone who does not agree that Jesus Christ saves sinners. The charge is a very old one. One of the very first nonbiblical references to the Christian faith came from the Roman historian Tacitus, who wrote in the early second century. When he related the story of Nero's reign, the fire of Rome, and Nero's execution of some Christians as the perpetrators of that blaze, Tacitus acknowledged that the Christians had not in fact started the fire. But he went on to say that no one in Rome was much troubled by Nero's actions against the Christians, since the believers were notorious "for their sullen hatred of the whole human race."[1] Historians of the period usually hold that Tacitus was referring to the way Christians had offended their peers both by claiming a unique salvation for themselves and by acting censoriously toward their fellow Romans who had not become Christians. Such charges concerning the propensity of Christian believers to alienate others by claims of their own unique relationship to God or by antisocial attitudes based on those claims have continued to the present.

The heart of this charge against Christianity as a malignant historical force is the assertion that whenever Christians have obtained power, they have transformed the conviction of their own spiritual superiority into attacks, acts, structures, and persistent patterns of violent aggression. This charge received a full airing in conjunction with the observances in the early 1990s commemorating Columbus's arrival in the New World. One of its sharpest statements came in a book by Forrest G. Wood entitled *The Arrogance of Faith: Christianity and Race in America from the Colonial Era to the Twentieth Century.*[2] In that work, Wood argued boldly that "Christianity, in the five centuries since its message was first carried to the peoples of the New World—and, in particular, to the natives and the transplanted Africans of English North America and the United States—has been fundamentally racist in ideology, organization, and practice." Moreover, Wood went on, "one can say that, good works notwithstanding, there has been no greater religious force in the dehumanization of humans than Christianity, the self-proclaimed religion of peace, brotherly love, and fellowship."

More specific instances of Wood's charge are actually more damaging for being more specific. For example, the fourteen-minute orientation film shown at the U.S. Holocaust Memorial Museum in Washington, D.C., which is called simply *Antisemitism,* contains enough material about historic Christian antagonism to Judaism that the impression can arise that the producers are assigning the primary blame for the Holocaust to Christianity.

The sobering thing for Christians with an interest in history is how much evidence there is to support such charges. For example, the record is anything but reassuring for three of the historical events most often enlisted in the indictment against Christianity—the Crusades, the European settlement of the Americas, and the Nazi persecution of the Jews.

The Crusades began with fully noble intentions. Pope Urban II (ca. 1035–1099) first called for a crusade in the year 1095. He had received an appeal from the Eastern Roman Emperor in Constantinople for assistance in protecting his territory from Islamic invaders. Pope Urban II reasoned that a military venture from Europe would assist his fellow Christians in the East and also ensure European access to holy sites in Palestine. Urban also hoped a crusade would provide some useful business for the younger sons of the European nobility, whose violent quarrels were a constant menace to European peace. So Urban urged his hearers to become soldiers for Christ, to "take up the cross," and to advance the kingdom of God through a crusade.

The result was a moral disaster. The various crusades of the next several centuries wreaked havoc almost everywhere. Rabble associated with the First Crusade in the 1090s could not wait to get to the Holy Land to strike out at "infidels," and so, as a kind of practice, fell violently upon Jewish communities in Germany and the Balkans. Once crusaders arrived in the Eastern Mediterranean region, they gave the Eastern Orthodox more grief than relief. Worst of all was the physical destruction promoted in the name of Christ. Here is the chilling account of Foucher (Fulcher) de Chartres (ca. 1059–ca. 1127), an eyewitness, in his *Chronicle of the First Crusade,* about what happened on July 10, 1099, when the crusaders finally breached the walls of Jerusalem:

> Then the Franks entered the city magnificently at the noonday hour on Friday, the day of the week when Christ redeemed the whole world on the cross. With trumpets sounding and with everything in an uproar, exclaiming: "Help, God!" they vigorously pushed into the city and straightway raised the banner on the top of the wall. All the heathen, completely terrified, changed their boldness to swift flight through the narrow streets of the quarters. The more quickly they fled, the more quickly were they put to flight. . . . Then some, both Arabs and Ethiopians, fled into the Tower of David. . . . Nowhere was there a place where the Saracens could escape the swordsman. On the top of Solomon's Temple, to which they had climbed in fleeing, many were shot to death with arrows and cast down headlong from the roof. Within this Temple about ten thousand were beheaded. If you had been there, your feet would have been stained up to the ankles with the blood of the slain. What more shall I tell you? Not one of them were allowed to live. They did not spare the women and children.[3]

This kind of Christian violence has not been forgotten. At least some Muslims to this day know what Christian so-called civilization is about because they remember the Crusades.

The European settlement of the Americas is every bit as much of a problem. Native American indifference to Christianity, or more generally Native American resistance to European settlement, became a reason for systematic destruction of the Indians. It was dreadful almost everywhere, with the exceptions rare, like the relatively benign approach of the Jesuits to Huron Indians in what is now Western Ontario and the pacific work of the Moravians among Indians in New Jersey and Pennsylvania. It is particularly painful for me to recite the attitude of Puritan Christians in New England, since I admire them so much for so many reasons. But the records are relentless.

For example, one of the main reasons Harvard College was established at Cambridge in 1636 was because of the godliness of Thomas Shepard, the minister of the Puritans' Cambridge church, whom everyone recognized as a person of rare compassion and winsome spirituality. Shepard, who had undergone a life of spiritual pain and much domestic stress, was renowned for his patient wisdom and his ability to guide troubled souls to security in Christ. The leaders of Massachusetts Bay figured that the college boys would need a lot of gentle nurture of this sort, and so they set up their college in Shepard's backyard.

Shift now, however, to the Puritan relationship with Native Americans. When in 1637 warfare broke out between the Puritan settlers and the Pequot Indians, Shepard acted as chaplain to the New England troops and shared in the successful campaign that subjugated the Pequots at the Great Swamp Fight in Connecticut. The dismaying thing for a modern Christian reading about Shepard and this battle is what he said after the Puritans surprised and then massacred an Indian settlement by burning their dwelling down upon their heads. For Shepard, this episode represented, in his own words, "the divine slaughter [of the Indians] by the Hand of the English."[4] Such attitudes were far from uncommon in Puritan New England. They represented a particularly appalling example of Christian demonization of the Other.

Christian responsibility for the Holocaust is, I think, a more complicated affair, though it is also a situation that brings no credit whatever to Christian believers. My own opinion on this extremely important, but also extremely complicated, question is similar to the opinion of six prominent Jews who recently wrote a letter to the U.S. Holocaust Museum protesting the content of the orientation film entitled *Antisemitism.*[5] The letter writers question what they say is the impression left by the film that Christians were the initial promoters of anti-Semitism and that there was a tight link between historic Christian antagonism against Judaism and Nazi efforts to exterminate the Jews.

About historic Christian antagonism to Judaism there can be no doubt. In fact, I am so repelled by harsh statements against the Jews by Christian leaders for whom I have otherwise the highest regard, leaders like the great preacher John Chrysostom in the early fifth century or Martin Luther in the sixteenth century, that I do not even want to repeat what they said. To be sure, such harsh statements have not been the only opinions expressed by Christians about Judaism; moreover, some Christian leaders who have railed against Judaism as a religion have also gone out of their way to repudiate violence against Jews. Nonetheless, the long history of Christian antagonism to Judaism and the record of social oppression attending that history is a moral scandal. It does seem to me that the Jewish leaders who have written to the Holocaust Museum are correct in suggesting that anti-Semitism did not originate with Christianity, that Nazi anti-Semitism arose more from pagan racial ideology than from Christian religious antagonism, and that part of Hitler's self-conscious strategy was to silence Catholic and Protestant forces who, if left to themselves, might have done something to defend those whom the Nazis targeted for destruction. Still, it is a very small consolation for a Christian believer to conclude that the Christian faith was "merely" one of the underlying forces paving the way to the horrific Nazi assault upon the Jews.

Allow me to summarize at this point: wholesale indictments of Christianity as a malignant force in history do not arise out of thin air. For anyone who makes the effort to study history carefully, especially Western history where Christianity has been so prominent, the role of Christians in promoting the destruction of others, while acting self-consciously in defense of what believers openly claim as Christian principles, cannot be denied. Similarly, there are also enough questionable activities taken or attitudes promoted by Christians to lend at least some plausibility to those who would link Christianity with the environmental crisis, with misogyny, and with the alienation created by unchecked capitalism.

When looking at the historical record as a whole, have Christians done more harm than good? At the very least, this is not a frivolous question.

At the same time, however, it is not a question that should shame modern believers into silence, for in fact there are things to say that provide substantial mitigation concerning the record of Christianity. These things are of two sorts. First, a fuller consideration of the historical record can dispel the idea that Christians have been the unique, the predominant, or even the main source of social evil over the last two thousand years. Second, and more importantly, a fuller consideration of Christianity itself can strengthen the credibility of the faith even while admitting that Christians have contributed, and sometimes contributed substantially, to the wrongdoing so obvious in the historical record. I do not offer these mitigations as exonerations, for there can be nothing but shame and repentance for much that we living Christians and our fellow believers in the past have done. But as mitigations they deserve to be taken seriously.

The first historical mitigation is the observation that much of the evil perpetrated by Christians in the past has arisen more from the general circumstances of particular cultures or individual historical epochs than from the specific application of Christian faith. In other words, it is possible to reduce the charge. A more objective and more comprehensive understanding of human history points, not to the conclusion that Christians have done more harm than good, but to the conclusion that Christians, like all other human beings, have often abused the power they have been given. Eugene Genovese wrote a scathing review of the book by Forrest Wood from which I quoted earlier, where Wood argued that Christianity was a uniquely evil force in the European settlement of America. To Genovese, this claim was historically myopic. Wood, Genovese charged, "goes to great lengths to show what he palpably cannot show: that Christianity and Western civilization indulged in horrors that other religions and civilizations would never have dreamed of. All that he does show (and it will not come as news) is that the great technological, economic, and military breakthroughs, the commercial and industrial revolutions that made world conquest possible, came in Christian countries, and with much church support. That rival religions would not have accommodated a Chinese, Indian, Zulu, or Malaysian conquest of the world may nonetheless be doubted. . . . The periodic bloodletting of Hindus, Muslims, and Buddhists in Southeast Asia might invite a speculation."[6] Genovese does not deny that Christians have engaged in the demonization of others, the abuse of power, and the exploitation of the marginalized. He asserts, rather, that these evils are part of the human condition rather than distinctive features of Christianity. No one can claim to be an expert on world history as such, but everything I have read in comprehensive texts on world civilization suggests that Genovese is right—all societies and the adherents of all religions have promoted the kinds of evil seen in Western Christian history, once they are given the chance.

The next mitigation carries Genovese's argument one step further. This mitigation is the observation that, however nasty have been some of the fruits of Christianity, the fruits of other, often explicitly anti-Christian religions or substitute religions have been worse. The most obvious evidence in support of this claim is the record of twentieth-century Marxist regimes, which, ostensibly to secure the dignity of the proletariat, unleashed death and destruction on an apocalyptic scale. A book first published in France in 1997 as *Le Livre Noir du Communisme* has engendered much debate because of the boldness of its claims concerning Marxist regimes.[7] The comparisons of the book are especially germane to our topic. This *Black Book* claims, for instance, that by the time Lenin and the Bolsheviks had been in power for only five months, they had deliberately liquidated—that is, murdered—more human beings than had been put to death by the czarist regime in the entire century before 1917. Similarly, any objective account of Stalin's Great Terror, of Mao's Great Leap Forward, or of the Khmer Rouge's rape of Cambodia must conclude that these Marxist regimes were responsible for arbitrary violence against persons and property on a scale vastly greater than any violence ever perpetrated anywhere on the face of the globe by any religious group of any sort. The followers of Jesus may have slain their thousands, but the followers of Marx have laid waste their opponents by the hundreds of thousands. Karl Marx himself penned an elegant attack on the church in *The Communist Manifesto* as supplying the holy water that the bourgeoisie sprinkle on their consciences as they go about exploiting the weak. The twentieth century revealed that the followers of Marx had no conscience whatsoever.

Comparisons with other religions can be invidious, but they nonetheless put into perspective our question. If Christians have sometimes promoted violence

in the name of Christ, so too have other world and local religions also perpetrated violence in the name of their deities—or perhaps to put it more accurately, if Christians have used the cloak of religious language to mask episodes
of tribal ethnic cleansing, so too have Turkish Muslims against Armenian Orthodox, Sudanese Muslims against the Christian Bor Dinka of the southern Sudan,
Azerbaijanian Muslims against the Armenians of Nagorno-Karabakh, and so
on. Likewise, if Christians have contributed to the racism and sexism of the
West, what should we say about the Hindu contribution to the glaring oppressions of the caste system on the Indian subcontinent? In addition, a good case
can be made that Hitler and the Nazis explicitly rejected Christianity in the
process of shaping their neopagan Aryan tribalism and therefore that the
unspeakable crimes of the Nazis were as much a protest against the restraint of
Christian ethics as in any meaningful way an expression of Christianity. This
second mitigation, in other words, is the claim that, if Christianity can be implicated in systematic social evil, such evil has been promoted even more cata-
strophically by other religions, ideologies, and substitute religions.

A third mitigation requires reflection on the very charge that Christianity
has done more harm than good. Here the observation is that without the legacy
of Christianity, the West would never have possessed the trajectory of moral
critique that could lead to an indictment of Christianity for its moral failings.
Where, in other words, did notions of the dignity of all human beings, the
rights of conscience, or the potential value of even the most humble life come
from? Certainly there were Greek contributions to such values, and parallel
expressions can be found in other world religions. But in the West, the long-
term, driving, omnipresent engine for a higher opinion of humankind has been
the record of divine revelation contained in the Jewish and Christian Scriptures. Again, allow me to quote the very good sense of Eugene Genovese on
this relationship: "The very concept of individual freedom, as generally understood and cherished even by our noisiest radicals, arose in the West on Christian foundations. . . . Christian doctrines provided the moral ground on which
the exponents of a doctrine of freedom could stand."[8]

Much more, of course, would need to be said to make any of these mitigations into a definitive response to the observation that Christianity has caused
a lot of damage in world history. But I hope I have said enough to suggest that,
even when it comes only to looking at the historical record fairly, there are serious objections to unequivocal assertions about the unique damage done by
Christianity in the human past.

But mitigations of the sort I have been outlining are only defensive reactions to this problem. Specific attention to the nature of Christian faith itself
makes possible a different tack—not an effort to contain the damage done to
Christianity by the record of evil perpetrated by Christians, but an effort to
show how the very evil done by Christians can serve as an indirect apology for
the truth of Christianity. Here I begin with a personal story from the noted

African-American clergyman of a previous generation, Howard Thurman. In 1935 Thurman was part of an American student delegation to what was then called Ceylon when he was quizzed closely by a Hindu scholar about how Thurman, an African-American, could in good conscience be a Christian. The questioning was sharp:

> More than three hundred years ago your forefathers were taken from the western coast of Africa as slaves. The people who dealt in the slave traffic were Christians. . . . The men who bought the slaves were Christians. Christian ministers, quoting the Christian apostle Paul, gave the sanction of religion to the system of slavery. . . . [Y]ou have lived in a Christian nation in which you are segregated, lynched, and burned. Even in the church, I understand, there is segregation. . . . I am a Hindu. I do not understand. Here you are in my country, standing deep within the Christian faith and tradition. I do not wish to seem rude to you. But, sir, I think you are a traitor to all the darker peoples of the earth. I am wondering what you, an intelligent man, can say in defense of your position.[9]

Thurman's answer took more than five hours to deliver personally; that response, in turn, became the seed for Thurman's book *Jesus and the Disinherited.* In that volume, Thurman began and ended with the person and work of Jesus Christ. To his Hindu interlocutor, he pointed out that Jesus was a Jew whose Jewishness Christian interpreters forget only to their loss. But not only was Jesus a Jew, he was also "a poor Jew" who by his poverty was thus linked to "the great mass of men on the earth." Again, however, Jesus was not just a poor Jew; he was in addition "a member of a minority group in the midst of a larger dominant and controlling group," the imperialistic Romans.[10] On this basis, Thurman then went on to say, "The basic fact is that Christianity as it was born in the mind of this Jewish teacher and thinker appears as a technique of survival for the oppressed. That it became, through the intervening years, a religion of the powerful and the dominant, used sometimes as an instrument of oppression, must not tempt us into believing that it was thus in the mind and life of Jesus. 'In him was life; and the life was the light of men.'"[11] Thurman was concluding, as he put it, that evil done in the name of Christ was not "a basic weakness in the religion itself" but "a betrayal of the genius of that religion."[12] With this distinction, Thurman attempted to defend the essential integrity of Christianity while still accounting for how it could have been used as a tool of oppression.

Thurman was on sound historical ground here, for it is possible to record innumerable examples where Christian believers have acted humanely, generously, kindly, altruistically, unselfishly, and charitably—and, moreover, have acted in this way on behalf of the powerless. The number and diversity of these examples raises the possibility that Christianity could be defended on strict historical grounds as a positive force in human history.

A Christian historian can find so many of such instances that it is hard to know where to begin, but as Thurman did, it is good to start with the life of Jesus as recorded in the Gospels. Thus, we find there a record of one who used his divine power and wisdom to dignify the status of women; to exalt the position of children to a much higher status than they normally enjoyed in the society of his day; to treat the Samaritans, who were ancient antagonists of the Jews, as persons worthy of full respect; to personally deal with the sick and even to touch the ones who suffered from the most loathsome diseases; and to honor the humble people of his society above the high and mighty. In other words, if records of the life of Jesus Christ are to mean anything in the definition of Christianity, that definition begins with remarkable solicitude for the weak, the despised, the oppressed, the Other.

Without denying that the religion originating in Jesus has been used for many nefarious purposes, the historical record fairly bulges with instances where the followers of Jesus really did follow him in deed as well as word. Examples cannot prove that Christianity has, on balance, contributed more good than evil to the world, but it is nonetheless important to take account of multitudinous positive examples. Thus, state-sponsored Christianity did eventually link the faith with the high and mighty, but one of the great attractions of the Christian church in its early centuries was its openness to slaves, gladiators, women, and "the nations," to the very ones upon whom Roman power looked down as beneath contempt. Yes, missionary activity has often enough been callously imperialistic to target cultures, but that is far from the only reality of missionary service. The early Christian missionaries to Ireland, for example, never rode on horseback because they did not want to exalt themselves above the level of ordinary people. In the thirteenth century, the Franciscan mystic Ramon Llull (Raymond Lull; ca. 1235–1316) intentionally traveled without weapons or the protection of military might in his missionary journeys among Muslims in North Africa. A couple of centuries later, the Jesuit Matteo Ricci (1551–1610) came to China and acted with a modern kind of sensitivity to the integrity of Chinese culture. In 1659, the Roman Catholic Church's Sacred Congregation for the Propagation of the Faith stated a principle that many more Christian missionaries have followed than is often recognized. In writing to its missionaries in the East, the Congregation said, "Do not try to persuade the Chinese to change their rites, their customs, their ways, as long as these are not openly opposed to religion and good morals. What would be sillier than to import France, Spain, Italy, or any other country of Europe into China? Don't import these, but the faith. The faith does not reject or crush the rites and customs of any race, as long as these are not evil. Rather, it wants to preserve them."[13]

Similarly, while it is true that Christianity was often employed to justify the subjugation of non-European peoples, it is also true that Christianity very explicitly provided the rationale for defending the integrity of non-Europeans as human beings as fully dignified in the sight of God as were the Europeans. Thus, among the first ones to speak out against European degradation of Native Americans were the Dominicans Bartolomé de las Casas (1474–1566) and Francisco de Vitoria (ca. 1486–1546), both of whom overcame much resistance to argue boldly for the full human dignity of the Indians.[14]

Equally, if Christianity was sometimes used as a rationale for slavery, it was also the most important source of antislave agitation, as has been recognized in the magisterial histories of antislave activity by such modern scholars as David Brion Davis and Roger Anstey. Thus, it was a group of Quakers and Mennonites in Pennsylvania in the 1680s who made the first public protest against slavery in the New World at a time when almost no one else in the British Empire had even given the issue a thought; it was John Wesley, the founder of Methodism, who jeered at the hypocrisy of the American Revolution and the American patriots' claim to be fighting tyranny by referring to the Africans enslaved in the land of the Declaration of Independence; it was William Wilberforce and other British evangelicals who took the lead in attacking Britain's participation in the slave trade; it was Congregationalists from New England and the Mid-Atlantic states who, at great risk to themselves, took steps like funding the defense of the *Amistad* Africans; it was a coalition of white and black Protestants who pushed hardest on Abraham Lincoln to expand the purposes of the Civil War from preserving the Union to freeing the slave; and it was a similar coalition that provided most of the practical support for the freed slaves after that war was over. This record of proactive opposition to slavery cannot obliterate the record of those who used Christianity to defend slavery, but it must be brought into the picture for any meaningful historical assessment.

The story is the same for Christian involvement with Native Americans. While the record is dismal of believers employing the faith to justify the displacement and even destruction of the Indians, it is nonetheless still the case that almost all efforts at defending, improving, and upholding Native Americans from the seventeenth century through at least the nineteenth century arose directly from the application of Christian faith. Thus, Roger Williams of Rhode Island, the Rev. John Eliot of nearby Roxbury, and successive generations of Mayhew clergymen on Martha's Vineyard were about the only New Englanders in the seventeenth century to even attempt to treat Native Americans as dignified human beings, and they did so explicitly from Christian motivation. The Moravians in the 1750s were the only ones to speak for the Delaware Indians when they were assaulted by American militia during the heat of the French and Indian War. In the 1830s, Baptist and Presbyterian missionaries, some of whom went to prison in acts of civil disobedience, were the only serious defenders of the Cherokee, when they were violently expelled from Georgia by the edicts of President Andrew Jackson. And on the American plains, the Belgian Jesuit, Pierre-Jean de Smet, was a notable force for humane treatment of Native Americans as well as an active missionary.

Christian efforts among Native Americans were never culturally sensitive by the standards of the late twentieth century, but as dreadful as the fate of American Indians has been, it is terrifying to think of what would have happened if many Christian workers, acting directly from their consciousness as Christians, had not been there.

And what can be said about the twentieth century, when moral standards concerning Western treatment of the Other have risen so high? Certainly not an exoneration of Christians using the faith to justify various forms of hegemonic oppression. But at the same time, the record of sterling Christian altruism is so thorough and so profound that, at the very least, it should make the game of moral accusation a lot more difficult than it often appears. It is probably not possible to develop systematically a case for the preponderance of Christian-inspired good over Christian-sanctioned evil for the twentieth century, but such a case would include at least the following matters.

It would include the arguments of Lamin Sanneh, the Gambian-born student of Islam who now teaches at Yale University, that efforts by missionaries to translate the Christian Scriptures into the languages of indigenous peoples have constituted the single most important factor in the preservation of indigenous cultures in the course of the last century.[15] Sanneh's argument contains its ironic twists, for he recognizes that the intention of many missionaries was to use translation of the Bible to make over indigenous peoples into good middle-class Americans. Nonetheless, Sanneh contends that the reduction of indigenous languages to writing along with the rise of Christian churches within indigenous societies has enabled many indigenous peoples to resist the various political, economic, and cultural imperialisms that have decimated so many indigenous societies in the twentieth century.

A full argument for the benefit of Christianity to the twentieth century would require also a careful reexamination of the Hitler period in Germany. While Christian complicity with the Nazis is a fact, so is it also a fact that most of the principled opposition to Hitler arose from either communist or Christian sources. If many Christians were silent during the Hitler horrors, other Christians like the Lutheran ministers Dietrich Bonhoeffer and Martin Niemöller, the Roman Catholics who made up the White Rose in Munich, and the Catholic Stauffenburg family that spearheaded the attempt to assassinate Hitler were powerful "signs of contradiction" inspired by their own appropriations of Christian faith.

Similarly with the story of communist regimes in the twentieth century. I am prepared to concede that the rise of state Marxism was facilitated by the failure of Christians to alleviate oppressive conditions that Marxists hoped to improve. Yet a Christian must also insist upon recognizing the heroism—there is no better word—of millions of Christian believers, of high estate and low, who resisted, often with their lives, when Marxist good intentions became

Marxist terror. I am thinking of the tens of thousands of Russian Orthodox priests who perished in the camps rather than renounce the Christian faith. Likewise, Aleksander Solzhenitsyn's untiring efforts to memorialize the victims of Soviet gulags are unthinkable without the grounding provided by his Orthodox Christian faith. I do not want to claim perfection for movements like Polish Solidarity, but the record of its patient resistance to communist tyranny is similarly unthinkable without grounding in the Roman Catholic faith. It is also worth considering the fact that it was in Leipzig's St. Nikolai Kirche, where in the eighteenth century the music had been provided by J. S. Bach, that East Germans met week after week for candlelit prayer vigils throughout the summer of 1989 and by that means, though always threatened by imminent reprisals, brought down the most powerful of the communist satellites, and did so without a single shot being fired.

Space fails to write of other matters, many of which actually involve complicated mixtures of motivations. But it would be a foolish historian indeed who paid no heed to the Christian root in the work of the Rev. Martin Luther King Jr. and the Southern Christian Leadership Conference in attacking racial discrimination in the United States, or who ignored the Christianity that bulks so large in the work of the Sisters of Charity founded by Mother Teresa, or who neglected the Christian factor in the peaceful transition of South Africa from apartheid to democracy. One last datum from countless others that could be mentioned is the statement released in 1998 by the Vatican to repent publicly for Roman Catholic failure to do more for the Jews during the Nazi era. I am not myself persuaded that this document says all that could be said, but I am very hard pressed to think of any other worldwide organization—whether governmental, religious, business, or cultural—that in the twentieth century took such pains to criticize itself as the Catholic Church did in this document. Nor am I aware of other statements that so nobly exhibit Christian ideals of realism toward personal failings combined with confidence in the purifying effects of the Christian gospel as Pope John Paul II's personal statement that accompanied the release of this Vatican study:

> As we prepare for the beginning of the Third Millennium of Christianity, the Church is aware that the joy of a Jubilee is above all the joy that is based on the forgiveness of sins and reconciliation with God and neighbor. Therefore she encourages her sons and daughters to purify their hearts, through repentance of past errors and infidelities. She calls them to place themselves humbly before the Lord and examine themselves on the responsibility which they too have for the evils of our time.[16]

One argument implied by merely listing such instances of Christian integrity, honesty, and altruism is straightforward. It is to suggest that, however much evil has been done in the name of Christ, the world would be in a much, much more dreadful situation if Christianity did not exist. Another argument is more indirect: it is the contention that one can discriminate, as Rev. Thurman did, between Christian behavior that is true to Christ and Christian behavior that betrays Christ. It can be argued, in other words, that some supposedly Christian behavior comes much closer to the religion of Jesus and the ideals of Christianity than other supposedly Christian behavior. This indirect argument contains an appeal for historical evaluation that goes like this: when you discover someone in the past referred to as a Christian, pause to inquire if the person or group is following the words of Jesus, such as, for example, those found in the fifth chapter of the Gospel of Matthew:

> Blessed are the poor in spirit, for theirs is the kingdom of heaven.
> Blessed are those who mourn, for they will be comforted.
> Blessed are the meek, for they will inherit the earth.
> Blessed are those who hunger and thirst for righteousness, for they will be filled.
> Blessed are the merciful, for they will be shown mercy.
> Blessed are the pure in heart, for they will see God.
> Blessed are the peacemakers, for they will be called sons of God.
> Blessed are those who are persecuted because of righteousness, for theirs is the kingdom of heaven. . . .
> You have heard that it was said, "Eye for eye, and tooth for tooth." But I tell you, Do not resist an evil person. If someone strikes you on the right cheek, turn to him the other also. And if someone wants to sue you and take your tunic, let him have your cloak as well. If someone forces you to go one mile, go with him two miles. Give to the one who asks you, and do not turn away from the one who wants to borrow from you.
> You have heard that it was said, "Love your neighbor and hate your enemy." But I tell you: Love your enemies and pray for those who persecute you, that you may be sons of your Father in heaven.[17]

If groups or persons known as Christian appear not to follow such guidance from Christ himself, maybe they are not truly Christian at all.

Any indictment of Christianity for the damage it has done in human history is dishonest to the core if it does not also pay attention to the good done by Christians. That good has been very consistent and very considerable throughout history.

At the same time, more needs to be said. It may, in fact, not be a particularly Christian way of defending the integrity of Christianity merely to show that there are probably more instances of human goodness done in the name of Christ than instances of human evil done in the same name. As a Christian historian, my conviction is that, objectively considered, the good far outweighs the bad. Yet that evaluation may not take seriously enough both the historical record and the Christian faith.

Merely counting examples, pro and con, is too simplistic, in the first instance, because of the ambiguity witnessed time after time in the history of Chris-

---

tianity. That ambiguity is the fact that good brought about by honoring the name of Christ has very often coexisted organically—in the same situation, in the same group, even in the same person—with evil carried out in the name of Christ. Think again of the Reverend Thomas Shepard, who by all contemporary accounts and in the opinion of almost all later historians was the very model of charity, and who yet could demonize the Native American enemies of Massachusetts as nonpersons. Or for a contemporary example, think of the way in which the South African Nationalist Party leaned on the Christian Scriptures to defend the system of apartheid at the same time that practical Christian energy was a massive factor in resistance to apartheid as well as in the relatively peaceful dismantling of apartheid.

The reality is that the Christian faith has been a plastic force in history. It has obviously inspired to great goodness, but it has also obviously been used for great evil. What is going on? Allow me to suggest that this historical reality of Christianity undergirding supernal goodness even as it countenances great evil is exactly what someone should expect who attends carefully to the nature of Christianity itself.

The Christian religion at its foundation is a religion of grace. It proclaims that Jesus Christ, the second person of the Trinity, entered into the human story that he had authored in order to save sinners. Moreover, almost all groups of Christians have maintained, while differing in details of how they express it, that humans are redeemed by God's grace rather than by the achievement of their own perfection. Again while differing in how they express it, the major traditions of Christianity have also said that the salvation offered by God to sinners through Jesus Christ is a gift that we do not deserve; it is not a reward that we can earn. This means that Christianity is a religion of redeemed sinners. The different branches of Christianity have different ways of talking about "saints," but all agree that saints are not perfect; they are only those who have begun the process of practicing in their own lives an imitation of the goodness that God, in his mercy, has shown to sinful humans. The cross is the central symbol of Christianity because it both calls unbelievers to heed God's act of mercy on their behalf and reminds believers of the constant need to repent of their sin. In these terms, we may say about the evidence of history that every self-sufficient effort by self-confessed Christian believers to promote the kingdom of Christ by violence, or by any other way that does not fully live up to the standards set by Christ himself, is another blow of the hammer nailing Jesus to the cross. But at the same time, every self-denying act by Christians to promote the kingdom of Christ by the sacrifice of self or by the offer of power to the powerless or by giving dignity to the despised is another sign of the resurrection of Christ.

Thus, even if Christians have acted according to the highest standards of Christianity only inconsistently, even if Christians often contradict in their lives the model of merciful holiness provided by Jesus Christ, there is nothing in that inconsistency which contradicts Christian faith. In fact, for Christians to recognize how poorly we and our fellow believers throughout history have so often acted is an essential step toward understanding the Christian faith as it really is.

SECTION TWO
PRACTICES

SIX

BEYOND COMPLICITY

The Challenges for Christianity after the Holocaust

VICTORIA BARNETT

Whatever our place on the theological spectrum, Christians have the understandable desire that our theology be consistent with our other beliefs and convictions. We aim to weave a garment of whole cloth, as it were, that gives our lives as people of faith in the world a coherence and consistency. Some of us tend to work from the worldly end, engaging in an ongoing critique and reworking of our theology on the basis of our lived experience. Others draw more upon a foundation of firm theological doctrine as both a starting point and as the measure for all subsequent perspectives and actions in the world.

The quest for such theological coherence is a daunting task, and there are certain events in history—such as the Holocaust—that push our capacity for it to its utmost limits. The Jewish thinker Arthur Cohen has described the Holocaust as a *tremendum,* a rupture in history so cataclysmic that it forces Jews and Christians alike to alter the way we think about evil and the way we understand faith itself. After the Holocaust, writes Cohen, our conceptions of "both God and man are in need of rethinking and redescription."[1] The history of the Holocaust confronts Christians with particularly painful dilemmas, for part of this history is its record of Christian complicity in violence, including incendiary church teachings and statements about Judaism and even active complicity in the Nazi persecution and genocide of the Jews.

Given the churches' bleak record between 1933 and 1945, some people have concluded that there is a direct causal relationship between Christianity and

97

the Nazi genocide of the Jews. They view Nazism as the logical outcome of centuries of Christian anti-Judaism. While there is indeed a connection, however, it is not a linear or straightforward one. To portray either Nazism or the Holocaust as the logical outcome of Christian history is false, both historically and theologically. One should raise the question, for example, of whether the church was led astray by Christian doctrine itself, or more by the churches' often problematic alliance, throughout history, with state authority. Moreover, while we must acknowledge the passivity and complicity of all too many church leaders, it would be wrong to disregard the record of those leaders and laypeople who drew upon Christian teachings and traditions in the fight against Nazism. And, despite occasional efforts by Nazi leaders to woo the churches, Nazi ideology itself was fundamentally anti-Christian, and the most fervent Nazis viewed the churches as a potential source of resistance and saw Christianity as an outmoded belief system that would die out.[2]

At the same time, while Christianity was not the sole reason for what happened, it remains part of the picture. The anti-Judaism in the Christian churches did not "create" Nazism, but it was part of the cultural and political milieu out of which Nazism emerged. It gave theological legitimation to racial anti-Semitism, which shaped the response of many Christians at the time and even led some church leaders to publicly defend the Nazi measures against the Jews. Even Christian leaders who were critical of some aspects of Nazism rationalized the persecution of the Jews or, at the very least, were reticent to criticize it publicly.[3] This complexity must be acknowledged if we are really to understand what happened in the Christian community, inside and outside Nazi Germany, between 1933 and 1945.

This ambiguous legacy has sparked debate about whether the history of Christianity during the Holocaust includes any insights into how Christians can avoid complicity in such violence—or whether it only offers, at best, a cautionary example of what *not* to do. Certainly one thing the Holocaust demands of Christians is a serious and critical confrontation with those parts of our theology and history that have been used to justify oppression and violence. At the same time, while acknowledging the problematic nature of this history, I believe that we can indeed find the theological and ethical resources within Christian teachings to go "beyond complicity." I remain convinced that Nazism and the Holocaust represent the antithesis, not the fulfillment, of Christian teachings, and that there are aspects of the history of the churches from 1933 to 1945 that can help us address the challenges raised by this history.

It is particularly important to define the kind of violence we are looking at here: political persecution and genocidal violence against a group defined as "other." For that reason it may be helpful to discuss Christian complicity in the Holocaust in juxtaposition with some reflections about the actions of those who were not complicitous: those Christians who resisted, particularly those who rescued Jews. I do not propose this as an "easy out." The stories of rescue—actions, we must recall, of a minority—neither undo nor excuse the complicity of other Christians. Yet what defined the acts of the rescuers was their capacity to help people who had been stigmatized and persecuted as outcasts, as the "other." Through their actions, they were able to step outside the dominant ideology that perceived Jews as subhuman and subversive enemies. What specifically Christian resources enabled them to do so?

One enigma that arises here is that there are no common factors (including religious faith) that characterize this group.[4] Rescue was usually the spontaneous act of individuals, a generous response to an unexpected appeal for help. Those who saved Jews came from all walks of life, from diplomats to rural farmers. Some of them—though not all—were Christians. More significantly, even among Christian rescuers, faith seems to have played an inconsistent role. Theologically, they were a very diverse group, ranging from the Huguenots of Le Chambon in France to Polish Catholics. Some of them were moved by a theologically grounded faithfulness to the Jewish people; others more by their political opposition to what Nazism stood for. Many of them—and this is true of rescuers as a whole—couldn't really say why they responded as they did.

To this group we could add the names of courageous Catholics and Protestants who were not involved in rescue, but who condemned what the Nazis were doing and gave their lives in protest: people such as the Berlin priest Bernhard Lichtenberg, who died en route to Dachau after praying publicly for the Jewish victims of Nazism, and the Rhineland Protestant pastor Paul Schneider, whose angry protests from his pulpit against the Nazis led to imprisonment, torture, and death in Buchenwald. Finally, we could include those Christians who moved into active political conspiracy and resistance, most notably Dietrich Bonhoeffer, who was executed in April of 1945 for his role in the conspiracy against Hitler.

At some point, most of these Christians attempted to weave the "whole cloth" of faith and worldly witness that I mentioned at the beginning of this chapter. That is: they thought theologically about what they were doing. The sermons, letters, and theological writings of Dietrich Bonhoeffer throughout the Nazi era are the most complete literary record of this process. Yet many of the Christian rescuers and resisters tried to understand their situation (either at the time or later) not just as citizens of Nazi Germany or Nazi-occupied Europe, but as Christians.[5]

The reason for including such people in a discussion of complicity is that both complicity and rescue are not so much single actions as processes. The nature of the process of rescue has been studied by David Gushee, who examined Christian rescuers of Jews within the greater faith context of their actions. Gushee concluded that some of these people were indeed shaped by "resources of Christian piety"—primarily by what he calls "a lived Christian spirituality."[6] To see this "lived spirituality" as a "process" means recognizing its circular dynamic. While it emerged from certain religious resources and beliefs, the act of rescue in turn deepened the strength and viability of these resources. It exemplified an ethic—the fundamental ethic preached by Jesus of Nazareth—in which conviction and faith both inform activism and strengthen it. We can see how this dynamic profoundly touched the lives of those rescued and continues to move those who read about such rescue today. Even during the Holocaust, the rescuers' actions had a profound effect upon their own lives and faith. Acts of goodness (like acts of complicity) alter both the protagonist and the recipient.

Both complicity and rescue, then, can be viewed not as individual actions but as steps along a continuum, leading those involved in separate directions. And, like rescue, complicity has a ripple effect that affects both the complicitous individual and the greater community.

In this chapter, I will address these phenomena in two stages. First, I will simply offer a historical overview of some kinds of Christian complicity during the Holocaust. Second, I will reexamine Gushee's notion of "lived spirituality," for it may be that we can gain a deeper understanding of complicity if we examine it in direct contrast to the religiospiritual dynamics of rescue. If a common feature among rescuers is their lack of complicity, what insights for today can we glean from their actions?

Christian Complicity in the Holocaust

A detailed study of Christian complicity in the Holocaust goes beyond the scope of this chapter, yet a series of "snapshots" of Christian behavior during the Holocaust illustrates the numerous forms that such complicity took:

- The most striking case of such complicity was that of the "German Christians" (the *Deutsche Christen*), a group within German Protestantism that sought a so-called Reich Church. In reality, this Reich Church was a Nazified church: one with new hymns and new liturgies that reflected the new "Aryan" spirit.[7] The German Christians wanted to excise the Hebrew Scriptures and selected portions of the New Testament from the Bible, including all references to Jesus' Jewishness. The more radical ones wanted to get rid of the cross, since they believed that no real "Aryan" hero would ever have allowed himself to be crucified. Above all, they sought a church that would be "racially pure," which meant setting up separate churches for converted Jews.

- Where did they come from? Another snapshot, from late-nineteenth-century discussions of the "Jewish question," reveals some of the roots of the German Christians' anti-Judaism and nationalism. Several issues of a mainstream Protestant newspaper carried an ongoing editorial debate that featured an exchange of views on whether Christian baptism could

turn a Jew into a German. The Jews being referred to, of course, were German citizens; and baptism brings new members into the Christian community, not a national one. Yet these essential facts seem to have eluded the educated Protestants debating the issue—an ominous early sign of the kind of thinking that fostered the rise of Nazism a half century later.[8]

- Early in the Nazi era, however, a Protestant group emerged in direct opposition to the German Christians: the Confessing Church. Its founding statement, the Barmen Confession, was written by the Swiss theologian Karl Barth, who would leave Nazi Germany in 1935 after refusing to take a loyalty oath for professors. The Barmen Confession was subsequently interpreted in different ways, but the church leaders who signed it in May 1934 viewed it as a protest against the totalitarian demands Nazism had placed on the church. By declaring that Christian faithfulness to God and the Scriptures superseded allegiance to worldly leaders, the Barmen Confession held the seeds of resistance against Nazism. At the same time, the Barmen Confession said not a word about the persecution of the Jews.

  Some of the most famous Confessing Christians became known for their resistance against Nazism, such as Dietrich Bonhoeffer and an outspoken Berlin pastor, Martin Niemöller, who was imprisoned by the Nazis in various concentration camps from 1938 to 1945. Yet the Confessing Church made a number of compromises with Nazi authorities, and even its most outspoken members did not necessarily begin as opponents of Nazism. Martin Niemöller voted for Hitler in 1932, and from his cell in Dachau he volunteered to fight for the German Wehrmacht in 1939.[9]

- Another snapshot further illustrates the caution within the Confessing Church regarding the persecution of the Jews. In September 1935, two weeks after the passage of the Nuremberg Laws, Confessing Church leaders convened at the Steglitz Synod in Berlin. Some of those present hoped to pass a church statement that would have offered tacit support for the Nuremberg Laws, which had seriously intensified restrictions on German Jews. At the illegal Confessing Church seminary in Finkenwalde, Dietrich Bonhoeffer and his students received a call urging them to come to Berlin and protest. The Finkenwalde group sat in the balcony of the church, booing and stomping their feet as the debate about the measure proceeded. They and the other opponents of the measure succeeded; the proposal was tabled. But another proposal to the synod—one that would have given public church support for the Jewish victims of Nazi persecution—didn't even make it onto the agenda. It was blocked by several bishops, including Bishop Hans Meiser of Bavaria, who warned his colleagues against "a martyrdom we bring upon ourselves."[10]

- Here are some other snapshots from outside Germany during the spring of 1933. Shortly after the April 1 boycott of Jewish businesses in Berlin, church leaders in Europe and the United States sent strongly worded protests to their colleagues in Germany, explicitly condemning the anti-Jewish actions of the German regime. In fact, there was a series of such protests, some of them powerfully eloquent, from the international Christian community throughout these years.[11] Some came from the Federal Council of Churches in New York, others from ecumenical leaders in Switzerland.

- The German response to such protests was defensive. German church leaders accused their foreign colleagues of not understanding the hope Germans had placed in their new Führer. Some went so far as to defend Nazi policies. In 1933, for example, Superintendent Otto Dibelius of Berlin—who as a leader in the Confessing Church would protest against the Nazi regime on other points—defended the April 1 boycott of Jewish businesses as the logical outcome of "justified" German resentment against the Jews.[12]

- Another snapshot comes in the wake of the so-called *Kristallnacht* of November 1938, when hundreds of Jewish synagogues, businesses, and homes were destroyed by the Gestapo, and hundreds of Jews were arrested. In Baden-Württemberg, Pastor Julius von Jan preached a powerful sermon the following Sunday, condemning the pogrom. Several days later, he was attacked and beaten by a group of Nazi thugs. His parsonage was vandalized and his family was threatened, and von Jan was finally arrested and imprisoned in a Gestapo jail. His bishop, Theophil Wurm, made sure that von Jan's family was cared for, and Wurm negotiated to reduce his prison sentence. All this took place behind the scenes. Wurm did not make any kind of public protest. When he finally did write a letter to Nazi Justice Minister Franz Gürtner, protesting the pogrom, Wurm added that he did not dispute the Nazi regime's right "to fight Judaism as a dangerous element." Years later, in his memoirs, Wurm wrote that he would regret those words "to the end of my life."[13]

- Here are more snapshots from outside Germany. In 1934, leaders of the Protestant Federal Council of Churches and the United Jewish Appeal opened an office in New York to help refugees from Nazi Germany. Most of these refugees were so-called "non-Aryan Christians"—Jews converted to Christianity. In Germany, because of the high degree of assimilation, this group was actually larger than the Jewish population; in 1933, there were 615,000 Jews and 1.5 to 2 million "non-Aryan Christians" in Germany. Eighty-eight percent of them were Protestant. By the end of 1934, U.S. Jewish organizations had raised $1,800,000 to support the refugee aid office. In contrast, the Protestant member churches of the FCC had contributed a total of $8,000. In the years that followed, this pattern was repeated in every Christian ecumenical agency that did refugee work. There was little Christian support for refugee work—even when the refugees were church members.[14]

- A final snapshot portrays the interfaith cooperation in Geneva, Switzerland, between Willem Visser 't Hooft, the Dutch pastor who led the ecumenical offices there; Adolf Freudenberg, head of the ecumenical refugee office; and Gerhardt Riegner, head of the World Jewish Congress. For four years, from 1941 to 1945, Riegner regularly passed on the messages he was getting about the murders of European Jews to Visser 't Hooft. Those messages were then conveyed to the international community— to the Archbishop of Canterbury, to leaders in New York, to diplomats, to the International Red Cross. The three men met once a week. They lobbied the Swiss government to take in more refugees, and they spoke with foreign diplomats to gain an international hearing as well. Riegner later described his work and friendship with these two men as "the only signs of light in the darkness that surrounded us."[15] And Riegner was personally and tremendously hurt in 1948, when the founding conference of the World Council of Churches in Amsterdam approved a statement about the church's relationship to the Jewish people, repenting of its failures to help them during the Holocaust—yet, at the same time, reaffirming the churches' commitment to evangelize among Jews: a statement that Riegner described in an interview with me as "after all that had happened, a slap in the face."[16]

A list of historical snapshots of Christian behavior during this period could go on for some time. Its many contradictory pictures raise a number of uncomfortable questions. They establish that the story of the Christian community's response to the Holocaust, inside and outside Nazi Germany, is a very complex one. Inside Germany, the complicity of the churches and their members with the Nazi violence was woven from many threads. Many of their motives had nothing to do with what people believed and how they thought theologically. Nationalism was a powerful force that united many Catholics and Protestants behind the Nazi regime, particularly in the early years. Anti-Judaism led all too many Christians to tolerate Nazi anti-Semitism. There was anti-Semitism in the churches that paralleled that found in Nazi propaganda. There was fear, as well. Some bishops and pastors were convinced that their role was not to resist but to work behind the scenes. There was apathy. There were assumptions about Christianity and German culture that led most Germans to view Jews—even those born in Germany—as outsiders. There was opportunism. There were leaders who felt that the future of their church depended upon whether it could get along with the Nazi regime. There were leaders who defended their public silence by saying that they were fighting for the very life of the institutional churches under the threat of Nazism. There were people who sympathized with Nazism. There were others who opposed it but never spoke up. Still others underwent remarkable conversion experiences, and moved from apathy to resistance and rescue. Sometimes it's hard to determine where one motive stops and another begins. We do not always know whether goodness reflects courage or something else, or whether complicity is the mark of a coward, an ideologue, or an opportunist. And the picture outside Nazi Germany is just as varied. There were some very eloquent condemnations of the Nazi regime from the international Christian community. There were other Christian leaders who remained silent.[17]

All this only underscores David Gushee's point that there are different "Christianities" and "Christian faiths." To this I would add that there are different levels of Christian existence, and very different interpretations of what the church is called to be and do during times of evil. A very central lesson that emerges from the complex history of complicity is that the church and its members do not remain unscathed when they encounter evil. As Dietrich Bonhoeffer wrote in *Ethics,* "When evil becomes powerful in the world, it infects the Christian, too. . . . [The reconciliation we find in Christ] is replaced by bitterness, suspicion and contempt for men and the world. . . . Thus a world which has become evil succeeds in making the Christians become evil too."[18] Bonhoeffer recognized that the nature of Nazi evil had affected everyone— whether they fought it, ignored it, or cooperated with it. Complicity, even when unconscious or unintentional, is an insidious process. By its very nature, as Bonhoeffer noted, it undermines our capacity for goodness and innocence. At one of the darkest points in his work for the conspiracy against Hitler, Bonhoeffer wrote, "We have been silent witnesses of evil deeds; we have been drenched by many storms; we have learnt the arts of equivocation and pretence; experience has made us suspicious of others and kept us from being truthful and open; intolerable conflicts have worn us down and even made us cynical. Are we still of any use?"[19]

Bonhoeffer's poignant question was addressed to his fellow conspirators, who had opted for the path of secrecy, silence, and caution in the hopes that their political conspiracy against the Nazi regime would succeed. Yet elsewhere, Bonhoeffer confronted his church with the same question—for all too often, the members and leaders of the German Evangelical Church were "silent witnesses of evil deeds." Because of its history of nationalism and subservience to state authority, the German Evangelical Church was ill-prepared to withstand Nazism. In some ways, it almost seemed preordained to succumb to it. Nonetheless, some members of that church were able to move beyond what they had been taught. Dietrich Bonhoeffer came out of this tradition, as did the Confessing Church itself. Despite the many flaws within the German Evangelical Church, some of its members, teachers, and leaders were saved because they took their theology and their faith seriously. This led them to rethink their faith and critique it. It enabled them to recognize the heresy of the "German

Christians," and it led a few, like Bonhoeffer, to look at what the Nazis were doing and oppose it in the name of Christianity.

The very act of taking a stand in the name of Christianity required the church opponents of Nazism not only to articulate certain theological truths, but to connect those truths with the life of the church in the world. This is where, as the slogan goes, the personal and political go together. The best people within the Christian churches recognized Nazism as a challenge not only to their church, but to themselves as individual human beings. The challenge that confronts us in any age is to make this theological link between our own lives—our essential humanity as people created by God—and our faith. One could argue that this is at the heart of what the incarnation is all about.

This link is very evident in the rescuers that Gushee studied. One of the most striking aspects of these people was their sense of immediate responsibility for those in need. This sense of responsibility—usually spontaneous and unreflective—is indicative of a kind of straightforward ethical simplicity. Such simplicity, of course, characterizes the Gospel accounts of Jesus' ministry, particularly the parables. Indeed, the radicality of Jesus' simple ethical demands sometimes confounded his listeners, as they have confounded Christians through the centuries. Years after the end of the Third Reich, Pastor Martin Niemöller said that his break with Nazism had come in the early years of the regime, when he saw the direction in which nationalism and ideology were driving his church and simply asked himself: What would Jesus do?

All too often, the simplicity of that question drives us in an inward, introspective direction. Yet the question "What would Jesus do?" impelled people like Niemöller out into the world, where they took risks and became involved in rescue and resistance. To return to the point I raised earlier, they took this question not as the issue about the state of their own theology or spiritual life, but as a challenge to recognize, in the Jewish "other," their neighbor. In times of genocidal violence, the response to the "other" is a theological act as well as an ethical one. "In encountering the stranger, one encounters a witness to the transcendence of God, one who, like God, cannot be domesticated in order to legitimate one's life, religion, or cultural-national identity—one who by his or her very differentness or otherness calls one's identity into question."[20]

While certain "resources of piety" may lay the foundation for our capacity to embrace the "other," the act of embrace is really a first step that opens the way to reevaluating our theology and our lived faith. Once embarked in this direction, people such as Dietrich Bonhoeffer began to rethink their faith in radical and unconventional ways. It is one of the ripple effects of rescue and resistance. The rethinking and critique of faith comes when that simplicity—the knowledge of the right thing to do—collides, in a sense, with the powers that be, be they political or theological.

Naturally, it is important that we wrestle with theological questions in the wake of the Holocaust. We must ponder our Christology, our notion of what it really means to carry the good news into the world, and our interpretations of Scripture. But I would add that this must be carried out at both the personal level of belief and, at the more communal level, in reflection about what it means to be the church in the world, and what it means to be a church for the "other." We must question the church's role when it legitimizes violence and undermines the work of those who resist. And, more than anything, we must not be afraid to articulate a Christian vision that combats violence and its violation of innocence in the world. Such an articulated vision—a lived spirituality—may bring us into conflict with the world. It may also bring us into conflict with ourselves and with one another, leading us to question certain theological and doctrinal precepts. Yet the Christian tradition includes the tools that help us to do that. Christians have strong traditions of prayer and discernment, repentance, forgiveness, and reconciliation, which we can draw upon as resources when we confront violence.

The fact is that all religions offer their members the tools and the capacity to see the world differently, to rethink, to critique, to resist, even to rescue. This is why dictators try either to co-opt religious groups or to eradicate them. When dictators and demagogues do succeed in getting religious leaders on their side, this leads to vicious, brutal, horrible situations in which religion explicitly sanctifies violence—as we have seen in all too many parts of the world.

But I don't think that's what happened during the Holocaust, which is an important historical distinction if we are to understand the nature of Christian complicity during that era. What we have during the Nazi era is not the leaders of the Christian world aligning themselves with Hitler to approve the persecution and murder of the Jews. Complicity during that era was constructed far more of Christian silence or passivity. The Christian failure to stand in solidarity with the Jewish "other" is a damning failure, but it remains possible to critique that failure from within the Christian faith—just as rescue and resistance drew upon both the language of faith and the understanding of how to witness to that in the world. During the Nazi era Christians, many in responsible positions, were sucked into the maelstrom of violence and used the language of faith either to legitimate that violence or to oppose it. As the rescuers remind us, it took a "certain kind of Christianity" to escape that maelstrom. The challenge to Christians in any era is not only to define that kind of faith, but to live it.

SEVEN

How Should We Then Teach American History?

A Perspective of Constructive Nonviolence

James C. Juhnke

Introduction

In the light of our concerns about violence, how should Christian historians think about, write about, and teach American history?[1] As thoughtful and faithful Christian scholars, we do not accept the autonomy of the secular disciplines, but attempt to apply Christian values to our scholarship and teaching. George Marsden in *The Outrageous Idea of Christian Scholarship* drew on the theology of St. Augustine to claim both a higher ultimate citizenship as well as a limited worldly obligation: "Even though they are pilgrims whose ultimate allegiance is elsewhere, Christians also owe limited allegiance to the regimes of their earthly sojourns. At the same time Christians should have no illusions about political institutions. Ultimately they reflect the flaws of human nature and, despite the good they do, are founded on principles of self-love or self-interest. They are created by bloodshed and maintained by force."[2] How shall followers of a nonviolent Christ tell the history of institutions created by bloodshed and maintained by force? Is it possible to write and teach history from the viewpoint that human institutions, even in some ultimate sense, have been also created and maintained by ideals?

The current climate of American historiography typically leaves us trapped between two options—triumphalist nationalism and radical cultural criticism. The triumphalist school sees a national history of freedom, albeit qualified by some ironical exceptions. In a democratic society, the people demand triumphalism. The American history textbook publishing business is hostage to a nationalistic market. Publishers must provide books that tell the story of America's rise to greatness. Nationalistic patriotism still owns the public square. In 1995 the Smithsonian Air and Space Museum backed down when its exhibit on the *Enola Gay* put the atomic bombing of Japan into a wider context than the American public could allow. Meanwhile the countercultural critics produce their own literature condemning the American nationalism for what it did to Native Americans, to slaves from Africa, to victims of neo-imperialism, to the environment, to women, to immigrants, and to religious and ethnic minorities. For the radical critics, Howard Zinn's *People's History of the United States* has served as the favored survey from the underside.

On one point, however, the triumphalists and the radical critics agree. They both adhere to the myth of redemptive violence.[3] They approve of warfare as a means of liberation. The one side believes American freedom is the product of wars fought and won for human liberation—from the American Revolution through the great wars of the twentieth century. The other side regrets that the truly dispossessed people—the Indians, the blacks, the oppressed workers, and the Filipinos who fought for their own independence after the Spanish-American War—were too weak and disorganized to turn the violence to their own liberation. Triumphalists and critics in different ways justify violence, as long as the good guys win.

Christian historians who honor the teachings and the example of Christ must find a way to cut through the prevailing consensus on redemptive violence. An alternative perspective that can chart a creative path between the poles of triumphalism and radical criticism may be given the label of "constructive nonviolence." The viewpoint of constructive nonviolence is constructive in that it affirms the civil order and the benefits of good government, while insisting that so-called "just wars" have left a legacy of death, destruction, and debt. Our violent warfare has perpetuated and intensified the violence of domestic poverty, racism, the workplace, and the home. The theological and historiographical foundations for the viewpoint of constructive nonviolence deserve sustained attention.[4] But given the limitations of space in this chapter, here it must suffice to offer a few principles with supporting examples on how to teach American history in a way that challenges the violence-affirming assumptions that pervade American historical consciousness. Quite practically, then, what may happen when we approach our national history from the viewpoint of constructive nonviolence?[5]

Teaching Strategies and Interpretive Options

Honor the Survival and Strength of Native American Cultures

American history begins with the original inhabitants of North America. A constructive question to guide analysis of Native American history is this: What enabled the Indians to survive as distinct peoples in the face of the devastating holocausts they suffered—infectious diseases, military defeat, economic dependence, and loss of self-rule? Generations of European Americans observed the results of their invasion and predicted that the Indians would tragically die and disappear—as represented by *The Last of the Mohicans,* the title of the nineteenth-century novel by James Fenimore Cooper, or by the tragic frame that John G. Neihardt imposed upon his famous narration of the story of Black Elk.[6] But Indian culture adapted and survived rather than disappeared. Today their numbers are growing. Their creative art and literature inspire the world. In our time thousands of rootless great-grandchildren of the Puritans, having lost their own spiritual heritage, beat paths to Native American teachers and plead, "Tell us how we can be whole again!" What accounts for the survival and vitality of Indian culture?

The master narrative in American history textbooks, Hollywood films, and History Channel specials offers little help on the question of Indian cultural survival. The original Indian communities, like humans everywhere, contained powerful impulses toward both peace and war. But unbalanced white American narratives lift up just one side. The heroes of the master narrative are the military warriors who rose up to resist the white advance across the continent—Metacomet (King Philip; ca. 1639–1676), Pontiac (ca. 1720–1769), Tecumseh (1768–1813), Crazy Horse (ca. 1842–1877), Geronimo (1829–1909). The textbooks pretend to honor the Indians by celebrating their warriors—a kind of political correctness paying its dues to the dispossessed and defeated. In fact this rhetorical strategy feeds the triumphalist myth by erecting heroes worthy of the white conquerors of the continent. It nourishes the cult of the warrior both among Native American cultures and among the dominant white culture, while obscuring the peacemakers on both sides of the tragic encounter.

Did the warriors save their peoples? No, the warriors perished in hopeless battles. Generation after generation of Native Americans sacrificed their sons to futile violent resistance. Meanwhile the unsung heroes of Native American history were those who resisted nonviolently. Native American culture was rescued and sustained by Indians who strove to avoid war and who picked up the pieces after repeated rounds of death and destruction. Indian ways of living survived because of the patient, persistent, and creative traditionalism of ordinary women and men, and because of the special role of charismatic prophets who set forth new visions for the life of their people. They had to make cultural adjustments and compromises, even as they found ways to sustain their identity. From the viewpoint of constructive nonviolence, the peaceable Wampanoag chief Massasoit (d. 1661) is a greater hero than his war-making son Metacomet. If the question is long-range cultural survival, the Seneca peace prophet Handsome Lake (d. 1815), who counseled his people not to take up arms in the war of 1812, is a worthier model than the warrior Tecumseh, who died in that war. By the same token, the Cheyenne peace chiefs White Antelope (d. 1864) and Black Kettle (d. 1868) must be honored above the flamboyant warriors who created the reputation of the "fighting Cheyenne."

Honor Nonviolent Alternatives Proposed but Rejected

A perspective of constructive nonviolence must give attention to moments in our national history when leaders made decisions for violence and war. Here the task is to grasp the reality of choice and to show that people had good reasons for and against different courses of action. Decisions for war in the American past were not inevitable, even though the master narrative of our textbooks typically makes it appear that way. Christian historians with a preference for peace need to lift up the voices of farsighted leaders who proposed reasonable alternatives to warfare.

We all know of the Boston Tea Party of December 16, 1773—an allegedly heroic event of extralegal violence that set the stage for the War for Independence. From the viewpoint of constructive nonviolence, the Boston Tea Party was a lamentable failure in conflict management. At the same time as the Bostonians resorted to violence, the city of Philadelphia resolved its tea crisis nonviolently. The Philadelphians refused the East India tea as firmly as did the Bostonians. The Quaker merchants and an impressive mass of protesting citizens persuaded Samuel Ayres, captain of the tea-bearing ship, to take the tea back to London. They smoothed the way by advancing funds to buy supplies for the journey. John Penn, the proprietary governor, treated the situation with benign neglect, unlike Thomas Hutchinson in Boston, who forced a showdown with Sam Adams and the anti-British hotheads. This Philadelphia success in conflict resolution is never honored in our national memory. Such events should be remembered, if only as reminders that apparently intractable conflicts can be resolved. As the late Kenneth Boulding once said, "If something happens, it ought to be viewed as historically possible."[7]

In the wake of the British response to Boston's violence, colonial leaders met in Philadelphia at the First Continental Congress. At that meeting Joseph Galloway, leader of the Quaker Party of Pennsylvania, proposed a bold plan to change the constitution of the British Empire. He called for an American Parliament, a "Grand Council," to share powers with the British Parliament over American affairs. The congress debated Galloway's plan for two days and then rejected it by the narrowest of margins, six colonies to five. Most delegates found the plan too radical in proposing that the separate colonies should yield some authority to an intercolonial legislature. They mistakenly believed that the British would back down if the congress got tough in its resistance. Galloway's vision for reforming the constitution of the British Empire was more insightful and expansive than the arguments of his opponents. Yet Galloway has been all but expunged from our national memory.

A constructive nonviolent perspective must investigate the critical moments leading to war throughout our history and ask the questions: Was this war necessary? Who was offering proposals to avoid the violence? What were the arguments for and against those proposals? What would the likely effects have been of their adoption? The point of such a teaching strategy is not to portray good and evil as clear-cut alternatives, or to argue that good motives and strong reasons were all on one side. If my experience is typical, many of our students will be drawn to such oversimplifications. The point is to engage history in its complexity and messiness, rather than excluding the proposals of peacemakers from the national story as our reigning myth of redemptive violence consistently does. Thus our history classes in covering the critical period after the election of 1860 could examine the arguments of those who counseled president-elect Abraham Lincoln to assert himself as a moderate national leader, not hostage to the radical wing of the Republican Party. Was there a strong case for cooperating with moderate unionists in the South, and for Lincoln to appoint one or more of their number to his cabinet? Might such a strategy have helped avoid the war? Or to jump forward to the twentieth century, in the case of the debate over U.S. entry into the European war of 1914–1917, we could give primary attention to the arguments of Secretary of State William Jennings Bryan, who saw that only genuine neutrality would keep the country out of war and that by entering the war the United States would not make the world safe for democracy.

To examine seriously the nonviolent alternatives proposed but rejected at critical points in our past can quickly lead to counterfactual considerations. What if nonviolent proposals had been accepted? What would have changed? Such questions are valid for our American history classrooms, I believe, for at least three reasons. First, when people in the past proposed nonviolent policy alternatives, they did so in reality. Exploration of their actual documented arguments is not itself counterfactual history. Indeed, as historian Niall Ferguson has pointed out, "what actually happened was often *not* the outcome which the majority of informed contemporaries saw as the most likely: The counterfactual scenario was in that sense more 'real' to decision makers at the critical moment than the actual subsequent events."[8] Second, American history as currently taught and debated is already enlivened with counterfactual scenarios and arguments. Military historians are especially fond of the counterfactual.[9] For example, the triumphalists argue that if we had not dropped the bombs on Hiroshima and Nagasaki in 1945, a land invasion of Japan would have been necessary and might have killed more people than did the bombs. That counterfactual hypothesis may be countered with the suggestion that Japan in the fall of 1945 was already militarily prostrate, had contacted the Soviet Union about conditional terms for surrender, and would likely have surrendered if the United States had offered the terms we eventually accepted—including that Japan could keep the emperor. Such counterfactual arguments can move beyond mere speculation if they force us back to investigate and evaluate critical sources. Third, it can be argued that the ability to imagine nonviolent scenarios is especially important if we are to live with reasonable hope for survival in a world in which nuclear weapons of mass destruction are not under international control and continue to proliferate. Today's students need to develop habits of imagining nonviolent alternative futures.

Honor the Antimilitary Idealism of the Founders

A perspective of constructive nonviolence will recognize that our nation has a usable peacemaking past. In the early decades of the republic, the country was more fervently committed to the ideal of peace than to the arts of warfare. This peace commitment was not at the fringes of national identity. It was near the core. Quaker pacifism had put a permanent stamp on the character of the middle colonies and states. A classical republican or "Whig" political ideology, imported from England and Americanized in the Revolution, saw America's mission in terms of peace. If there was no nationwide "peace movement" in the United States before 1828, it was because the national mission seemed to make it unnecessary. The experiment in democratic republicanism was itself a peace movement, an updated and more secular version of the earlier holy experiments in Pennsylvania and New England.

Central to the new republic's antimilitarism was hostility to "standing armies." From the scholars of the French Enlightenment, and from the English Whig opponents of monarchy, early American leaders learned to assume that the making of war belonged to kings and their conspiracies with ruling aristocracies. The common folk did not make war. Wars rather resulted when reigning monarchs (and in the English case, the king-in-Parliament) established alliances with their national military forces, which were run by an elite corps of aristocrats. Royal governments granted offices, titles, and money to the aristocratic corps in exchange for loyalty and obedience. This alliance of the monarchy with the military resulted in standing armies, which were a perpetual threat to peace, as well as a threat to the basic freedoms of the people. In America it would be different. Here the people were free citizens, landowners who had a stake in society, virtuous citizens who hated standing armies but would freely volunteer as members of well-regulated local militia in case of threat to the community.

The perspective of constructive nonviolence will take this American antimilitarist heritage seriously, rather than dismissing it as misguided romantic innocence. To be sure, the classical republican ideology may have functioned to obscure the violence of the American mind and society. But the ideology also bore some remarkable fruit. Above all, it led national leaders to decisions against war in situations when warfare seemed imminent and justifiable. In February 1799 President John Adams took a bold initiative, against the clear will of his Federalist Party, to make peace with France rather than to call for a declaration of war. Adams's decision to end the so-called "Quasi-War" with France was clearly prompted by his distaste for a standing army; a "many-bellied monster" he once called it. His decision for peace was costly. It helped to split the Federalist Party so that Adams was not elected for a second term in 1800.[10]

In the summer and fall of 1807 President Thomas Jefferson, like Adams eight years earlier, chose a strategy of peace in the face of a crisis that could just as well have produced a war. This time the prospective enemy was England, which was at war with France, violating American neutral shipping rights, and allegedly impressing American seamen into the British navy. Jefferson in 1807 could have had a popular war against England, but he chose as an alternative to initiate a total embargo—a prohibition on all exports to all countries from American ports. The embargo was not popular, but it did succeed in avoiding war. Nevertheless, typical American history textbooks treat the embargo as a near total failure, and the 1812 war of James Madison, Jefferson's successor, as a partial success. Jefferson's critics doubt his idealism and blame him for national military weakness.[11]

The perspective of constructive nonviolence proposes to turn the prevailing interpretation on its head. In the light of the costs of the war the United States might have fought in 1807–1808—the killing of thousands of people, the wasting of fortunes and property, the empowering of nationalistic militarism—the country got a good bargain. Jefferson, a so-called "half-way" pacifist, acted upon ideals that were central to American national identity.[12] Our students today need to encounter those ideals, and to understand that classical republican antipathy to "standing armies" is an authentic American ancestor of late-twentieth-century concerns about the military industrial complex.

Honor the Human Conscience against Killing

The perspective of constructive nonviolence will honor the human conscience against killing. The principled religious pacifists who conscientiously objected to military service have been a negligible minority in United States history. Even so it is appropriate, especially for Christian audiences, to tell stories such as that of Christian Good (yes, that was his real name), who was conscripted into the Confederate army but refused to fire at the Yankees in battle. When his captain reprimanded him, Good said, "They're people; we don't shoot people."[13] Christian Good was exceptional in his ability and courage to articulate his nonviolence. But in his basic refusal to kill he belonged to a larger majority. S. L. A. Marshall, a U.S. Army brigadier general, conducted postbattle interviews with

World War II soldiers, which became the first authoritative and convincing evidence for the high percentage of nonkillers in the ranks.[14] When they were part of a team action or when they were firing at a general distant target, as in an artillery unit or aerial bombing, they were willing to kill. But when they could see an individual enemy in their sights, most soldiers could not pull the trigger. Deadly "sharpshooters" were a small minority. More recently an army psychologist, Lt. Col. Dave Grossman, has deepened the analysis of the psychology of killing. Grossman demonstrated, with analysis of inventories of discarded muskets at the Battle of Gettysburg, that Marshall's statistics were valid also for Civil War infantrymen.[15] Therefore, although precise numbers cannot be known, it is likely that eighty to eighty-five percent of rifle-bearing infantrymen refused to fire their weapons directly at enemy soldiers in all American wars through World War II. This estimate so contradicts the national myth of redemptive violence that it remains buried under mountains of remembered military courage—the stories of heroic fighters acclaimed on the so-called "History Channel," in untold volumes of military history, and in thousands of speeches each year on Memorial Day and the Fourth of July. If faced honestly, it would transform the narration of American battle experience.

Christian historians who wish constructively to address the issue of violence can use the evidence and arguments from Marshall and from Grossman to help students critique the heroic popular images of military combat. For those who seek nonviolent solutions, persuasive evidence of the hardwired human resistance to killing can be a sign of hope.

Christian historians who wish to teach from a perspective of constructive nonviolence must give special attention to strategies for teaching about the human experience of war. In recent years the old heroic treatment of military battles with glorious generals exposing themselves to fire has given way to more realistic portrayals of the actual boredom, confusion, misery, and horror experienced by soldiers.[16] Yet the challenge is made more complex by the way the mass media have heightened the horror of graphic portrayals of military combat. The escalations of graphic violence do not add up to antiwar statements. In 1998 Steven Spielberg's R-rated film *Saving Private Ryan* managed to set new standards for horrific portrayal of combat. Yet this film's central moral message was that the violence of World War II was redemptive. Such portrayals ironically make it increasingly difficult for Christian historians to teach the ultimate truth of Jesus' saying that "All who take the sword will perish by the sword" (Matt. 26:52). The message is rather that those with the sharpest swords—and the most ruthless and murderous courage—will triumph.

Honor the Role of Voluntary Communities

In recent decades the vistas for the perspective of constructive nonviolence have been magnificently expanded by an explosion of research and writing in social history, in peace movement history, and in the role of religion in United States history. The tyranny of conventional political-military history has been successfully challenged. It has become increasingly possible to see how the course of national history has been shaped by the life of small communities, of voluntary associations, and of religious groups. We can sense afresh the significance of creative minorities in history as well as the hidden people's movements that sway the future despite the apparent power of generals and presidents.

Just one example, among a myriad of possibilities, from this new social history is the way historian Mary Hershberger brought together the reform efforts of American women, of Native Americans, and of evangelical denominations in her study of the struggle against removal of Indians from Georgia in the 1830s.[17] The anti-removal movement had its base in the new women's religious charitable organizations and in the new denomination-based periodicals of the 1820s and 1830s whose circulation far outstripped the traditional party and secular periodicals. Jeremiah Evarts, a lawyer and commissioner of the American Board of Commissioners for Foreign Missions, protested the removal in a set of essays known as the "*William Penn*" *Essays*. Evarts's essays were "more widely distributed and read in the summer of 1829 than any political pamphlet since Thomas Paine's *Common Sense*." According to Hershberger the struggle against Indian removal led these religious reformers and their communities to reconsider the popular reform ideal of recolonizing American slaves in Africa. The evolving reform movement to abolish slavery thus owes much to the prior struggle against Indian removal. The new social history enables us to see how ordinary people, operating out of newly created religious voluntary organizations, mounted significant challenges to the violence implicit in oppressive social institutions and legislation. The reformers were not necessarily successful in achieving their goals, nor did they remain consistently nonviolent. Nevertheless, a perspective of constructive nonviolence is more interested in affirming the agency of such creative and nonviolent movers of history than in rendering judgment on their relative success or failure.[18]

Honor the Opponents of Total War

A perspective of constructive nonviolence will seek ways to teach honestly and realistically about the course and the consequences of modern total war in the twentieth century. The concept of "total war" can help organize our understanding and teaching about modern war. Twentieth-century warfare has vindicated the biblical wisdom "All who take the sword will perish by the sword" (Matt. 26:52). American participation in World War I did not make the world safe for democracy. Indeed, total military victory by the Allied powers in that war created the conditions which led to the rise of totalitarian states in Germany and the Soviet Union and to the outbreak of World War II. More than sixty million people died in the Second World War, most of them civilians. The result of that awful bloodletting was a protracted Cold War polarization and nuclear arms race between the United States and the Soviet Union.

For the two great world wars, "total war" meant the mobilization of all the energies and resources of the fighting nations—spiritual as well as material. All citizens, civilian and military, conscientious objectors and combatants, were inescapably involved. By the end of the century, however, "total war" had come to mean the prospect of total nuclear destruction—a possibility from which ordinary people were distanced and alienated. Today, despite some faltering steps toward disarmament in the 1980s and the collapse of the Soviet Union in the 1990s, the United States and Russia each have over five thousand thermonuclear armed missiles in place aimed at the other side. Each of these weapons has the potential to explode into a fireball a mile in diameter, to set fires in a diameter of twenty-four miles, and to cover 700 to 800 square miles with radiation. Today we remain ready to kill in a few hours more than ten times the number of people who died in World War II. In the past decade we have made no progress in nuclear disarmament. We have been unable to stop the proliferation of nuclear technology to new countries—with India and Pakistan the most recent entrants into the nuclear club. We are now in a second nuclear age, an age made considerably more dangerous than the first nuclear age because of the rapidly increasing capability of more and more nations to build nuclear weapons if they wish to do so.

In view of the place to which the history of twentieth-century total warfare has brought us, constructive Christian teaching about warfare in the twenty-first century cannot responsibly treat that history as a sequence of great triumphs. To be sure, in a narrow military sense the United States "won" World War I, World War II, and the Cold War. But every victory brought its own dark shadow. The escalating military means for each of those devastating military triumphs contributed to the coming of another greater cataclysm. The twenty-first-century prospect of nuclear terrorism is the natural outcome of the earlier events and technologies out of control. We need to stop using the language of victory and triumph for events that were failures in conflict resolution. The stories of how the United States helped stop Prussian autocracy, Nazi Germany, Hirohito's Japan, or Soviet Communism must be seen in the context of a larger looming tragedy.

Is it possible to teach the history of twentieth-century warfare without dissolving into cynicism, anger, and despair about the human prospect? For those who think clearly about the relationship of means and ends, the celebration of military and technological triumph will be no antidote to despair. Nor will the guilt-producing denunciations of angry critics meet our need. If we are to find hope in history, we must find it in the witness of people who testified that there were alternatives to total war, and who worked to implement those alternatives. Alongside our assigned textbook readings of the triumphalist master narrative of American history, we need to assign readings such as *The Peace Reform in American History* by Charles DeBenedetti, *The Struggle Against the Bomb* by Lawrence Wittner, and *Unarmed Forces* by Matthew Evangelista.[19] People such as Jane Addams, Randolph Bourne, A. J. Muste, Henry Wallace, Linus Pauling, Martin Luther King Jr., Randall Forsberg, and the host of other peace leaders who challenged the prevailing military mythology can inspire more hope than the heroic deeds of generals and their armies.

Constructive Nonviolence, Salvation History, and the Ideal of a Master Narrative

In conclusion I would like to shift to a more confessional mode. As an Anabaptist-Mennonite historian, two of my theological mentors have been John Howard Yoder and Gordon Kaufman. Yoder offered fresh understandings of the politics of Jesus, and Kaufman undertook an imaginative reconstruction of the doctrine of God. When I was in college I first read Kaufman's *Relativism, Knowledge, and Faith,* a book whose Christian historicist perspective remains important for me.[20] Kaufman argued that the meaningfulness of history depends upon a process in which crucial events are interpreted to shed light upon other events, and in which one event ultimately becomes the center of history. A Christian historian is one for whom the Christ event is the normative center. The life, teaching, death, and resurrection of Jesus constitute the event in terms of which all human events, including the events of American history, are to be judged. The narrative structure of American history will itself be shaped according to the values represented by Jesus, a man who embodied suffering love. American history, and the history of all other nations, must be told in terms of a larger story.

The dominant master narrative of American history, which sacralizes the state and the fruits of its violence, contradicts the Christ-centered story. Recent decades have seen a postmodern scholarly assault on all master narratives, as well as on the very assumption that events of the past bear any relationship to each other apart from the mind of the historian. As an Anabaptist-Mennonite I have welcomed some of the results of this deconstruction, especially as it has tended to undermine the myth of redemptive violence. In this welcome I join other historians who represent once-marginalized groups and who applaud the discrediting of outworn absolutisms that once excluded them.[21]

I also believe that the gospel of Christ calls us more foundationally to the work of construction than to that of deconstruction. The constructive task of Christian historians has its ultimate authority in Christ, but external efforts to impose the lordship of Christ from the outside upon the world, or upon the world's history, will surely fail. Fortunately the history of the nations includes signs of hope and of blessed community, for God has been active within history. The signs of God's purposive action in history are events that actually happened and that we can know at least in part. To be sure, we will never comprehend the mind of God. From where we now stand, the possibility of fashioning a master narrative of salvation history, and relating that history to the unfolding course of the nations, may seem impossibly difficult and remote. But we must faithfully endeavor to reconstruct historical understandings in the light of the kingdom of God, which we can see by God's revelation in Christ to be a nonviolent kingdom. As heirs of St. Augustine, we must insist upon our ultimate allegiance to the city of God, as well as upon the limited nature of our allegiance to worldly kingdoms. We also must disabuse ourselves of the illusions of the myth of redemptive violence. I believe the perspective of constructive nonviolence has a significant role to play in that effort.

EIGHT

CHRISTIAN DISCOURSE
AND THE HUMILITY
OF PEACE

KENNETH R. CHASE

Upon receiving the Centennial Nobel Peace Prize in Oslo, December 10, 2001, Kofi Annan spoke for many when he contrasted the forces of exclusion and absolutism with the spirit of dialogue.

> The idea that there is one people in possession of the truth, one answer to the world's ills, or one solution to humanity's needs, has done untold harm throughout history—especially in the last century. Today, however, even amidst continuing ethnic conflict around the world, there is a growing understanding that human diversity is both the reality that makes dialogue necessary, and the very basis for that dialogue.[1]

For many observers of the human condition (but not, thankfully, for Secretary-General Annan), Christianity is implicated in the first sentence of this passage. After all, Christians adhere to a single proclamation of truth in Jesus Christ, and we believe that the world's ultimate need is to turn to Christ alone in confession and repentance. Many critics of our faith operate under an oft-stated suspicion that our commitments to truth and evangelism undercut our expressed interest in peace. Indeed, so the suspicion runs, our commitments also facilitate our participation in violence.

If our age is one of dialogue, then what is the contribution of Christian discourse to the task of peace?

119

I will argue that faith in God's truth about Jesus and about divine judgment enables Christian discourse to promote peace in a violent world. To develop this argument, I will sketch two theological principles for Christian talk that serve to highlight specific practices for peace within the New Testament. I hope to show that these principles rooted in Christian teachings not only distance the Christian advocate from violence, but engender a discourse celebrating a peace that extends even to one's enemies.

A Rhetorical Situation

Prior to discussing these theological principles, though, I must consider directly the notion that any Christian theological formulation is morally suspect due to its complicity with violence. Given the supposed causal connection between exclusive and absolute beliefs and violent actions (such as we find in Kofi Annan's statement), how could a Christian discourse that purports to be peaceful be anything other than a charade? Are principles rooted in exclusive and inviolable religious claims inherently complicit with the "world's ills"? Is Christian doctrine morally flawed no matter what its explicit proclamations?

A moment's reflection will tell us that simple causal arguments linking absolute and exclusivist religious claims with violence cannot hold. The connection between religious belief and the coercive use of force is always historically and sociologically complex, involving a large number of variables, such as economic, political, psychological, and ideological factors. This complexity ought to preclude facile judgments about the dangers of Christian belief. For instance, David Martin, retired sociologist from the London School of Economics, argues that Christianity is typically a minor or nonexistent factor within the complex of causes for most wars.[2] And Robert Bates, in a recent book on the economic and political development of states, identifies violence and coercion as integral to social organization. Growth comes not from the elimination of violence, he argues, but from the economic and political control of violence so that investors can confidently anticipate a return on their capital expenditures. Although he makes but scant reference to religion, Bates's analysis would lead to the conclusion that religion contributes only marginally to development. Thus, within any current political arrangement, the presence or absence of religious absolutes is not a key causal factor in the presence or absence of violence.[3] Of course, the studies by Martin and Bates do not conclusively eliminate Christian belief as a factor in state violence, or even in wars. Yet, these studies ought to remind us that violence has many causes, and that holding to exclusive religious claims produces no necessary connection with many of the most obvious sorts of harm that come through state development and advancement.

Furthermore, Christianity as practiced is not independent of culture and society, but in any given historical moment may be as much affected (or infected) by its social reception as it is a causal factor affecting that reception. The historically specific location in which a Christianity develops, then, may be of more relevance to violent practices than a blanket suspicion cast toward Christian exclusiveness would allow. I can illustrate this briefly through T. Richard Snyder's examination of how specific Christian theological understandings shape attitudes toward punishment in the United States (in *The Protestant Ethic and the Spirit of Punishment*). On the one hand, Snyder places Christian teachings, such as sin and guilt, within the causal mix leading to our extraordinarily high incarceration rate. It is not the sole cause, of course, but contributes by "preparing and fertilizing the ground."[4] Yet when Snyder delves into his analysis, he eventually acknowledges that Christian teaching may have been influenced, in turn, by culture: "In spite of its devotion to the words of the Bible, contemporary Protestantism has succumbed to the hyper-individualism of the culture."[5] At the core, this is a chicken and egg problem. To what extent has Christian theology established the foundations for U.S. hyperindividualism? And to what extent has U.S. hyperindividualism adversely affected Christian theology? The intertwining is enormously complex, so drawing clear causal lines between Christian theological premises and social harm demands, at the least, charitable and cautious judgments.

To link a Christian's adherence to exclusive truth claims with violence, therefore, one must reduce an enormously dense social complex into a coherent narrative featuring a relatively straightforward causal motif. Thus, the historical narrative connecting belief and violence always is *made,* not given; the critic of religious belief functions as an advocate who strategically constructs causal relationships to accomplish certain purposes. Thus, positing a connection between Christian theological principles and violence is a rhetorical phenomenon.[6]

Given this understanding of complex relations between Christian teaching and social action, one might wonder if any causal connection ought to be made about any sort of social action, including peace. If the connection between doctrine and violence is so difficult to determine, is there any reason why one ought to proclaim a connection between doctrine and peace? Yes. For Christians, theological formulations are testimonies of God. We must speak in ways that honor God's name and that foster reflection on the goodness of God's salvation. Furthermore, a purported complicity between Christian belief and violence may be that which precludes a nonbeliever from giving a moment's notice to Christian claims about new life in Jesus. Developing a discourse of peace grounded in Christian teaching, therefore, is a matter, at the least, of removing unnecessary offense from the gospel. Affirming the Christian commitment to peace also is a requirement of the present age, when violence in multiple and insidious forms ravages the hopes of humankind. Although the affirmation of Christian peace through discourse cannot be a solely efficacious cause of halting violence, it will function as one factor within the social complex that may prompt some to glimpse God's eternal goodness within an evil circumstance.

Thus, to encourage Christian-based discourses of peace, I will develop two theological principles that ought to generate and guide Christian advocacy. My approach here is not the only rhetorical option available when faced with a challenge from Christianity's critics linking our faith with violence. Christians could, for instance, develop a vigorous apologetic that diffuses and/or rebuts any historical connections. Or, we could acknowledge the many instances in which Christians have acted violently and offer sincere apologies to victims and, perhaps, the watching world. Indeed, Christians have offered these discourses in recent years, and we ought to nurture further efforts. In this essay, though, I outline a third discursive response, constructing a counterdiscourse of peace generated by theological principles.[7] The task with such discourse is both to testify on behalf of and to enact the forgiveness and charity Jesus brings to broken relationships and hostile interactions.

These principles are applied within specific historical moments, keyed kairotically (i.e., at opportune times) to particular exigencies and articulated according to shifting demands of people and their expectations. Given the inevitability of changing circumstances, all communicators are in the rhetorical position of always having opportunity to say more. The prevalence of violence within our world provides Christians ample opportunity to say more about God's peace, again and again. Christians need to saturate our lives with these restatements, with these incessant resayings of our pasts and our futures in light of God's salvation and judgment. The task I outline here, then, is to be a rhetor of peace.

Theological Principles

Overview

The New Testament is, of course, a central text for supplying the Christian's orientation toward peace and violence. It provides the critical apparatus—the resources for critique and for affirmation—crucial for saying again the disjunction between Christianity and human violence and the conjunction between Christian practice and the pursuit of peace. Preeminently, the gospel is the good news that Jesus Christ, through his death and resurrection, offers to humanity peace with God. This relationship of peace must extend directly to our relations with one another. Christians, therefore, ought to eschew violence.[8] The New Testament supports this claim by profoundly and compellingly narrating the life and teaching of Jesus Christ. He taught peace, even in the face of enemies; he promised peace, even in the midst of a violent world; and he lived peace, even in the throes of his own trial and death. The New Testament ethic of human relationships insistently urges Christians to live peacefully with all, to be content in all circumstances, and to share the attitude of Christ as he suffered quietly under the violent gaze of his enemies. In contrast to those who dismiss Christianity because of its complicity with violence, the New Testament portrays Jesus and his followers as those who need not advance their beliefs using the weapons of war, or of revenge, or of intimidation.[9] Therefore, today's Christians face the challenge of rhetorically structuring our talk and our lives in ways consistent with the redemptive work of Jesus. To do so is to undermine our complicity with violence and promote the practice of peace.

Yet, Christian discourses of peace through Jesus also must acknowledge that this peace is presented as the work of a God who promises wrath and judgment against those who reject the gospel. Hebrews 12:14 is an exemplary text in this regard: "Strive for peace with everyone, and for the holiness without which no one will see the Lord."[10] The writer here, and throughout this epistle, does not attempt to hide the threat of God's judgment hanging over the head of those who deny Jesus. For the author to declare that "without [holiness] no one will see the Lord" is, in context, to hold forth a most unappealing consequence of rejecting the Christ. This is not merely a missed opportunity to see God, as if we are in the wrong place the day a celebrity or high government official passes by our street, but a declaration of ultimate destruction. The chapter closes with the sobering claim, repeated from Deuteronomy 4:24, that "God is a consuming fire" (12:29). We ought to pursue holiness, and the attendant practice of peace, because if we do not we subject ourselves to the judgment of a perfect God. To have peace with this God, the God of consuming fire, is so extraordinary (and life-giving) that we ought to live that peace with all, regardless of personal harm incurred or cost expended (Heb. 10:32–34). The seriousness of this command stems from the character of the God who commands it. Thus, the judgment of God secures our motivation to live peacefully.

There is little benefit, then, in retelling the story of Jesus and peace without also narrating the judgment of God. A simple waving of the hand cannot disconnect Christianity from violence and reconnect Christianity with peace. We must be people of peace, even while serving the God who consumes. We must practice the peace commanded of us under the specter of divine judgment shadowing our world. Only as we hold these two together—human peace and divine wrath—will we be able to live truly as peacemakers. We must repent of our hate, our prejudice, our covetousness, our arrogance, our self-satisfaction, and our coercion. We must embrace peace as people under God's rule, which means that we wed peace with humility. The two theological principles sketched below provide a generative frame for an ethic of Christian discursive action that takes seriously New Testament teaching on peace within the broader narrative context of God's work with and through violence as redeemer and judge.

Principle 1: Depend on the Sufficiency of Christ's Death

Christian discourse should depend on the finality and sufficiency of Jesus' sacrifice. Returning to Hebrews 10, the text clearly and definitively locates Jesus' sacrifice as the only sufficient and effective mechanism of divine-human reconciliation. The sacrificial system of Jewish law, involving animals presented by priests, was not sufficient to overcome our separation from God's judgment: "But in these sacrifices is a reminder of sin every year. For it is impossible for the blood of bulls and goats to take away sins" (10:3–4). The sacrifice of Jesus, though, ends this epoch of annual sacrifices: "And it is by [God's] will that we have been sanctified through the offering of the body of Jesus Christ *once for all*" (10:10, emphasis added). Thus, we can do nothing to secure our peace with God that has not already been done by God himself; nothing else need be sacrificed, neither human nor beast. The Christ sacrifice is fully sufficient for life with God and, thus, all of life itself. Anything elevated to the status of sacrifice is a rival of the Christ and ought to be eschewed by Christians. To see salvation in any other sacrifice is to reject God's gracious solution to the demands of his own holiness.

What would these discourses look like? What must we do to celebrate the sufficiency of Jesus?

For starters, we must avoid locating and recommending alternative sacrifices that would purportedly bring forth human fulfillment or enduring peace. Rhetorical practice frequently promotes the analogical construction of ideal human experience on the other side of some sacrifice. Thus, a U.S. president urges the nation to war by constructing the nation *as* a nation at peace and in prosperity *after* the enemy has been eliminated (e.g., such as Saddam Hussein, or Osama bin Laden, or Al Qaeda—each offered up for the good of the collective order). To accept the sufficiency of Jesus' sacrifice, we must challenge this typical rhetorical practice. This is not to say, though, that all national war efforts are unacceptable (the moral acceptability or unacceptability of war requires an argument exceeding the scope of this essay). Nor is this to say that any rhetorical practice of placing blame or assigning responsibility for wrongdoing is to be avoided. I simply mean that Christians ought to avoid and, if necessary, challenge the sacrificial mechanism through which the destruction of victims becomes a rationale for achieving social health, personal wholeness, and civic well-being.

Kenneth Burke, whose insight into rhetorical practice is legendary, famously diagnosed this sacrifice-based discourse practice in Hitler's *Mein Kampf.* As Burke explains, Hitler developed a "noneconomic explanation of economic phenomena,"[11] and this explanation involved symbolic constructions of purification through scapegoating leading to symbolic rebirth. The Jews, of course, served as the scapegoat. The elimination of the Jews would purify the Aryan race, he claimed, giving new birth to the Aryan goal of world supremacy. As Burke rightly notes, this rhetorical construction is a gross perversion of the

Christian story. Hitler relied on fundamentally religious patterns of reasoning to generate his horrific vision. Yet Burke insists that Christianity is not to be faulted for Hitler's perversion: "There is nothing in religion proper that requires a fascist state. There is much in religion, when misused, that does lead to a fascist state." Burke relies on the Latin proverb *"Corruptio optimi pessima,"* to absolve religion of its complicity: "And it is the corruptors of religion who are a major menace to the world today, in giving the profound patterns of religious thought a crude and sinister distortion."[12] The perversion of sacrificial logic is an extreme rhetorical danger.

Yet Burke locates the danger of the sacrificial logic not in the logic per se, but in its particular application in Depression-era Germany. He accepts the inevitability of the logic in all human motivation. Thus, Christianity is not the origin of the logic that is later perverted by fascists, but one particular instance of a logic that can be applied in ways to promote fascism. Therefore, Burke sees Christian notions of sacrifice as part and parcel of a universal symbolic pattern through which humans are motivated for change and restoration. Whenever humans live according to a preference for social order—and for Burke this is inevitable—humans will struggle with the reality of disorder. Both order and disorder are necessarily symbolic, since they require a conception of how things ought to go and how things can go wrong. The invoking of a moral order, involving positives and negatives, depends on the existence of language. Therefore, we can expect to find within discourse the rhetorical mechanisms for restoring order after a lapse, or redemption after a fall. Burke describes: "If order, then guilt; if guilt, then need for redemption; but any such 'payment' is victimage." So the act of invoking a scapegoat to serve as the sacrificial victim is not due to a particular religious origin, but is "a device natural to language here and now."[13] Because of its inevitability, we are, in a sense, trapped within this logic. Human societies function within it, and human discourse necessarily reproduces it. There is no escape from this cyclical pattern; we only can be aware of its particular malevolent invocation. To be aware is not, though, to be outside its functioning or superior to its mechanisms. Our awareness springs from a comic attitude that "demystifies" the logic: "the comic frame should enable people *to be observers of themselves, while acting.* . . . One would 'transcend' himself by noting his own foibles" (emphasis in original).[14] Burke's social hope relies not on the end of sacrificial logic but on the triumph of irony rooted in an awareness of futility. (For good reason some have suggested that Burke prefigured postmodernism by decades!)

Burke's view of sacrifice, then, differs from the view in Hebrews. In Scripture, Jesus' sacrifice is fully and permanently sufficient. Accepting his sacrifice frees humanity from the cycle of violence involving repeated scapegoating and a merely temporary redemption. Social hope, therefore, need not depend on the wry perspective of a postmodern archness, but on our divinely granted release from the burdensome task of maintaining social order through rituals of victimage. Certainly, Burke is helpful in urging that we not see Christianity blamed for the atrocities committed according to the sacrificial logic of symbol systems. Yet, ironically, Burke manages his own corruption of Christianity when he contains it within the perpetual cycle of scapegoats and redemption identical with pagan religious practices. Jesus breaks the cycle; he is not a mere participant.

René Girard, who shares with Burke a capacity for inventive literary criticism sensitive to anthropological research, has done us the enormous service of identifying a specific difference between merely religious sacrificial systems and the Christ event. Girard, like Burke, sees similarity between mythological structure and the structure of biblical stories. Yet he differs from Burke in noting a fundamental difference between the Bible and myth. Scripture, he argues, exposes the violence driving mythical action. Thus, both myth and Scripture portray violent acts resulting from covetousness, but only Scripture exposes the violence as a hidden power that relies on the murder of a scapegoat to resolve social conflict.[15] Indeed, for Girard, the difference between Scripture and myth is so striking that Girard refuses to see the Christ event as an instance of sacrifice at all.[16] Rather, Scripture provides an exposé of the collective violence (rooted in mimesis and contagion) by which an innocent victim is treated as a scapegoat. Thus, Girard sees the crucifixion of Christ as putting into motion the end of what Burke describes as the guilt cycle. Now, by virtue of Jesus' death, the whole world has laid plain before it the gross injustice of using violence against a scapegoat to purify conflict and restore social health. The end of the cycle is made plain, and we turn compassionately toward the victim and away from violent contagion. No sacrifice remains satisfactory. Social hope rests here, in the unveiling provided by the Gospels.

Girard, then, in contrast to Burke, would urge us to abandon scapegoats in our discourse, not merely to avoid amusing ourselves with their presence, but to abandon our dependency on them altogether. Yet, with Burke, we might wonder if this is at all possible. If scapegoating is an inevitable mechanism of language, can we ever really break free? Ultimately, Girard must trust that the retelling of the Jesus story will open eyes and challenge the myriad of social structures built on the residues of collective violence and victimage.[17] The motivation of compassion must dismantle the motivation of symbolic order (with its attendant practices of guilt, sacrifice, and purification). Does Girard provide a sufficient account of this productive power?

Despite the enormous insight into Scripture Girard provides, his explanation comes at a cost. He readily acknowledges that he is treating the divine work from an anthropological perspective. Thus, he is expanding the social scientific discourse to encompass topics that had been typically the province of spiritual and theological mystery. Where the theologian sees sin, Girard sees mimetic desire. Where the theologian sees Satan, Girard sees the hidden power of violent contagion. Where the theologian sees the Holy Spirit, Girard sees the narrative unveiling of sacrificial logic.[18] Where the theologian sees Jesus as the ultimate scapegoat, upon which God places the sins of the world, Girard sees not a divine sacrifice but a refusal of sacrifice.[19] For Girard, God simply cannot be the judge, the consuming fire, so Hebrews is inconsistent with his anthropological reading of the Gospels.

Yet without the just judgments of a sovereign God, the social hope for ultimate peace is unsecured, shifting in the winds of human frailty. Girard's reading of violence in social life is simply unable to overcome the warring passions driving covetousness and violent desire. Without God as judge, Burke's diagnosis may very well trump Girard's, leaving us with a postmodern cynicism toward Girardian peace: We see our own destruction, and we look coyly upon it with a gaze of comic distance.

In contrast to Girard, then, we must retain the God of Hebrews. Girard is right in that Christianity ends the cycle of victimage with the death of Christ, yet the work of atonement that Girard abandons is necessary for transforming the human passions that drive the social engine of contagion.

James's epistle provides a diagnosis of human violence that allows us to see a more complete portrait of the human condition. We see here, with Girard, that human violence derives from the mimetic processes. Yet we also see something more:

> What causes quarrels and what causes fights among you. Is it not this, that your passions are at war within you? You desire and do not have; so you murder. You covet and cannot obtain; so you fight and quarrel. You do not have, because you do not ask. (4:1–2)

By obeying desires that place us in conflict with others, James is saying, we quarrel and battle. Violence emerges from the desire to eliminate any obstacles preventing us from gaining the object of our desires. James continues: "You ask and do not receive, because you ask wrongly, to spend it on your own passions" (v. 3). By linking violence with the pursuit of pleasures, James strips pleasures of their presumed innocence (as if they are pure motives of peaceful gain) and exposes their conflicted and competitive nature.

Yet the solution to human violence is not merely exposing the desires, but bringing those desires before God. Thus, the desires must be purified through dependency on God's provision. This purification process is not at all the result of violent self-sacrifice on our part, but a submission to God's grace.[20] James continues by quoting Proverbs 3:34: "God opposes the proud, but gives grace to the humble" (v. 6). God comes "near" to us as we "draw near to God" (v. 8). The awareness of how violence arises in our experience is not sufficient to quell violent action. We need to transform these impulses by bringing them under the authority of a God whose work through Jesus' death enables peace to abolish the sacrificial logic.

Linking Christianity and peace, therefore, requires that we abandon discursive scapegoating. Accepting the full sufficiency of Jesus' death enables us

to move outside of a sociological guilt cycle through which we covet and compete with others for scarce resources. Rather, through Jesus, we are empowered
to break free from the motivations that lead to the violent dismissal of others
for the sake of personal or social satisfactions. Christ's "once for all" sacrifice
alters our relationships with others, including our enemies. We take on the
character of Christ's own behavior, reaching forth to others in forgiveness,
mercy, generosity, and love. As we abandon the egocentric spiral of covetousness and quarrelling, we are pulled by Christ's spirit outward to relieve suffering and oppression; we celebrate justice and compassion and resist revenge and
hatred. Our discourse models peace.

Principle 2: Anticipate the Justice of God's Judgment

Christian discourse should anticipate God's ultimate judgment in which
the triumph of justice is eternally secured. This principle emerges directly from
the realization, conveyed throughout Scripture, that the people of God frequently suffer at the hands of enemies who act unjustly. The proper response
to these unfortunate circumstances is not to seek revenge—as if our violent
reactions right the wrongs—but to entrust the circumstances to the righteous
action of God.

Christians who construct discourses built upon the redemptive and sufficient sacrifice of Jesus have not always been met with enthusiastic and accepting responses. We should not find this surprising; after all, Jesus himself suffered death at the hands of those who rejected his message of peace with God.
Can we really expect that our representation of Jesus' message will be received
without contest? Has two thousand years been enough time for the world to
abandon its murder of the Christ?

In his bracing review of contemporary global practices, Wolfgang Huber
sees a surfeit of assaults and degradations that humans inflict on each other.[21]
Humans practice violence unrelentingly, and it reaches into our entertainment,
our recreation (such as professional sports), and our relationship with nature.
We must add to Huber's survey the reports that violence against Christians, in
particular, has been horrendous in recent years.[22] Suffering under physical and
emotional threats, torture, and murder, how ought Christians respond to this
violence against them? Do we fight for our peace?

On the contrary, we must practice peace in the midst of violence. To fight
back is to succumb to the "domination system," to use Walter Wink's phrase,
in which we seek victory over enemies, not their repentance.[23] Therefore, our
discourse must promote a sustaining peace, not merely an occasional effort.
What is the hope that sustains? What allows the wholesale rejection of domination logic? It is the ultimate and perfect judgment of God.

The author of Hebrews, again, sets our course. Returning to chapter 10, the
text moves from the sufficiency of Christ's sacrifice to the command that believ-

ers persevere. Again, the context is God's awesome judgment, for we ought not drift. Yet the motivation for our endurance is not entirely negative but positive, rooted in God's supremacy over all possible circumstances: "Let us hold fast to the confession of our hope, for he who has promised is faithful" (v. 23). So why persevere through violence? Because obedience to the one who judges all violence is preferable to taking matters into our own hands. Hebrews is very specific at this point:

> But recall the former days when, after you were enlightened, you endured a hard struggle with sufferings, sometimes being publicly exposed to reproach and affliction, and sometimes being partners with those so treated. For you had compassion on those in prison, and you joyfully accepted the plundering of your property, since you knew that you yourselves had a better possession and an abiding one. Therefore do not throw away your confidence, which has a great reward. For you have need of endurance, so that when you have done the will of God, you may receive what was promised. (10: 32–36)

To fight violence with violence is to abandon trust in God. This is the antithesis of faith and marks one who "shrinks back" from hope in God's ultimate provision for suffering (vv. 38–39).

The logic here is quite simple. God's ultimate capacity to determine life and death, to rectify the wrongs and honor the righteous, motivates the practice of peace in everyday life. To pursue peace in the face of violence demands a confidence that God's system is preferable to the domination system. Our example here is Jesus himself, who "endured the cross" willingly, because he knew of "the joy that was set before him" (Heb. 12:2).

The confidence of reward here is not to be trivialized according to banal sensual or material pleasures. Rather, we anticipate what Oliver O'Donovan characterizes as a "fulfilment from beyond [our]selves, a fulfilment that is recognisable and yet unknown."[24] We must have confidence that wrongs will be judged justly, that evil and violence will not ultimately succeed, and that we will be completed in righteousness. Our reward is that we will receive the completion of who we are designed to be. This promise of reward demands that God have sufficient authority to see the difference between right and wrong, between love and hate, between the oppressor and the oppressed. God's authority to make a *final* judgment secures the promise to provide ultimate peace for those who suffer in faith against unjust attack.

Two contemporary theologians, each writing from divergent political and ecclesial perspectives, coalesce on this point to provide theological support for this final guarantee. One is O'Donovan, whose project is to situate human political acts within the kingship of God. He accepts the possibility that governments may use violence in their God-appointed role of performing judgments concerning malevolent and benevolent behavior within society. Yet this task of political action is decidedly not the practice of the church. Rather, the church speaks caution and self-discipline to governments, as a testimony against the imperial tendencies that lead governments to step outside their appointed tasks. Importantly, the church demonstrates the ultimate kingdom rule of God in which peace is the practice and the violence of earthly political arrangements is obsolete. In this capacity, the church lives out the commands of Jesus to be "unmeasured and uncalculating" in its love and generosity within its community. The contrast between secular authority and ecclesial authority sets the terms for Christian testimony in the world: "The secular authorities . . . deal only in provisional and penultimate judgments. By embracing the final judgment of God, Christians have accepted that they have no need for penultimate judgments to defend their rights."[25] God is the one who deals in ultimate judgments concerning rights, so the church lives peace in the confidence that nonretaliation is the anticipatory "fulfillment" of its existence.

Miroslav Volf is the second theologian. Although his Anabaptist leanings contrast sharply with O'Donovan's defense of government violence in its military and police functions, he shares, with O'Donovan, the theological insight that anticipating God's judgment motivates and justifies Christian perseverance in love and peace. Volf's project is to establish the theological warrant for embracing others in such a way that the otherness of the other is preserved (and not reduced to the identity of the one embracing). The practice of exclusion is reserved for God alone, and it is precisely this capacity that secures our vigorous commitment to nonviolence. First Peter 2:21–23 is an exemplary text for Volf: Christ suffered because he "entrust[ed] himself to him who judges justly." Volf notes that the New Testament repeatedly associates human nonviolence with God's vengeance: "The certainty of God's just judgment at the end of history is the presupposition for the renunciation of violence in the middle of it."[26] Humans cannot overcome violence by simply denouncing it; the passions of vengeance and of hatred are too strong. The only possibility, therefore, is to transfer the violence elsewhere, to let go of it by giving it to transcendence—placing it in the hands of the God who is perfectly just and wise.

Strikingly, Volf moves this theological insight into a bold apologetic move. Without God as ultimate judge, earth is doomed to perpetual violence. Christians not only rely on God's ultimate judgment to motivate perseverance, but *need* God's ultimate action against brutality to preserve any hope in the world. As Volf states: "God *must* be angry. A nonindignant God would be an accomplice in injustice, deception, and violence."[27] Christians also insist on God's truth as distinct from the multiple truths that compete for human allegiance. It is a truth that demands human peace, charity, and forgiveness. Without this truth, there can be no check on the inevitably violent manipulations of power by which local truths are secured.[28] Christian commitment to the ultimate judgment of God, then, is not a commitment that fosters violence, but a commitment to step aside, to turn the cheek, from the temptation to secure one's temporary satisfaction at the expense of others. God's truth and judgment are not a threat to peace, but its down payment.

The Christian's discourse of peace, then, emerges from a confidence in God's future action to bring about eternal peace and justice. It rests in a full dependence on God's authority over time. This means, practically, that Christians exhibit patience and endurance when faced with suffering. This also means that we understand hardship as a temporary condition mitigated by the abundant resources of God's comfort, resources that are mediated partly by the church. Thus, Christian discourse must encourage the application of the full resources of generosity and care to those who are suffering. Indeed, Christian discourse must be itself a mode of care, providing encouragement and assistance.

Yet, Christian discourse has an additional responsibility. Because violent retribution is disavowed as a solution for personal injury, the comfort offered by the church might not resolve human injustices. At times, the enemy might crush our offers of forgiveness and care. The church still must respond.[29] The discourse at this point anticipates God's ultimate judgment by speaking of the suffering as a witness to God's superior kingdom. In other words, Christian discourse articulates martyrdom.

William T. Cavanaugh's provocative study of torture during General Pinochet's military dictatorship in Chile, from 1973 to 1990, provides a valuable resource for conceptualizing this responsibility. In his book *Torture and Eucharist,* Cavanaugh argues convincingly that the state used torture to remove the voices of its subjects and, hence, to dis-integrate the body, both physically and spiritually. Torture left the church voiceless, without identifiable shape and without a living testimony to God's sovereignty. Cavanaugh notes, however, that this was a temporary condition, for the church regained its voice in the strength of the Eucharist. Remembering the body and blood of Christ focused the church on the sacrificial suffering of its members. To participate in the Eucharist is to identify with God's redemptive work in opposition to the state's destructive work. Church members who "disappear" due to violent actions of the state police are not merely gone, but martyrs for the "counter-politics" of Christ's kingdom. These are witnesses testifying to "the end of victimization." Whereas the state relies on victims to feed its dominance, the church's remembrance of Christ's sacrifice provides an alternative logic. "Martyrs offer their lives in the knowledge that their refusal to return violence for violence is an identification with Christ's risen body and an anticipation of the heavenly banquet."[30] Christian discourse, then, speaks openly and boldly of its persecuted victims, situating them within the long tradition of martyrs whose faith leads them to anticipate the coming of divine justice.

Discourse in Practice

I have recommended two theological principles that ought to generate Christian discourses of peace: the sufficiency of Christ's death and the ultimate justice of God's judgment. In the above explanations, I have identified some general discourse practices flowing from these principles. Some additional comments about practice are warranted. Of course, the exact practices need to vary from context to context, depending on human need and spiritual discernment, yet further elaboration will provide additional guidance. I will return to James, from whom we gleaned the nature of human violence above, because this practical epistle provides a convenient framework on which to hang a list of discursive practices motivated by the two theological principles. Also, relying on James at this point deepens the New Testament support for discourses of peace.

After urging believers to live faith, in chapter 2, not merely to speak it, James begins chapter 3 with cautions about the proper use of the tongue. I will enter his text following his turn to peace in 3:9: "With [the tongue] we bless the Lord and Father, and with it we curse those who have been made in the likeness of God. From the same mouth come blessing and cursing. My brothers, these things ought not to be." The practical advice tumbles forth in chapters 4 and 5. I will follow the text's sequence of verses and pull five recommendations; the first three recommendations flow from our acceptance of Christ's sufficient sacrifice, the latter two from our anticipation of God's justice.[31]

First, our discourse of peace is dependent on God's grace, demonstrated supremely through the death of Jesus and extended into our lives as wisdom "from above" (3:17–18). One practical implication of grace is that we listen carefully to one another, not treating our desires as having merit or priority over those of others. Furthermore, this means that we must extend grace to others by offering forgiveness and by providing charitable interpretations of others' actions (4:11: "Do not speak evil against one another"). Second, we express contentment in our material provisions and activities. Since human sufficiency comes through the sacrifice of Christ, we ought not celebrate the gain of material riches or boast about our plans in ways that deflect our trust away from God's provision. We must avoid talk that fuels the development of passions operating outside of God's resources; this protects us from the wrangle over resources and status that is a root of violence (4:16: "All such boasting is evil"). Third, we support the voices of the poor and the oppressed. As Girard notes, Jesus' death uncovers the injustice done against the weak and the marginalized in the name of social harmony. As Christians seeking to speak peace under God's rule, we must challenge the social pathology that denigrates and destroys others. James vehemently rebukes the rich for their complicity with oppression: "Behold, the wages of the laborers who mowed your fields, which you kept back by fraud, are crying out against you, and the cries of the harvesters have reached the ears of the Lord of hosts" (5:4). James continues by directly naming their violence: "You have condemned; you have murdered the righteous person" (5:6). Our discourse, too, ought to call out the violent oppressor and trumpet the voice of the victims. Fourth, we urge patience toward one another and toward trying circumstances. This means, practically, that we avoid complaining: "Do not grumble against each other, brothers, so that you may not be judged" (5:9). This implies, as well, expressions of gratitude for God's provision. As an analogy for Christian lives, James offers the farmer: "See how the farmer waits for the precious fruit of the earth, being patient about it, until it receives the early and the late rains" (5:7). James coaxes us to be steadfast as we wait for God. The urgency of rhetorical appeals—an urgency that often is used to motivate incautious action—must be tempered by a patient anticipation of deliverance. Fifth, we speak of the blessings to those who persevere, for they receive God's "compassion and mercy" (5:11). The honor bestowed on the prophets serves as our exemplar; "we call blessed those who showed endurance" (5:11).

The epistle closes with an appeal to prayer, which once again urges a dependence on God's work, and an appeal to do the work of an advocate, "bring[ing] back a sinner from wandering" (5:20). James does not shy away from the rhetorical practice of seeing one another analogically *as* people who are subject to God's peace and judgment.

Although admittedly only a selection of guidelines for a rhetoric of peace, these five work well together to shape discourse that avoids the violence of sacrifice while anticipating the judgment to come. The impetus for rhetorical action derives from the sinfulness of humanity and the injustice of social oppression, yet this action is channeled through a humility that precludes a violent solution. Thus, a humble dependence on God saturates one's vigorous pleading. We speak with passion, yet with caution so as not to fuel a violent contagion that would kill in order to achieve its goal.

Peace and Humility

Because Christians live between two advents, our unmistakable call to be peacemakers is carefully circumscribed by the parameters of God's relationship to violence: Jesus' birth was accompanied by the violence of Herod slaughtering the boys of Bethlehem; Jesus' death was a violent result of complex political and religious motives; and Jesus' resurrection enables his victorious execution of ultimate judgment, the violent sweeping away of death itself. As Volf describes, "A Christian perspective on violence must be won by reflecting on attitudes to violence in this whole drama of Jesus Christ's coming into the world, living in it, and judging it."[32] The situation in which we find ourselves called to peace is humbling indeed.

In effect, situating peace within God's divine relationship to violence protects us from using peace as a justification for war or an excuse for indifference. At one extreme, aggressively seeking a peace outside of God's truth will turn peace into a rationale for domination. Many wars have been fought in the name of peace, and many rulers have held high the banner of peace in order to subjugate or obliterate those who are unacceptably bellicose. At the other extreme, seeking a peace in which everyone is left alone to pursue his or her own interests leaves little motivation for engaging the injustices and violences experienced by those other than self. This is not peace, but merely a rationalization for abandoning care and neglecting the burdens of others.

A Christian peacemaker, though, has no justification for either extreme. Since peace originates from God, it ought not be worshiped as an alternative god. Thus, it cannot be idolized as something to be fought for or something to be preserved at the expense of the other. Christians avoid the other extreme by recognizing that we have been rescued from habits of covetousness and greed; we are freed from the chains of egoism and enabled to live charitably and generously. So, Christian peacemaking actively engages the needs and the injustices of the world. Yet, Christian peacemaking will not use a discourse of domination to correct the wrongs. The peacemaker would rather suffer than inflict suffering on others. This is our witness to the God of justice who suffered and died so that we may live beyond death.

In this essay, I have suggested that a Christian discourse of peace is generated through a firm commitment to theological principles; this position contrasts with the suspicion that such commitment to exclusive doctrines (especially doctrines involving judgment and sacrifice) fosters violence and hatred. The task for Christian rhetors, then, is to take their own theology with utmost seriousness. Christians who enter a global dialogue on peace ought not to soften their commitment to theological principles, but to strengthen it, such that the full implications of New Testament teaching on sacrifice and judgment saturate their discourse. Suspicions directed toward Christian exclusivism, then, will be misplaced, for the Christian rhetor worships the God who commands the rhetor to love.

Yet, the God who commands our love is not only the God who *is* love, but also the one who someday will judge the world for the rejection of love. Indeed, it is not the Christian advocates who are to be feared, but the one who has authored peace itself. This fear is not a cause of violence in the world, but is the beginning of wisdom.

NINE

JESUS AND JUST
PEACEMAKING THEORY

GLEN STASSEN

Recently in class, a student said, "Just war theory is so much better than the ethic expressed by members of my church—the American nationalistic ethics of 'Let's kick butt.' Every time the United States has bombed another country recently, some of my church members have celebrated: 'We kicked butt, didn't we!' It would be great progress if they would adopt just war theory, let alone pacifism." And I add, it would be great progress if they would mean "we Christians" more than "we Americans" when they say "we." Or perhaps I should just say, "It would be *Christian* if their identity were defined in terms of following Jesus rather than American nationalism."

Like my student, I have much respect for the two dominant paradigms of Christian ethics on war and violence, pacifism and just war theory. But they almost always drive the debate to the question where they disagree: "Is it ever justified to make a war?" Or "Is it right to make this war?" The other important question gets overlooked: "What initiatives should we push for that can prevent war?" As a result, the debates are like two persons in a rowboat drifting rapidly toward a waterfall, arguing whether to protest against the fall or to justify taking part in the catastrophe. The force of the drift toward war is powerful, and arguing whether it is right is not enough to prevent it. We need a third person in the boat who asks early about initiatives to change the direction toward the shore while there is still time.

So I wrote a book developing a third paradigm that focuses on initiatives that prevent war.[1] The initiatives are based on practices taught in the Sermon on the Mount and on Paul's letter to the Romans, and analogous practices in our time. The new paradigm caught on: twenty-three interdisciplinary and interdenominational scholars took up the idea and worked together for five years to develop a consensus just peacemaking theory: *Just Peacemaking: Ten Practices to Abolish War* (Cleveland: Pilgrim Press, 1998). They identified and described ten peacemaking practices that have developed since World War II, when the world realized we must not have another world war, or even worse, a nuclear war. Their goal was to develop a new peacemaking ethic that can be supported by persons of other faiths as well. Accordingly, they based just peacemaking theory more on empirical evidence about what peacemaking practices actually prevent wars than on biblical teaching about what peacemaking practices we are commanded to do. They saw that not only is each practice preventing some wars, but that the ten practices are working together to prevent many wars. Their identifying these effective war-preventing practices means that now we know where to put our shoulders to the wheel, and which direction to push, in order to abolish many wars and save death and misery for millions of children, women, and men whom God loves. And in a debate on whether to bomb Kosovo, or whether to attack Iraq, or how to prevent terrorism, now we can see the context from the perspective of the ten peacemaking practices that can prevent unneeded disasters.[2] For example, while Kosovo was being bombed, 200 students participated in a forum at Fuller Theological Seminary to discuss the bombing. One speaker supporting the bombing asked for a straw poll: "Raise your hands if you support the U.S. bombing of Kosovo." Not one student favored the bombing. Yet the question remained: "What is the alternative?" That is what just peacemaking theory helps us answer.[3]

So we now have not two but three paradigms for the ethics of peace and war. The new paradigm, just peacemaking, points debates not only to the permissibility of making war, but to the peacemaking practices for preventing war. Henceforth if you ever teach or discuss the ethics of peace and war with only the two old theories, I hope you will feel out of date and incomplete.

Just peacemaking theory also opens up a new perspective on biblical study. Guided by the debate between the two other paradigms, biblical study on war and peace has tended to ask only the permission question and not the prevention question. Does the Old Testament support military action? Yes (the conquest of Canaan and the concept of Holy War) and no (Isaiah, Jeremiah, Hosea, Micah, Jonah). Does Jesus? No, Jesus opposes it. So then just war theory often proceeds by marginalizing Jesus as not relevant for such questions, and then follows some other lord, or develops an ethic based not on Jesus but on some other norm. (I urge just war theorists not to make that marginalizing argument, and instead to put their just war theory under the lordship of Christ as an effort at least to reduce and restrain violence.)[4] But guided by the questions posed by just peacemaking theory, rich new biblical resources open up. What did God mean by telling Cain he could do the right thing? Jesus answers it in Matthew 5:23–26: "Go, first be reconciled to your brother."[5] What initiatives did Joseph take to make peace with his brothers, and Jacob to make peace with Esau? What initiatives did the prophets say were the will of God in order to avoid the destruction of war?[6] What peacemaking initiatives did Jesus command? When Paul wrote all his letters as calls to peace based on grace, what kinds of peacemaking initiatives did he urge?

I want to add strong guidance from the words and deeds of Jesus to the argument in *Just Peacemaking: Ten Practices for Abolishing War*. I shall call attention to several important recent studies of the way of Jesus in the New Testament, and a few theologians, showing how they support the ten practices of just peacemaking: N. T. Wright, David Garland, Richard Hays, John Howard Yoder, Clarence Jordan, Donald Shriver, Miroslav Volf, Dietrich Bonhoeffer, Walter Wink, William Klassen, and others.

The brilliant recent book on the historical Jesus, *Jesus and the Victory of God*, by N. T. Wright, opens by saying we must root our church practices, our discipleship, and our Christian faith in the real Jesus or we turn our faith into a feather—a thin, soft feather that blows with the wind and conforms its shape to whatever group interests it comes upon. I could not agree more. I love Wright's opening statement, itself rooted in history:

> Käsemann, aware (as in all his work) of the dangers of idealism and docetism, insisted that if Jesus was not earthed in history then he might be pulled in any direction, might be made the hero of any theological or political programme. [He] had in mind, undoubtedly, the various Nazi ideologies which had been able, in the absence of serious Jesus-study in pre-war Germany, to construct a largely un-Jewish Jesus. Without knowing who it was who died on the cross, he said, there would be no solid ground for upholding the gospel of the cross in all its sharpness.[7]

Conflict Resolution

I want to point to the work of John Howard Yoder on Matthew 18 and Jesus' teaching on the practice of binding and loosing,[8] as well as to Jesus' teaching in Matthew 5:21ff. on resolving conflict with antagonists. Jesus commands us to drop our gift at the altar, go make peace with whoever is hostile, and only then come back and offer our gift. And he adds: "Quickly make peace with your accuser while you are on the way to court" (Matt. 5:25).

The analogous practice in our time is conflict resolution.[9] This practice of just peacemaking theory is preventing some wars. For example, some in the Clinton administration were beating the war drums against North Korea, charging that they were diverting plutonium produced by their nuclear power reactors into bomb fuel. Former president Jimmy Carter went to North Korea and worked out the agreement that they would switch to light-water reactors that would not produce bomb fuel. He listened to their valid concern that they could not afford to buy the new, light-water reactors, and got South Korea to pay for it, and to their face-saving concern that the reactors should not be labeled "made in South Korea." And North Korea listened to U.S. concerns, allowing U.S. senators to inspect the locations where bombs or missiles were allegedly being produced, showing that this was not happening. Recently, Cuba was accused by some in the Bush administration of making chemical or biological weapons, at the very time when President Carter happened to be there, and Fidel Castro invited him to inspect any location he wanted. The drums of war were stilled. Senator George Mitchell was sent to Ireland to practice conflict resolution in that age-old, historically intransigent, hate-filled conflict, and Northern Ireland now has a peace government. On the other hand, conflict resolution was not tried before the Gulf War and before the bombing of Kosovo, and the results have been tragic for millions of people. Similarly, President George W. Bush began his presidency by announcing disengagement from conflict resolution processes in Korea and in the Middle East. But the resulting escalations of antagonism in those two places persuaded the Bush administration that it needed to reengage in conflict resolution. This practice of just peacemaking is demonstrating its usefulness in preventing war, and therefore governments are obligated to try it. Engagement in the process of conflict resolution between Israel and Palestine is a crucial way of combating terrorism, because Arab anger against the steady expansion of Israeli settlements, bypass roads, and checkpoints throughout Palestinian land is a major cause of terrorism.

Nonviolent Direct Action and Independent Initiatives

For these two practices of just peacemaking, I want to point to Jesus' teaching in Matthew 5:38ff., in the Sermon on the Mount. To understand this teaching rightly, we need to correct the error of idealism, which turns the Sermon on the Mount into high ideals or hard teachings. Therefore, I want to demonstrate briefly that the sermon, from Matthew 5:21 through 7:12, is not structured as dyadic *antitheses*, as if they were prohibitions, or hard teachings, or high ideals, in antithesis to the realism of the Old Testament. Rather, the structure is triadic *transforming initiatives*.[10] The pattern is that first Jesus identifies a traditional prohibition. Second, he identifies a vicious cycle that causes the problem named in the traditional teaching. Third, and climactically, he commands a transforming initiative that participates in the way of deliverance from the vicious cycle. This is the way of realistic deliverance, and it is based on the grace of God's compassionate deliverance.

For example, consider the teaching we just referred to, Matthew 5:21ff. First comes the *traditional teaching*: "You shall not kill." Second comes the *vicious cycle*: Continuing in anger, or calling your brother "fool," makes you liable to judgment. This is not a command in the Greek, it is a participle: it is a diagnosis of a vicious cycle that does lead to judgment and destruction. The third member is where the five commands come, and where the emphasis comes. It is the grace-based way of deliverance, the *transforming initiative*: Go, make peace with your brother, and with your accuser. This is the way of grace that God has taken toward us in Christ, taking a grace-based transforming initiative to come to us in Christ and make peace. When we go to our brother or our enemy, talk things through, and make peace, we are participating in the way of grace that God takes toward us in Christ. And this is not optional. It is an imperative, a command. It is not "If you think the one you are angry at, or who is angry at you, is good enough, deserving enough, open-minded enough"; rather, it is a *command* from Jesus: "Go, make peace." There is no guarantee of success, but there is the clear direction in which we are to go.

Matthew 5:38ff. is another triadic teaching. The *traditional teaching* is "An eye for an eye and a tooth for a tooth." Scholars agree widely that this teaching did not mean you should seek revenge, but rather that you should desist from the escalatory violence that had been practiced in a kind of Hatfields versus McCoys cycle of revenge. The *vicious cycle* is usually translated "Do not resist evil." This hardly makes sense: Jesus regularly resisted evil, confronting it directly. The translation gets the Greek wrong. As Walter Wink, followed by N. T. Wright, points out, the Greek word translated "resist" means violent and revengeful resistance.[11] And as Clarence Jordan points out, Greek grammar says the dative word translated "evil" can equally well be translated as the instrumental dative, "by evil means." The context determines which translation is correct. The context in Jesus' practice is Jesus repeatedly confronting and resisting evil. It got him crucified. But he did not do so by the evil means of hate, violence, revenge, domination, or self-righteous exclusion. He rejected violent defense in the Garden. Therefore the context clearly favors "Do not resist revengefully by evil means."[12] This translation is confirmed by Romans 12:14–21, where Paul gives us Jesus' teaching as "Never avenge yourselves. . . . Do not be overcome by evil, but overcome evil by good."

As expected in the triadic pattern, the *transforming initiatives* come next: turn the other cheek, give not only your coat but also your cloak, go not only one mile but two, and give not only to the one who begs but also to the one who borrows. Analogously, Paul gave two transforming initiatives in Romans 12: feed your enemy when he or she is hungry, and give a drink when he or she is thirsty. The trend in New Testament scholarship is to interpret these as transforming initiatives—creative ways to confront hostile action, include in community, assert dignity, and ask for peacemaking—rather than keying only on what is renounced. One can see this in the commentaries by Hans Dieter Betz, David Garland, Donald Hagner, Clarence Jordan, Pinchas Lapide, Ulrich Luz, Walter Wink, and N. T. Wright. The whole sermon consists of grace-based transforming initiatives that are the way of deliverance from the vicious cycles that we get stuck in, and that bring us to judgment and destruction.[13]

For example, Jesus' teaching on the second mile has its meaning in the context of being compelled by a Roman soldier to carry his pack one mile. Jesus does not emphasize what we are not to do, such as pull out a knife and kill him, or comply sullenly, breathing resentment all the way. Rather, he emphasizes the transforming initiative of carrying it a second mile, and, if it is combined with 5:23ff., making peace while walking together. Similarly, Jesus' teaching on the left cheek has its context where a person in that shame-and-honor culture is slapped with a demeaning, backhanded slap on the right cheek. Turning the left cheek is a nonviolent confrontation of the wrong; it says, "No more backhanded slaps." It turns the cheek of dignity and equality, while raising the possibility of peacemaking. Jesus' implicit emphasis is on a nonviolent direct action of confrontation and peacemaking.[14] The structure of the whole central section of the sermon from 5:21–7:12 strongly supports placing emphasis on the third member of each triad, and interpreting each not primarily as a negative prohibition, but as a transforming initiative. This supports the trend toward emphasizing the transforming initiatives of peacemaking in this pericope.

So Jesus is here teaching, as Paul says in Romans 12, that we are to take an initiative of nonrevengeful confrontation that seeks to overcome evil with good. The well-known just peacemaking practice in our time that implements this teaching is nonviolent direct action, as practiced by Gandhi and Martin Luther King Jr. It is nonrevengeful, it is confrontation, and it seeks to overcome evil with good. And it was practiced in Jesus' time. John Howard Yoder reports two cases in Jesus' time of collective nonviolent direct action that were successful in changing Roman policy toward Israel.[15] They happened shortly before and after Jesus' ministry, all within the same ten-year span. Crossan reports seven nonviolent demonstrations by Jews against Roman policies. "All those demonstrations were nonviolent, all had very specific objectives, and four out of the seven achieved those objectives without loss of life."[16] This shows that transforming initiatives of nonviolent action were not unthinkable or undoable in Jesus' context. They were what Jesus was calling for, instead of the violent, revengeful resistance that led to Rome's destruction of Jerusalem and the temple in 70 A.D.

The just peacemaking practice of *independent initiatives* is less well known. Yet it has been the key to getting rid of the most destabilizing nuclear weapons of all, the weapons most likely to start a nuclear war, the medium-range nuclear weapons. It also has been key to getting rapid actions and agreements to remove nuclear weapons from surface ships and to reduce the number of long-range nuclear weapons from 17,000 on each side to 3,500 or 2,000. The strategy works like this:

1. Take an initiative that decreases distrust and threat perception by the other side, by decreasing some offensive threat, but not significantly

reducing defensive capability, such as a halt to testing of nuclear weapons, or Gorbachev's removing half the Soviet tanks from Eastern Europe, or Ehud Barak's finally handing over the Lebanese territory that Israel had occupied.

2. Announce the initiative in advance, clearly explaining you are hoping for some reciprocal initiative, and that if it works, you will take more initiatives, because you want to shift the context from escalation toward deescalation.

3. Be sure to take the initiative on schedule, punctually, even if some hostile words or events occur; the point is to decrease distrust so the other side can take some initiatives.

4. Make the initiative clearly visible and verifiable by the other side; the point is to overcome distrust.

5. Take the initiative independent of waiting for the slow process of negotiations; afterwards it can be worked into a treaty.

6. Take initiatives in a series; it will take more than one to overcome deep distrust.

7. If the other side reciprocates, reward them with additional significant initiatives; if they do not, keep the door open by continuing with a series of small initiatives.

Both nonviolent direct action and independent initiatives, as well as conflict resolution, implement the strategy of transforming initiatives:

1. They affirm that the enemy is a member of God's community, loved by God, with some valid interests, even while confronting unjust actions of the enemy.

2. They are proactive initiatives of grace and peacemaking, not simply passive resignation.

3. They confront the other with an invitation to make peace that includes justice.

4. They are nonviolent and nonrevengeful.

5. They are historically embodied practices, not merely ideals.

6. They acknowledge the log in our own eyes and take responsibility for peacemaking rather than simply judging the other.

How can these two just peacemaking practices deepen the struggle against terrorism and make it more effective? Palestinians can be encouraged to shift to a strategy of nonviolent direct action rather than terrorist violence. This will decrease the threat to Israel's security and Israel's polarization against Palestine. Christians can give support to the centers in Palestine that teach nonviolent direct action, and can themselves participate in nonviolent initiatives like Christian

Peacemaker Teams. We can urge Israel not to exile Palestinians who teach non-violent action and not to block nonviolent observers from entering Palestine.

When the Palestine Authority takes initiatives that halt most terrorist violence, Israel can respond by desisting from further attacks on Palestinians and instead halting settlement expansion. When Israel pulls out from occupying Palestinian territory, Palestinians can respond by sincerely seeking to halt terrorist violence. But what initiatives can the United States government take besides pressing for such initiatives? Let us think with a bit of imagination such as Jesus suggests. The main source of anger for Palestinians is the steady increase of Israeli settlements in Palestinian territory, combined with bypass roads that carve up their land and that Palestinians may not use, and checkpoints that keep them from traveling within their own land. The settlements are lavishly subsidized by the Israeli government, so that settlers receive extensive financial awards for occupying housing in Palestine. The U.S. can earmark a small portion of its aid to Israel for purchasing settlers' homes at attractive prices, provided that they then move to Israel. Palestinians will then see the trend turning toward decreased settlements rather than ever-increasing settlements, and their hope can return. Israel will then receive the money as real estate investments in Israel, and will receive decreased terrorism and greater security.

The strategy of *acknowledging responsibility for conflict and injustice, and seeking repentance and forgiveness* hardly needs justification as a key part of the way of Jesus Christ. Jesus teaches, for example, that we are not to be judging others, in the sense of condemning them, but rather to be taking the log out of our own eye (Matt 7:1–5). He teaches that if we forgive others, our heavenly Father will also forgive us, but not otherwise (Matt. 6:14f.). When Jesus was crucified, while he was in the process of dying, nailed to the cross, he prayed for forgiveness for those who were killing him.

Elegant new work is being done on the meaning of forgiveness and repentance for large-scale peacemaking. Donald Shriver has argued eloquently in his book *An Ethic for Enemies* that forgiveness in Jesus' teachings and way of organizing the disciples was not just an individual matter but a social practice for the society as well.

> Like many a narrative in the Hebrew Bible, the Gospel stories are full of political references: Roman occupiers, Jewish kings, powerful high priests—all of them seeking to control a society none of whose members knew anything about "separation of church and state." Indeed, in spite of the politically "tamed" final versions of some of the Gospel narratives, Jesus' challenges to powerful politicians and institutions come through clearly in many passages.[17]

Shriver points to five regular practices that Jesus taught and modeled, all of which built forgiveness into the practice of the community: healings that brought outcasts into community membership; eating with outcasts that similarly brought outcasts into community; prayer that not only emphasized forgiveness but that he taught would not be effective if those praying did not forgive those who offended them; the community practice of forgiving enemies like Zacchaeus and other tax collectors, Roman soldiers, and those who executed him and, later, those who executed Stephen; and the practice of restorative justice that he taught the community.[18] Similarly, Christopher Marshall, in *Beyond Retribution*, writes profoundly of New Testament teaching on restorative justice as no one else has done.[19] Desmond Tutu, in *No Future Without Forgiveness*, thinks theologically about the experience of the Truth and Reconciliation Commission in South Africa, which he chaired.[20]

For centuries realists have argued that we could not expect rulers of nations to repent or give forgiveness; they would lose face, and it would weaken them in their competition for power and interest. So wars are fought over unconfessed injustices that still fester from as long ago as 1389. But a new practice has arisen out of Dietrich Bonhoeffer's writing a confession of his and Germany's guilt during the Nazi period.[21] Churches in Germany started making confession on Germany's behalf. Christian war resisters from Germany volunteered their alternative service in other nations that Germany had injured; three of them have lived in our home during their times of service. The organization is called, if translated literally, "Action Atonement-Symbol, Peace Service." After the churches had prepared the way, Willy Brandt, Germany's chancellor, went to the Warsaw Ghetto in Poland and presented a wreath in memory of Jews and Poles slaughtered by Germans there. He was deeply moved, and he sank onto his knees in tearful prayer. Poland was moved; the world was moved. Brandt announced that Germany would accept the shrunken border of Germany at the Oder-Neisse River, and never try to get formerly German territory back from Poland. Then German President Richard von Weizsäcker delivered an address in the German parliament concretely naming German sins during the Nazi period, and expressing German repentance for its sin. The words are powerful; Shriver quotes them at length. The outcome has been repentance and forgiveness between Germany and many of its former enemies, and a present-day Germany that has been transformed into an influence for peacemaking. The prime minister of Japan has finally apologized concretely and in writing to Korea for Japan's atrocities against Koreans. Korean President Kim Dae Jung responded that this was what Korea had been waiting for, and now cultural and social exchanges could finally take place.

Recently, at the annual conference of International Global Exchange, the speaker from Rwanda told of the shocking massacre of 800,000 human beings in eight weeks, and of church efforts to rebuild civic culture afterwards. He was asked whether he feared that the bitterness, resentment, divisiveness, and anger after such a shocking massacre might lead to yet another massacre in revenge. He replied in words like this: "Since the massacre, President Clinton came and apologized for U.S. inaction, and the British prime minister then came and also apologized, and Kofi Annan, the secretary-general of the United

Nations, also apologized. Our own Rwandan leaders have apologized. This has helped greatly to heal the resentment and turn the drive for revenge into a drive for rebuilding. The churches are working to foster the spirit of forgiveness and rebuilding. So I am optimistic that we will rebuild, not seek revenge." It is a remarkable new practice of peacemaking that can lance festering boils that threaten to erupt in violence and war. Shriver describes it eloquently. So does the brilliant Croatian-American theologian Miroslav Volf, in his moving book *Exclusion and Embrace.*[22] The practice of repentance and forgiveness, so clearly taught and practiced by Jesus, is now spreading among nations and is acting to control emotions that cause wars.

President George W. Bush asked, "Why do they hate us so much?" Perhaps we could study the history of imperialism in the Middle East, where Western nations first dominated and then carved up the Arab nations, breaking promises along the way. Likewise, we could study the history of U.S. support for dominating governments that resist calling democratic elections and that many people feel are oppressive; and U.S. support for Israeli governments that keep expanding settlements in Palestinian territory without using that support to curtail the settlements and the occupation. And then perhaps our leaders could apologize. Can we picture the response if the Israeli government, the leadership of the Palestinian Authority, and the U.S. government would each issue apologies for their part in the immense suffering?

Democracy, Human Rights, and Religious Liberty; Just and Sustainable Economic Development

Jesus cared deeply about justice; we can see this in a myriad of ways. New Testament scholars are paying new attention to Jesus' prophetic attack on the temple system. William Telford, Ched Myers, David Garland, Richard Horsley, E. P. Sanders, N. T. Wright, and John Dominic Crossan, among others, are focusing new attention here. They are seeing it as a major clue to why Jesus was crucified, and what he understood his mission to be.

N. T. Wright points out that in five different passages, Jesus prophesied the destruction of the temple: Mark 14:58; 15:29–30; John 2:9; Acts 6:14; Thomas 71.[23] He disagrees with Crossan on much, but here he says that Crossan comes very close to the right answer on the cross: "Crossan thinks, and I fully agree with him, that Jesus' action in the temple was a symbolic destruction; that some words of Jesus about this destruction are original; and that these words and this action followed with a close logic from the rest of Jesus' agenda, the programme enacted in healings and meal-sharings. . . . I think . . . that at this point we are on very firm historical ground indeed."[24]

David Garland writes that it was neither an act of violent revolution nor merely a "cleansing" or reform of the temple, but a symbolic prophetic action of protest against injustice and its cover-up. Why would Jesus try to reform the temple when he predicts it will soon be destroyed? "If sacrificial animals cannot be purchased, then sacrifice must end. If no vessel can be carried though the temple, then all cultic activity must cease." And if money cannot be made, then the financial support for the temple and the priests will be gone. "Jesus does not seek to purify current temple worship but symbolically attacks the very function of the temple and heralds its destruction." His hostility to the temple emerges as a charge at his trial (Mark 14:58) and as a taunt at the cross (Mark 15:29).

Jesus cited two passages from the prophets as he carried out this prophetic action. Isaiah 56:7, "My house shall be called a house of prayer for all the nations," is part of the declaration in Isaiah 56:1–8 that God's purpose is to bless all who are being excluded—the foreigners, eunuchs, and outcasts. "During his entire ministry Jesus has been gathering in the impure outcasts and the physically maimed, and has even reached out to Gentiles. He expects the temple to embody this inclusive love. . . . In Jesus' day the temple had become a nationalistic symbol that served only to divide Israel from the nations."[25]

Jeremiah 7 says, "Do not trust in these deceptive words, the temple of the LORD, the temple of the LORD, the temple of the LORD." But if you "truly amend your ways and your doings, if you truly act justly one with another, if you do not oppress the alien, the orphan, or the widow, or shed innocent blood, . . . and do not go after other gods to your own hurt, then I will dwell with you in this place, in the land that I gave of old to your ancestors." But because you have done all these injustices, and have made the temple "a den of robbers," I will cast you out of the land, "I will cast you out of my sight" (Jer. 7:3–15). The temple is functioning as a cover-up for injustice, what Bonhoeffer called "cheap grace" that does not call for changing our ways and our loyalties. If we continue to practice injustice and claim God is on our side because we have the temple of the Lord, God will destroy the temple and cast us out of God's sight. By quoting from Jeremiah 7, continues Garland, Jesus attacks "a false trust in the efficacy of the temple sacrificial system. The leaders of the people think that they can rob widows' houses (Mark 12:40) and then perform the prescribed sacrifices according to the prescribed patterns at the prescribed times in the prescribed purity in the prescribed sacred space and then be safe and secure from all alarms. They are wrong."

Some Christians claim God has given the land of Palestine to Israel, and therefore they pressure the U.S. government to support all Israeli policies and to oppose those who demand justice for Palestinians. But the book of Deuteronomy and the prophets of Israel say again and again that if Israel does injustice, if Israel oppresses the alien, the orphan, the widow, and sheds innocent blood, then the land will vomit them out, or God will drive them out of the land.

Christians who take Jesus' confrontations of injustice seriously, who take God's caring for justice to the weak and powerless seriously, and who care for Israel's security, will urge that Israel do justice to Palestinians and that the U.S. government urge justice for Palestinians. That is a crucial just peacemaking step to curtail terrorism.

A third quest of the historical Jesus is underway. The best book is by N. T. Wright, *Jesus and the Victory of God*. Wright begins with the thesis that has emerged out of his massive study: "I shall argue, first, that Jesus' public persona within first-century Judaism was that of a prophet, and [second] that the content of his prophetic proclamation was the 'kingdom' of Israel's God." "The prophetic aspect of Jesus' work is often surprisingly ignored," but Wright gives a synopsis of the verses seeing him as a prophet mighty in word and deed.[26] What we all surely know is that the prophets of Israel again and again announced that God wills justice to the powerless—the orphans, widows, poor, and foreigners (or immigrants). The four Hebrew words for justice occur 1,060 times in the Bible. Hardly any other word is repeated so often. We are often handicapped in recognizing this if we do not read Hebrew and Greek, because two of the Hebrew words are often translated as "righteousness" and "judgment" in various versions, but they mean the kind of justice that delivers the powerless from their oppression and bondage into covenant community with provisions of justice.[27]

In the Synoptic Gospels, I count forty-eight times, not including parallels, when Jesus confronts the hierarchy or the wealthy for injustice, such as seeking prestige and wealth and not lifting a finger to lift the burdens of the poor and oppressed. By "the hierarchy," I mean the Sadducees and the representatives of the temple hierarchy (including Pharisees), who were the day-to-day authorities that Jews encountered, plus the Herods and Pilates and Roman rulers. I see four themes running through his confrontations over injustice. Jesus opposed the injustice of violence, domination, oppression of the poor, and exclusion of the outcasts from community.[28]

The prophets clearly say again and again that our injustice causes the destruction of war, and that when we repent and practice justice, peace will follow. Jesus fulfills this prophetic witness to God's compassion for justice. And so our just peacemaking theory has two practices of justice. One is *Democracy, Human Rights, and Religious Liberty*. Jimmy Carter, a faithful Baptist, was determined to express his faith in a way that could be translated into public language shared by others. When he became president, he had already stood courageously for human rights in Georgia's struggle to overcome racial discrimination and segregation. He announced that U.S. foreign policy would examine the human rights record of other countries, and our foreign aid would be contingent on it. He got Congress to pass this annual review as law. It has continued ever since. The Roman Catholic Church had already committed itself to work for human rights, especially when Pope John XXIII was pope, and when the Second Vatican Council completed its work in 1965. Other denominations also pushed for human rights around the world. Partly as a result of these forces, those nations in Latin America that had been military dictatorships all officially became democracies with recognized human rights, although some are still working through the transition.[29] And democracy is spreading in many previous dictatorships formerly behind the Iron Curtain, and in South Korea, Taiwan, and Indonesia; democracy has existed in India from independence in 1947. When we participate in churches that encourage this spread, and join human rights groups like Amnesty International or Witness for Peace, we strengthen this trend. And here is the remarkable fact: not one democracy with recognized human rights fought a war against another democracy with recognized human rights in the whole twentieth century. When we push for human rights, we strengthen the force that is creating whole zones of peace. Some question this sweeping claim, but the data sources from the discipline of international relations are provided by Bruce Russett in his essay "Advance Democracy, Human Rights, and Religious Liberty."[30]

Terrorists usually come from nations that lack democracy and human rights. They feel voiceless and resentful, and see no alternative to terrorism for expressing their resentment and anger. Often they see the United States as imperial supporter of the dictatorships in their countries, and they resent both their own government and the U.S. support. For example, the U.S. government encouraged the government of Algeria to cancel its national elections in 1992 when it became clear the populist and more radical Muslim party would win the election. The United States has military relationships with several of the authoritarian governments in the Middle East, and military support moved into Saudi Arabia during the 1991 Gulf War. According to scholars, this is the event that convinced Osama bin Laden to become a terrorist. Just peacemaking suggests that if the U.S. government wants to decrease terrorism, it should support trends toward human rights and democracy a bit more and military alliances that strengthen antidemocratic forces a bit less. This is especially true in Indonesia, where the military supported the antidemocratic massacres in East Timor and threatens the weak democracy at the time of this writing.

David Bronkema, David Lumsdaine, and Rodger A. Payne also indicate that *just and sustainable economic development* focusing on building local communities and civic society is crucial for peacemaking.[31] I think of Carl Ryther, Baptist agricultural missionary, whose methods were crucial in transforming Bangladesh, perhaps the poorest nation in the world, into a self-sustaining food producer. I think of Musheshe and the Uganda Rural Development Training (URDT) project, which he leads and which I have visited, transforming the lives of rural Ugandans in the western part of the country, and I pray that the war in the Congo is not disrupting it. I think of Bread for the World, and of Ron Sider's book *Rich Christians in an Age of Hunger*, which students in my classes have read for over twenty years now. I want to recommend Michael

Edwards, *Future Positive: International Co-operation in the 21st Century,* for its broad-based wisdom, distinguishing what kind of economic development works and what kind does not. The key, in a nutshell, is that development that focuses on building community organization and grassroots development, rather than top-down concentration of economic power, and that involves aid-giving organizations in long-range relationships with community organizations rather than short-range projects, is what works—in the experience of many nations and many communities. The same conclusions, plus a few more, are what we show works in *Just Peacemaking: Ten Practices to Abolish War.* And we show that this practice is one key to reducing civil war and terrorism. Palestine, Egypt, Serbia, and Colombia have experienced economic dys-development, and they have accordingly produced group- and state-supported terrorism. If the coalition against terrorism is to succeed, it must focus major efforts on sustainable economic development. Hence President George W. Bush announced that the United States would focus efforts on economic rebuilding in Afghanistan, and would increase its economic aid to developing nations by $5 billion over the next three years. Many Americans think the United States is already quite generous in giving economic aid, but Ronald Sider, in *Rich Christians in an Age of Hunger,* provides data demonstrating that U.S. economic aid is a lower percentage of our income than the comparable percentage in the other twenty-one wealthy nations. Just peacemaking calls Christians to join Bread for the World and give the political encouragement for those needed increases in economic aid—and to do it in ways that are effective. Bread for the World, a Christian organization, is pushing for the kind of policies that our own research and Michael Edwards's experience indicate is effective.

The Final Four Practices—Community

Jesus' understanding of justice involved the important element of being included in community, and not being cast out. We think of the poignant story of the cripple at the pool of Bethsaida, who had no one to move him into the water. He lacked community and so was powerless. Jesus healed him and restored him to community. In healing outcasts and bringing them back into society, he often touched people whom no one would touch, like lepers or women with a flow of blood or the dead, or they touched him. Sometimes he instructed the healed person to submit to the priests, so as to be certified as includable in community, or to go back to their community. Furthermore, his healing was often connected with forgiveness (Mark 2:5–9), where forgiveness means not only wiping out past sins but embracing in community.

For a first-century Jew, most if not all of the works of healing, which form the bulk of Jesus' mighty works, could be seen as the restoration to membership in

Israel of those who, through sickness or whatever, had been excluded as ritually unclean. The healings thus function in exact parallel with the welcome of sinners, and this, we may be quite sure, was what Jesus himself intended. He never performed mighty works simply to impress. He saw them as part of the inauguration of the sovereign and healing rule of Israel's covenant God, [and] bestowing the gift of *shalom*, wholeness.[32]

"We have, in the last forty years, 'discovered' that Matthew, Mark, Luke, and John—and even, according to some—Q and Thomas—had a great interest in 'community.' It ought to be just as clear, if not clearer, that Jesus himself was deeply concerned about the social and corporate effects of his kingdom-announcement." It was corporate and personal, not individualist or collective. "A good deal of evidence indicates that Jesus fully intended his stories to generate a new form of community, and that this by itself ought to be sufficient to call into question any unthinking acceptance of the old dogma of the imminent expectation of the end of the cosmos."[33]

And what all agree is that Jesus revolutionized the understanding of who is to be included in community. Jesus' teaching that "You shall love your enemies" is affirmed by even the very skeptical scholars to be Jesus' authentic teaching, and his decisive innovation. It is Jesus' commentary on Leviticus 19:18— "You shall not take vengeance or bear a grudge against any of your people, but you shall love your neighbor as yourself: I am the LORD." The question was "Who is my neighbor?" (Luke 10:29). Jesus answered by telling the parable of the compassionate Samaritan, and by pointing to God's practice of including all in the community of God's care. God gives sunshine and rain to friends and enemies alike, and we are to participate in God's grace, including our enemies in our community of love (Matt. 5:43ff.). This is symbolized dramatically in Jesus' including Zealots and a tax collector in his community of disciples. He practiced a justice that clearly went beyond the justice of the Pharisees, and even of the prophets. He died to save those who crucified him!

As Jesus revolutionized the way we are to relate to enemies or those we have disagreements with, bringing them into community and making them fellow members, we are called to learn from him. How can we bring national adversaries into community with us? How can we build them into structures that give incentives for regular practices of conversation, mutual learning, cooperative efforts, and affirmation of valid interests even though we disagree on some interests? This is the question that untold numbers of persons asked after World War II. They were determined to begin processes of mutual engagement that together would prevent a repeat of World War II or other wars. They were thinking realistically of the real forces that influence nations' interests and incentives to engage cooperatively with each other. They began to nurture cooperative forces that would bring varieties of nations into community with each other as fellow members.

The result is two practices of just peacemaking: *Work with cooperative forces in the international system; and strengthen the United Nations and international efforts for cooperation and human rights.*

Paul Schroeder may be the most respected historian of international relations in the United States. In *Just Peacemaking: Ten Practices*, he writes:

> Four separate but inter-related trends in international history, marked since the early nineteenth century and increasingly powerful and accelerating in the latter twentieth century, have sharply altered the nature of the international system. These are:
>
> A. The decline of the utility of war, that is, a steep rise in the costs and dangers of major war as a tool of statecraft, and a corresponding decline in the applicability and potential benefits of even a successful use of large-scale military force as a way of solving major problems, securing either order or freedom.
>
> B. The rise of the trading state, that is, the priority now placed by most modern states on success in trade and the economy, as opposed to success in war, as the key to domestic order, welfare, and legitimacy. Where it used to be said that war made the state and the state made war, it is now becoming more true to say that trade makes the successful state, and the successful state makes trade. . . .
>
> C. A dramatic increase in the volume, density, and speed of international exchanges, communications, and transactions of all kinds, and the increasing integration of these exchanges into organized, complex international, supra-national, and transnational networks, corporations, and other institutions. This has now developed to such a degree that the domestic economics, politics, and culture of individual states cannot be isolated from them or do without them. Along with this has gone an equally startling increase in the number, scope, durability, and effectiveness of international organizations of all kinds, both governmental and non-governmental, which both modern governments and non-governmental groups must pay attention to and must use for their particular purposes.
>
> D. A gradual, uneven, but unmistakable ascendancy of one form of government, liberal representative democracy, as the dominant legitimate form of governance of modern states, and of one kind of economic system, market-oriented capitalism (whether of the welfare-state or a more laissez-faire variety) as the dominant form of modern economic development.
>
> . . . These four trends combine not to insure general international peace (nothing can do that), but greatly to enhance the possibilities of just peacemaking within the existing system. Some of the ways they do so are fairly obvious and frequently discussed—the great rise in costs and risks of large-scale war or military coercion and decline of its perceived benefits, together with the greater importance of . . . commercial competition in comparison to . . . military and power-political competition. . . . The dramatic rise in international transactions and organizations means far greater interdependence among states, and at least potentially greater incentives for cooperation and disincentives for overt conflict.[34]

Bruce Russett, Professor of International Relations at Yale University, who specializes in careful statistical studies of factors that decrease the likelihood and frequency of war, is also one of the authors of *Just Peacemaking: Ten Practices*. He concludes that trade—economic interdependence—decreases war:

> Economic interdependence gives countries a stake in one another's well-being. War would mean destruction, in the other country, of one's own markets, industrial plants, and sources of imports. If my investments are in your country, bombing your industry means, in effect, bombing my own factories. Just the threat of war inhibits international trade and investment. Economic interdependence also serves as a channel of information about each other's perspectives, interests, and desires on a broad range of matters not the subject of the economic exchange. These communications form an important channel for conflict management. Interdependence, however, is the key word—mutual dependence, not one-sided dominance of the weak by the strong.
>
> Interdependence in the last fifty years has importantly contributed—above and beyond the influence of joint democracy, wealth, and alliances—to reducing conflict among states so linked. When countries' trade with each other constitutes a substantial portion of their national incomes, violent conflict and war between them are rare. . . . The combination of democracy and interdependence is especially powerful. States that are both democratic and economically interdependent are extremely unlikely to initiate serious military disputes with one another.[35]

Russett's research also indicates that engagement in international organizations, including not only the United Nations but also the many other less well-known international organizations, engages nations in processes that work to prevent war. He writes:

> International organizations . . . may mediate among conflicting parties, reduce uncertainty in negotiations by conveying information, expand material self-interest to be more inclusive and longer term, shape norms, and help generate narratives of mutual identification among peoples and states. Some organizations are more successful than others, and in different functions. But overall, . . . they do make a difference.[36]

In another paper Russett continues in this vein:

> An extension of the quantitative empirical analyses referred to above makes the point. The same kind of analysis that first established an independent and significant influence of democracy in reducing conflict between countries, and then added evidence for an additional meliorative influence of economic interdependence, has been carried out on the effect of international organizations. We have collected information on the number of intergovernmental organizations (IGOs) in which both of any pair of countries is a member. This "density" of IGO membership varies from zero for some countries to over 100 for some pairs of European states. Adding this information to the previous analysis, we find that it too contributes an additional, independent, statistically significant effect

in reducing the probability of international conflict. The thicker the network, the fewer the militarized disputes.[37]

I would like to write personally of my own father—something I have not done before. As an active youth in Riverview Baptist Church (West St. Paul, Minnesota), in what used to be called the German Baptist Convention (now North American Baptist Convention), he grew up during World War I. His parents' German immigrant roots, leaving Germany when it became more militaristic and authoritarian under Bismarck, must have made him especially aware of the devastation of the First World War. And his strong Christian commitment as a follower of the Prince of Peace also influenced him. He became a national leader of Baptist youth, and eventually president of the American Baptist Convention. As a teenager he made a commitment to work realistically for peacemaking, which meant, he thought, entering into politics. He became governor of Minnesota, the youngest governor in the history of the United States, and was twice reelected. When he saw World War II coming, he spoke against the isolationism that had killed the League of Nations as an effective organization and had contributed to yet another world war. He called for the creation of a United Nations, this time with U.S. support and greater effectiveness, in order to prevent yet another world war. He resigned his governorship and entered the navy, where he fought against the Japanese in the South Pacific, eventually rising to the rank of captain. President Roosevelt had heard him speak and was impressed, and decided to call for a United Nations. He needed bipartisan support this time, and so he appointed my father as a Republican delegate to the charter-writing assembly of the United Nations in 1945 in San Francisco. Still in the navy, Dad came to San Francisco, dedicated to his Christian commitment to do what he could for peace. Only now he had seen the devastation of world war firsthand, and was all the more deeply committed to do what he could so that we would not have another world war. He gave all he had to the cause, working diligently to bring together the different nations, with their different interests, including the Russians, to agree to an effective United Nations Organization. When the charter-writing assembly was concluded successfully, the representatives of the press from around the world held a vote on who, of all the delegates from the nations of the world, had done the most for the success of the charter. It was a tie between the ambassador from Australia and my father.

My father was only one of very many who had experienced the unbelievable devastation of World War II, with fifty million human beings killed and so many more wounded, including the only use of atomic weapons in war, and who then got to work building institutions and practices that so far have worked to prevent World War III. The United Nations is one of those key institutions.

Michael Joseph Smith, professor of international relations at the University of Virginia, writes in *Just Peacemaking: Ten Practices* that just peacemaking theory requires "support for the United Nations and associated regional international organizations so that, collectively, we can develop the capacity to identify, prevent, and, if necessary, intervene in conflicts within and between states that threaten basic human rights." He writes that "Repeated polls have demonstrated that the American people believe the United Nations to be the most appropriate agency for peacekeeping and, despite some notable UN-bashing from American politicians, hold the UN in much higher regard than the US Congress." Between 1988 and 1994,

> the UN initiated nearly twice the number of peacekeeping missions as it had in its entire history until then. The budget for peacekeeping operations rose from $230 million in 1988 to $3.61 billion in 1994. In 1994, seventy-six countries contributed police and military units for seventeen peacekeeping operations that involved some 75,500 personnel.
>
> At the same time, it is widely recognized that the capacities of the United Nations are in no way equal to the magnitude of the needs.[38]

In the struggle to prevent terrorism, the U.S. government was forced to recognize that an international coalition was needed. Terrorism is an international network; only a coalition of nations can combat it. Gathering the needed information about terrorists requires the cooperation of many nations. Stopping the flow of money that finances terrorists requires the work of many nations. Therefore the Bush administration, which began by announcing its intention to disengage from many international efforts and treaties, rightly realized it must work with cooperative forces and must obtain U.N. approval. Secretary of State Colin Powell worked energetically and effectively to develop the needed international coalition. The first priority for very many Arabs was justice for Palestinians, and therefore it was necessary to reengage in peacemaking efforts in the Middle East. This, too, required international cooperation.

There was internal debate about how much to work with the United Nations and international forces, and how much to "go it alone." Our closest European allies, and our needed Islamic allies, were strongly critical of unilateral actions. Millions of Arabs and Muslims expressed great anger at U.S. "imperialist power," acting against advice from other nations. It was not clear whether U.S. policy would evolve more toward cooperation with international networks and the United Nations, or whether it would act in a more "go-it-alone" way. The Bush administration had declared itself against, or had withdrawn from, the anti-ballistic missile treaty, the comprehensive test ban treaty, the Kyoto Accords, and the International Criminal Court, and was bypassing the United Nations in its decisions on the war against terrorism.[39] A high-powered panel of thirty-five business and media leaders, scholars, and former diplomats gathered by the Council on Foreign Relations released a report July 30, 2002, saying, "There is little doubt that stereotypes of the United States as arrogant, self-indulgent, hypocritical, inattentive, and unwilling or unable to engage in cross-cultural dialogue are pervasive and deeply rooted." Other nations are saying the U.S. government is not listening to them. The U.S. government responded by creating a new office to communicate U.S. positions, so that other nations will listen to us.[40]

In the time after the attack on the Twin Towers and the Pentagon, people want security. If the empirical data that support just peacemaking theory are relevant, then security is decisively greater when we work with the international networks and the United Nations. International cooperation decisively reduces war and terrorism. But if the United States is seen as acting on the basis of its own military power and against the will of other nations, then terrorist anger increases. Security is not to be had by flying in the face of the international networks. Acting in what is seen as imperialist dominance will cause yet more antagonism, and result in yet more terrorist attacks.

The ninth practice of just peacemaking is to *reduce offensive weapons and the weapons trade.* Jesus entered Jerusalem as the Prince of Peace, coming not on a warhorse but on a colt, the foal of an ass, fulfilling the prophecy of a Messiah of peace in Zechariah 9:9 (Matt. 21:1–9 and parallels). When the mob sent by the high priest came to arrest Jesus in the garden, and his disciple drew his sword and cut off the ear of the high priest's slave, Jesus said, "Put your sword back into its place; for all who take the sword will perish by the sword. Do you think that I cannot appeal to my Father, and he will at once send me more than twelve legions of angels?" (Matt. 26:52f.). John Howard Yoder's *The Politics of Jesus* and Richard Hays's *The Moral Vision of the New Testament,* chapter 14, demonstrate Jesus' commitment to nonviolence. The twenty-three just peacemaking scholars, most of whom support just war theory rather than pacifism, agree that reducing offensive weapons and weapons trade has been demonstrated to reduce war.

At the time of this writing, a Palestinian terrorist has just detonated a bomb in the cafeteria of the Hebrew University in Jerusalem, and Palestinian terrorism continues to harden and polarize Jewish support for military occupation of Palestine, which in turn hardens and polarizes Palestinian parties that promote terrorism. This is what is meant by "vicious cycles." One side needs to take the initiative to call off its offensive attacks. And then the other side needs to reciprocate, with a reduction in occupation rather than with new attacks. The U.S. government needs to push in this direction in an evenhanded way, and U.S. Christians need to push the U.S. government in that direction of just peacemaking.

And that—Christians pushing for evenhanded peacemaking practices— brings us to the concluding practice of just peacemaking: *Join in grassroots and church peacemaking groups.* Jesus did not simply wander as an individual philosopher, but developed a grassroots group of disciples who would spread the message, and he gave them the mission of spreading the message. Furthermore, he founded cells of followers in different villages, like planting mustard seeds that would sprout and grow new communities.[41] Christians in the Middle East are forming peacemaking groups that work to spread the practices of nonviolence and just peacemaking. They fear that war policies are driving Christians, and the Christian witness, out of the Middle East. The advocacy group Churches for Middle East Peace is pleading for Christians elsewhere to join together in groups and push for peacemaking practices. Christians are ineffective in pushing for peacemaking practices unless they strengthen each other by joining in groups. They are ineffective if they do not follow Jesus' model.

From the perspective of just peacemaking theory, I believe we do have extensive biblical guidance and extensive empirical evidence that these ten practices are crucial for curtailing terrorism. They get at the roots of terrorism and of the causes that recruit people to become terrorists. They are the route to security, and security is what people want. If the response to terrorism is military repression of terrorists and unilateral action, it will increase the frustrated and resentful anger of those who feel powerless and turn to terrorism. Such a policy has not stopped terrorism in the Middle East, and it will not do well for the United States. Further terrorism will result. Is it not time to turn the thought and discussion of the churches, and then of the nation, to "the practices that make for peace"? (Luke 19:41–42).

> For the palace will be forsaken,
>   the populous city deserted;
> . . . .
> until a spirit from on high is poured out on us,
> . . . .
> Then justice will dwell in the wilderness,
>   and righteousness abide in the fruitful field.
> The effect of righteousness will be peace,
>   and the result of righteousness, quietness and trust forever.
> My people will abide in a peaceful habitation,
>   in secure dwellings, and in quiet resting places.
>
>   Isaiah 32:14–18

SECTION THREE
THEOLOGIES

TEN

VIOLENCE AND THE ATONEMENT

RICHARD J. MOUW

It has become a fairly common practice in recent years for scholars to criticize traditional Christian doctrines for the ways in which they purportedly
promote and reinforce unhealthy human practices. This mode of critique is
especially attractive to those thinkers who like to probe beneath the surface of
what to many of us are the obvious meanings of theories and stories, for what
they insist are the "subtexts" in which the operating motives and projects are
made plain. Marxism has long thrived on this kind of analysis. Its adherents
have insisted, for example, that while oppressed people who sing hymns about
the afterlife may sincerely believe in a glorious future heavenly existence, what
is "really" going on is that they have internalized a story that is designed to
make them passively accept the political-economic status quo. The Freudians
employ a parallel strategy for understanding religious belief, insisting that, for
example, the desire for divine forgiveness is a conscious effort to resolve an
unconscious Oedipal conflict. And it is not unusual these days to encounter
folks who reject, say, the doctrine of the virgin birth, not on the grounds that
it is "unscientific" to believe in a miracle of that sort, but because it promotes
an image of passive and servile femininity. Or the idea of divine transcendence
will be attacked for the way in which it reinforces "hierarchicalism" in human
relationships and in the way we treat other species.

The topic that I will be focusing upon here, the classical Christian formulations concerning the atoning work of Christ, has come in for special attention in this regard. Specifically, the suggestion is made that the story of a divine
Father punishing his Son on the cross features imagery that promotes violent
relationships among human beings. Obviously, such a critique is directed toward

what many of us see as a central theme in biblical orthodoxy. It is important, then, to think carefully about this way of analyzing theological motifs.

There are at least two good reasons for doing so. First, we need to be clear about the fact that the things critics of Christian orthodoxy claim to find in the "subtexts" of Christian teachings are often very bad things. We ought to be genuinely disturbed if, for example, we really are encouraging the poor to remain in their squalor, or promoting the subjugation of women by reinforcing models of passive femininity. The same goes for the exploitation of nature. It is a bad thing to encourage such patterns, and we ought to be willing—even eager—to check out any possible connection between Christian belief and such programs of unrighteousness.

And, second, there can be no denying that the actual record of the Christian community is not pure with regard to such programs. Christians *have* in fact often been on the wrong side of important moral issues. We owe it to our critics to admit our sins and to explore seriously any ways in which we have misused Christian teachings. As José Miguez Bonino once observed about the need for Christians to take the accusations of Latin American revolutionaries seriously: we are not ultimately accountable to our secular critics—only the Lord is our judge. But while our critics cannot sit in judgment over us, we do need to allow them, in the presence of that Lord, to take the witness stand and to present their evidence against us.[1]

Just War Spirituality

The need to listen carefully to our critics is nowhere more obvious to me than in our Christian dealings with the topic of violence. That subject has consistently been high on my own agenda during my career as an ethicist. My entry-level concerns on this subject were shaped by my very personal struggles during the Vietnam war era. And while I have always found a thoroughgoing pacifism to have some moral attraction, my basic convictions on the subject have been consistently formed and expressed within a just war perspective. I have never been happy, though, with the way many just war theorists have concentrated almost exclusively on the patterns and processes of *military* strategy, to the neglect of the more general patterns of violence and abuse in human relations. My own sense is that it is especially important to pay close attention to issues of *moral character,* a focus that clearly comes to the fore as we think about the very urgent question of what it means for us to address the crisis of our increasingly violent culture.

I have regularly drawn my inspiration on this topic from John Calvin. In his comments in the *Institutes* about the use of military violence, he links just war considerations to underlying issues of spirituality. When civic leaders are planning military actions, Calvin says, it is the duty of all magistrates here to guard particularly against giving vent to their passions even in the slightest degree. Rather, if they have to punish, let them not be carried away with headlong anger, or be seized with hatred, or burn with implacable severity. Let them also (as Augustine says) have pity on the common nature in the one whose special fault they are punishing. Or, if they must arm themselves against the enemy, that is, the armed robber, let them not lightly seek occasion to do so; indeed, let them not accept the occasion when offered, unless they are driven to it by extreme necessity. . . . [And] let them not allow themselves to be swayed by any private affection, but be led by concern for the people alone. Otherwise, they very wickedly abuse their power, which has been given them not for their own advantage, but for the benefit and service of others.[2]

Calvin is clearly disturbed here by the arrogance with which leaders often deal with the questions of military violence. Anyone considering the use of force, he is saying, must engage in a careful process of self-examination. To put it in simple terms, we must look honestly at our own sinful capacity for self-deception, and we must reflect deeply on the humanness of the people toward whom our violent remedies would be directed. Calvin is very aware here of the fact that because of our depraved natures we are inclined to do exactly the opposite of what he is proposing: we tend to exalt our own motives and to devalue the humanity of our opponents. So, as a spiritual corrective, we sinners need to be diligent in paying special attention to our own faults, while constantly reminding ourselves of the humanity of those with whom we disagree. In Calvin's scheme, the just war doctrine must also serve as, we might say, an instrument of spiritual formation.

Of special significance for this way of looking at issues of violence is the important Christian teaching that all human beings are created in God's image. This is the basis for Calvin's insistence that rulers must "have pity on the common nature in the one whose special fault they are punishing." St. Augustine, whose authority he appeals to at this point, is equally insistent in emphasizing this important element of theological anthropology. In Augustine's letter to Marcellinus, to which Calvin is referring, Augustine warns that in punishing evildoers rulers run the risk of defeating their external enemies only to be destroyed by "the enemy within" as they pursue their violent campaigns with "depraved and distorted hearts." To avoid these consequences, Augustine urges, we must cultivate "those kindly feelings which keep us from returning evil for evil." If we can manage to do so, "even war will not be waged without kindness, and it will be easier for a society whose peace is based on piety and justice to take thought for the conquered."[3]

Again, Augustine and Calvin—two prominent defenders of the just war perspective—are probing important underlying issues of spirituality. And needless to say, they are raising questions about the uses of violence that apply to a much broader moral and spiritual territory than the "official" conduct of armies and police forces. They are insisting that we cannot think morally about the proper use of violence without thinking about the kinds of *persons* we are in the process of becoming. Their pastoral concerns can be extended to the question of what kinds of *societies* we are living in, and what sorts of *patterns* of human interaction we as Christians want to model and espouse. We live in a culture in which the currents of violence run very deep. It is convenient for us to call for more regulation and control of those whom we can most easily identify as the perpetrators of lawlessness and abuse. But no effective Christian critique of our violent culture can ignore "the enemy within"; we are obliged to probe deeply into the violence that resides in our own souls, even as we reflect compassionately on the created humanity of those whose actions and attitudes we find it easy to judge.

But Augustine and Calvin are also known for their insistence that the only effective cure for the depravity that afflicts us as individual human beings is the personal appropriation, by the power of the Holy Spirit, of the atoning work of Jesus Christ. Thus, they take it for granted that a proper grasp of what the atonement is about will serve to *curb* violence, and not to reinforce a tendency *toward* violent activity. This is the way of viewing the situation that I will be defending here. But we do need to take a careful look at the contentions of those who think that a teaching like that of classical atonement theory is designed to reinforce a propensity for violent attitudes and actions.

"Promoting" Violence?

No writer has been more straightforward in rejecting Christian atonement doctrine because of what it allegedly reinforces in human relations than the feminist theologian Joanne Carlson Brown. "Christianity," she insists, "is an abusive theology that glorifies suffering," and if the Christian faith can be transformed into a force for genuine human liberation, "it must itself be liberated from this theology. We must do away with the atonement, this idea of a blood sin upon the whole human race that can be washed away only by the blood of the lamb." The "blood-thirsty God" who presently "controls the whole Christian tradition" rules over a pervasively patriarchal system. "We do not need to be saved by Jesus' death from some original sin. We need to be liberated from this abusive patriarchy."[4]

What can we say in defense of atonement doctrine in response to this critique? How would we go about deciding whether the classical Christian formulations regarding the atonement actually "promote" violence and abuse? What would it take to test the accuracy of such a charge, or of a defense *against* the charge?

Well, let me begin with some rather obvious ways of answering these questions. I have a pretty good idea, I think, about how I would decide whether, for example, Mennonite views of the atonement promote violence and abuse. As I read Mennonite theologians I regularly find them formulating their understandings of the atoning work of Christ in a way that explicitly rules out any espousal of violence and abuse. The cross is, according to the Mennonite thinkers that I read, a paradigmatic display of nonviolence. To understand the atoning work of Christ properly is, in a very direct way for them, to reject any Christian involvement in practices of violence and abuse.

I also think I could come up with an intelligent response to the question whether Roman Catholic theologies of the atonement promote violence and abuse. For example, I have read newspaper articles about Catholics in the Philippines who during Holy Week have themselves nailed to crosses. These seem to me clearly to be acts of self-inflicted violence and abuse. Furthermore, they also seem to be directly linked to the ways in which these Catholics think about the atoning work of Christ. Of course, I know that such practices are not advocated by Catholic academic theologians. But I do think one could make a case that there are motifs in Catholic thought that lend themselves to such acts, even if they are distortions of those motifs. Self-crucifixion, along with, say, the valuing of stigmata, certainly makes more sense in a context shaped by Catholic theology than it would in, say, a Lutheran or a Quaker setting.

Now, I do not think that many evangelical Christians connect their understanding of the atonement with issues of violence and abuse in either of these ways. Most evangelical theologians do not typically say, in the manner of Mennonite thinkers, that because of what happened on the cross our attitudes toward violence and abuse ought to be such and such. Nor do grassroots evangelicals think that they should punish their bodies in a way that reflects the suffering of Jesus on the cross.

But I know that those rather quick observations do not prove much. Certainly my Mennonite friends will insist that my Reformed view of the cross also deals with issues of violence and abuse in a paradigmatic manner. If it is true, as traditional Reformed theology has put it, that the transaction of the cross necessarily required that Christ experience the wrath of the Father, then Reformed thought does indeed insist that violence is an essential feature of the atoning sacrifice of Christ—an insistence, they might go on to point out, that has clear implications for questions about the permissibility of violent activity. And any Catholic who knows the history of popular Reformed attitudes— and, more generally, popular evangelical attitudes—about violence will rightly suggest that it is not fair to contrast "high" evangelicalism with "low" Catholicism. Evangelical Christians have often been militantly violent, and in such a way that their violence has obviously been shaped by theological motifs.

These are appropriate responses. It is certainly true that the evangelical way of understanding the work of the cross does have implications for our perspectives on violence, and that popular evangelicalism has often encouraged violent practices in a way that has been shaped by the evangelical way of thinking about God's dealings with humankind. I do want to suggest, however, that it does not follow from these concessions that the evangelical views about the atonement *as such* promote violence and abuse. Let me explain this by focusing briefly on the violent attitudes often associated with my own Calvinist tradition.

Calvinists have often not been very nice people. They have been intolerant, sometimes to the point of abusive and violent actions toward people with whom they have disagreed. The record of Calvinism in its cruel treatment of the Anabaptists is an obvious case in point in this regard. I think we must also acknowledge abusive practices in family contexts. Calvinist husbands and fathers have often been unspeakably cruel to their wives and daughters—this fact was well documented, for example, in an empirical study of the topic commissioned several years ago by the Christian Reformed Church.[5]

It is important to ask, though, whether these practices are in some sense "promoted" by Reformed understandings of the atonement. It would be interesting to find out, for example, whether, say, Old Amish fathers and husbands have also often abused their wives and daughters. If so, we might have to explore the possibility that abusive practices occur in theologically shaped cultures in spite of what those cultures might teach regarding the implications of a theory of the atonement.

Let me make it clear that I am not denying that Calvinist patterns of violence and abuse are related to theological motifs. On the contrary, it seems obvious that theological influences are at work in Calvinist nastiness. But I am not inclined to look for those influences in the area of *atonement* theology in particular. My own sense is that the attitudes toward violence and abuse in popular Calvinism have less to do with a view of what happened on the cross as such than with a more general picture of a God who has often been experienced as a very "distant" divine authority figure who is fundamentally and unalterably angry, from all eternity, with an identifiable subgroup of the human race.

For example, when I have used the above-quoted passage from John Calvin in teaching about just war theory, I have often detected a puzzlement in students of traditional Reformed persuasion. How does this emphasis square with other important Calvinist beliefs? Doesn't Calvin also teach that the human race is divided into two classes of people, elect and reprobate? And aren't unsaved persons the objects of God's wrath? Why, then, are we so concerned to "have pity on the common nature" that we share with them when God looks at them with full knowledge of the very different—and *un*common—destinies of the two groups?

There are at least two strategies for responding to these questions within a Reformed perspective. One is to point to the simple fact that we are not God. We do not operate with a clear sense of who the elect and reprobate actually are—which means that we need to proceed with an awareness of our finitude. Vengeance is the Lord's business. Our task is to treat even apparent reprobates as potential members of the elect people of God.

An even more basic response, however, is that God has made it clear that he continues to regard created humanness as valuable, even in persons who are not heading for a heavenly destiny. God's ethical directives to us do not make a clear distinction between how we are to treat the saved and how we are to treat the lost. This is what Calvin is getting at in his insistence that even in dealing with enemies we must "have pity on the common nature" that we share with them.

It is because of this conviction about the moral value of what God has created that Calvin and other defenders of the just war perspective have insisted that violence is permissible only within certain clearly defined moral limits. As John Howard Yoder and others have argued, just war teaching originated not in an argument with pacifists, but out of a desire to place moral restrictions on the use of violence as over against the unbridled militarism of pagan cultures[6]— and I am convinced that the Reformed version of the teaching fits this pattern.

It is an interesting and important exercise to think about how these moral restrictions apply to the phenomenon of *domestic* violence. Calvin's advice to magistrates—quoted above—can also be addressed, say, to parents, spouses, and siblings. In our family relationships too we ought not to "be carried away with headlong anger, or be seized with hatred, or burn with implacable severity"; here too—in our relationships with our own kinfolk—we should cultivate "pity on the common [human] nature in the one" whom we may be tempted to attack, either physically or verbally.

It is also interesting to think about how the notion of moral restrictions on violence applies to the atonement itself. To the degree that the transaction that took place on the cross does contain some element of violence—a matter I will soon address directly—we should expect that it too would fit within the moral limits associated with these guidelines for the proper use of violence. And the case for the atonement can be spelled out in terms of those guidelines. Thus, in sending Jesus to the cross, God is engaging in a "last resort" remedy for the ravages of human depravity; the punishment is proportionate to the end being sought, and so on. Furthermore, God is not being carried away by the kinds of illicit passions against which Calvin warns. There seems to be nothing here, then, that would "promote" the kind of gratuitous abusive behavior that is associated with, for example, domestic violence.

The important emphasis in classical theology on the "once-for-all" character of the atoning work of Christ must also be considered in our attempts to explore the possible links between atonement theory and our own patterns of violence. My own sense is that as a general rule Reformed Christians in particular have not been very attracted to the *imitatio Christi* models of spirituality or ethics. This certainly seems to be true with respect to any notion of specifically imitating the work of the cross. The Calvinist pattern here stands in stark contrast to both the Mennonite and Catholic examples that I mentioned earlier. Calvinists are not inclined to see the helplessness element of Christ's atoning work as a thing to be imitated. The once-for-all theme in the Reformed understanding of the atonement—which I am suggesting has a kind of ethical-inimitability corollary—suggests that *even if* there was an element of the kind of violence on the cross that, if it were to show up in human relationships, would be deemed highly abusive, there is no reason to think that Calvinists would be quick to pick up on that imitative possibility. When Calvinists have been abusive, I suggest, they have taken whatever theological cues that have motivated them from some other area of Reformed thought, and not from their understanding of the atonement proper.

Christ's Suffering

But we must explore some of these themes in more depth. What *about* the apparently violent-abusive themes that seem to be associated with a picture of the atonement in which notions like divine wrath and satisfaction figure prominently? Doesn't such a view feature punishment as an essential element in the atoning work of Christ? Take, for example, the way the case is made in the sixteenth-century Heidelberg Catechism. The requirements of divine justice are such, the catechism states, "that sin, which is committed against the most high majesty of God, be also punished with extreme, that is, with everlasting punishment both of body and soul." But—the argument proceeds—because we humans "daily increase our guilt," we cannot satisfy these requirements by our own efforts, to say nothing of bearing the burden of divine wrath on behalf of others. This could be accomplished only by the Lord Jesus, the incarnate God who "by the power of his Godhead" was able to "bear, in his manhood, the burden of God's wrath, and so obtain for and restore to us righteousness and life."[7]

There it is: a punishment inflicted on body and soul is an important element in God's solution to the problem of sin—an account that certainly seems to contain an element of divine violence. While I do accept this formulation set forth in the Heidelberg Catechism, others may try to avoid the difficulties by opting for some other strand within the larger Christian development of atonement theory. One cannot avoid, though, the sort of criticism lodged by Joanne Carlson Brown simply by embracing one of the "softer" theories of the atonement. She insists that all versions of atonement theory—not only the "satisfaction" account that I endorse, but also those spelled out, for example, in terms of "Christus Victor" or "moral influence"—glorify suffering and victimization. Atonement theory as such, on Brown's reading, makes the suffering of Christ a necessary means to our salvation from sin, and thereby commends imitative suffering on the part of Christ's followers. No matter how we explain the redemptive significance of Christ's suffering, says Brown, we are still left with "the same answers to the question: how shall I interpret and respond to the suffering that occurs in my life? The only answer is: patiently endure; suffering will lead to a greater life."[8]

A helpful move in responding to Brown is made by Margo Houts, who counters Brown's claims by pointing to the important distinction between redemptive and masochistic suffering. She uses this distinction to argue that Brown's rejection of "suffering *in itself*" leaves her with a position that, as Houts puts it, "undercuts what the Bible teaches is the key to the undoing of patriarchy, namely Jesus' victory over the powers through his death and resurrection."[9]

Still, Brown is right to insist that we think about the fact that all atonement theory requires a suffering Savior. Satisfaction theology, however, might seem to be a special case because of its insistence that the suffering of Christ on the cross was in some sense *directly* inflicted by the Father. But—and here we must keep Brown's point in mind—once we allow that Christ's suffering was necessary for our redemption, then the question arises for the other views as to why God would even *indirectly* will the Son's suffering. The "Christus Victor" theory, for example, sees the demonic principalities and powers as inflicting violence upon Jesus—a transaction that God allowed in order to demonstrate the inability of those powers to destroy Jesus, since he emerged victoriously from the tomb even after the powers had unleashed their full fury upon him. The "moral influence" theory, on the other hand, emphasizes the ways in which Jesus suffered violence at *human* hands—with the redemptive significance of that suffering being manifested in the way that Jesus selflessly forgave his enemies. Thus, while the satisfaction theory may be unique in seeing Jesus as in some sense directly experiencing the wrath of the Father, *all* of the views see Jesus as taking suffering upon himself in order to fulfill a divinely ordained redemptive mission.

But now we need to pay a little closer attention to the terminology that we use in describing atonement views. I have observed that the satisfaction theory *appears* to require a kind of violence that the Father inflicts upon the Son. Strictly speaking, however, the theologians who propound the satisfaction view of the atonement do not typically use the word "violence." The standard terminology used to describe what Christ suffered on the cross is *punishment* and *wrath*. How are we to understand this notion that Christ experienced the wrath of God, suffering punishment on our behalf? This is a large topic, and I can only touch briefly here on a few matters that strike me as productive issues to pursue.

Experiencing Wrath

When contemporary critics accuse satisfaction theory as featuring "divine child abuse," they assume a picture of God the Father somehow directly inflicting pain on the Son. The actual descriptions given of the nature of Christ's suffering in satisfaction theology, however, do not focus primarily on the physical pain he experienced on the cross as being the primary feature of the redemptive transaction. Jan Rohls emphasizes this fact in his recent study of Reformed confessions. In the Geneva Catechism, Rohls observes, Christ's "substitution for us lies not just in the fact that he *died* for us," but in the fact that "he was *condemned* to death." The important thing is that "Christ takes on himself the *curse* that lies upon human beings," that he experienced "an *accursed* death." Thus the Geneva Catechism's declaration that "he hanged on a tree to take our curse upon Himself and acquit us of it (Gal. 3:13)." In his condemnation by "an earthly judge" we are "acquitted before the throne of the celestial Judge."[10]

Here the suffering of Christ consists in the way in which his being condemned to death by Pilate also *counts as* a condemnation by God the Father. The key factor here is the *quality* of his physical suffering, his experience as an innocent one—as *the* Innocent One—of the cursedness of all the guilty ones in whose place he is being condemned.

This notion of cursedness is treated more expansively in the Heidelberg Catechism. In its exposition of the Apostles' Creed the catechism asks what it means to say Christ *suffered.* The answer given begins in this way: "That all the time he lived on earth, but especially at the end of his life, he bore, in body and soul, the wrath of God against the sin of the whole human race."[11] And at another point, the Heidelberger explains the ways in which Christ suffered the agonies of hell on our behalf by referring to the "inexpressible anguish, pains, and terrors which he suffered in his soul *on the cross and before*" (emphasis mine).[12] What is interesting here for our purposes is how these formulations insist that the way that Christ "especially" bore the divine wrath at the end of his life is nonetheless continuous with his experience of that wrath, both "in body and soul" throughout "*all* the time he lived on earth," both "on the cross and before." This echoes an important theme in the depiction of Christ's sacrificial ministry in the Epistle to the Hebrews, the primary biblical source for satisfaction theory: "In the days of his flesh, Jesus offered up prayers and supplications, with loud cries and tears, to the one who was able to save him from death. . . . [H]e learned obedience through what he suffered" (Heb. 5:7–8). What all of this seems clearly to imply is that Jesus was already experiencing the wrath of the Father in his infancy, in his teenage years, and during his earthly ministry. And yet it is not very easy to think of those stages in his life as times when he was being directly punished by the Father.

These formulations, then, locate the redemptive significance of Christ's suffering, not so much in pain that can be thought of as being actively inflicted upon him by the Father, but rather in his profound experience as the innocent one of the cursedness of being *abandoned* by God on behalf of those who do deserve that abandonment. Thus the greatest redemptively significant agony that he experienced on the cross, on this view, is not when he gasped in pain when they pounded the nails into his flesh, or when he pleaded that his thirst be quenched, or when he heard the mockery of onlookers, but when he cried out in utter forlornness, "My God, my God, why have you forsaken me?" (Mark 15:34).

There is one very good reason to emphasize this forsakenness as being at the heart of Christ's experience of God's wrath on our behalf. In his redemptive suffering, Christ was experiencing the agonies of *hell* that we deserve as sinners. If we were to understand hell to be God's actively inflicting violence on sinful persons, then it would indeed be important for Christ to take on that kind of violence as our substitute. But if we see hell—as I think to be theologically appropriate—as a state of radical separation from God, then it was not necessary that Christ be actively punished by the Father; rather it was fitting that he experience something far worse. It is a terrible thing to be punished violently by someone who is capable of loving us but who instead turns upon us in anger. But it is even worse to have so provoked that person's wrath that he or she simply gives up on us and turns away. This is the hellish abandonment that Christ experienced when he hung as our substitute on Calvary.

This way of viewing the significance of what has traditionally been seen as the penal substitutionary work of Christ has an important implication for our present discussions of violence. If the forsakenness, the experience of cursedness, is what is in the most basic sense the redemptive significance of Christ's substitutionary work, then there is something important about Christ's suffering that cannot be imitated, namely, the experience of being abandoned by God. To be sure, we Christians may be called to suffer in Christ's name. I think John Howard Yoder was right when he insisted, in *The Politics of Jesus,* that the only sense in which the New Testament calls us to imitate Jesus is in his suffering. But I also think he overstated himself in making his case: "Only at one point," Yoder wrote, "only on one subject—but then consistently and universally—is Jesus our example: in his cross."[13] The important point that Yoder *was* making is that there is no open-ended "Do what Jesus would do" mandate in the Scriptures: it is not appropriate for us to ask, "What would Jesus do?" when we are confronted, for example, with 5,000 hungry people at a religious gathering where no one bothered to prepare a lunch for the crowd, or when we are standing on a beach and we see some friends in a boat out in the lake, and we wonder how we can go out to meet them when we can't swim that far and we have no boat of our own.

But because there is, even in the clear call to imitate the sufferings of Christ, an element in those sufferings that we cannot imitate, I am troubled a bit by Yoder's insistence that the New Testament calls us to imitate the work of the cross "consistently and universally."[14] Oscar Cullmann began his wonderful essay on the Greek version of the biblical conception of the afterlife by drawing a stark contrast between the death of Socrates and the death of Jesus.[15] After a calm philosophical discussion with his friends, Socrates takes the hemlock in a seemingly cheerful anticipation of the separation of his soul from his body. Jesus, on the other hand, sweats drops of blood in Gethsemane as he pleads with the Father to allow the cup of suffering to pass from him. And then on the cross he cries out in agony over his abandonment by God. Cullmann rightly explains this contrast by spelling out the important differences between the Platonistic and the Christian understandings of sin and death.

Many of my Christian friends, though, have faced their deaths more in the spirit of Socrates than of Jesus. And this is appropriate. We do not have to—we *ought* not to—imitate Jesus' approach to dying. His suffering is in significant ways inimitable, because he bore the wrath of our cursed existence precisely in order that we do not have to suffer under that wrath. And this is important to emphasize with reference to the kinds of examples raised by those who worry that the Bible's depiction of the atoning work of Christ might encourage, say, women to think they must patiently endure spouse abuse. In such cases, the most basic consideration for a woman in that kind of situation is to know that Christ has suffered the abandonment and abuse on her behalf, and that she does not need to endure those experiences in order to please God.

Divine Agency

In his fascinating study of how the sacrificial rituals of ancient religions are motivated by the desire to solve the problem of violence, René Girard makes it clear that he doesn't think any intelligent human being today can believe in the literal efficacy of religious sacrifice. But Girard does insist that these "primitive" religionists were onto something that we have not been able to retain in our more sophisticated perspectives on reality. In the ritual sacrifice, Girard argues, people "fed" their "bad violence" to the gods, thereby allowing it to be transformed by the gods into "stability and fecundity." While we cannot enter into this worldview today, says Girard, if we choose to ignore its "mythic" power we will simply "persist in disregarding the power of violence in human societies."[16]

Those of us who believe in the efficacy of Christ's substitutionary sacrifice are certainly not compelled to endorse all that is associated with the "primitive" practices that Girard describes. But we can see those rituals as pointing in some profound way to the one true sacrifice that occurred at Calvary. The problem of human violence can only be solved by having our violence "taken up" into the life of the Triune God, to be transformed there into something good that is then given back to us as a gift. One way to spell this out is in terms of the concept of *power*. In the biblical scheme, power is not intrinsically bad. Its badness takes the form of violence and manipulative coercion—patterns that came into being as a result of our fallenness. These patterns were very visible in the scenario at Calvary, when the Son of God bled and died to save us from the ruin that we brought upon ourselves. But, having suffered the wounds that are inflicted by this kind of power, the resurrected Christ makes available to us a new kind of power, the power of reconciling love: "You will receive power," he says to his disciples just before he ascends to heaven, "when the Holy Spirit has come upon you; and you will be my witnesses" (Acts 1:8).

It is important to emphasize the fact that the work of the cross—which makes this transformation of bad power into good power possible—is itself an integrated act of the Triune God. John Stott rightly warns us against adopting any picture of the atonement in which the Son is a victim who stands *over against* a Father who is in turn "a pitiless ogre whose wrath has to be assuaged." Says Stott: "Both God and Christ were subjects not objects, taking the initiative together to save sinners. Whatever happened on the cross in terms of 'God-forsakenness' was voluntarily accepted by both in the same holy love which made atonement necessary." While the words "satisfaction" and "substitution" must never "in any circumstances be given up," Stott argues, we must also be very clear that "the biblical gospel of atonement is of God satisfying himself by substituting himself for us."[17]

The power that makes it possible for us to find a new kind of reconciled unity is made available to us out of the unity of the Godhead. This, of course, leaves us with much to ponder. The very same God who pours out the divine wrath is the One who experiences the wrathful forsakenness of divine abandonment. God, in the unity of the divine being, is both the violated One and the One who counts that violatedness as satisfying the demands of eternal justice. Charles Wesley's wonderful lines point to the mystery of this divine single-mindedness:

> Amazing love! How can it be
> That Thou, my God, shouldst die for me?

In the death on the cross God also took our violent impulses upon himself, mysteriously absorbing them into his very being in order to transform them into the power of reconciling love; and then he offers that love back to us as a gift of sovereign grace. One of the wise, but difficult, lessons taught to me by my presidential predecessor at Fuller, the late David Allan Hubbard, is this: *leaders do not inflict pain, they bear pain.* This is a lesson, as I see things, that is illustrated most profoundly in the atoning work of the Son of God. In the incarnation we see a supreme example of what James MacGregor Burns defines as "transformational leadership," where a leader so *engages* his or her followers that both leaders and followers are changed by the experience.[18]

When God drew near to us in Jesus Christ, God did indeed engage us in a way that God himself was deeply affected by taking on our frailties and temptations. This includes God's making himself intimately familiar with a most pervasive symptom of our sinful condition, our propensity to get ensnared in webs of violence. Here too our only hope is that "he was wounded for our transgressions, crushed for our iniquities; upon him was the punishment that made us whole, and by his bruises we are healed" (Isa. 53:5).

ELEVEN

EXPLAINING CHRISTIAN NONVIOLENCE

Notes for a Conversation with John Milbank

STANLEY HAUERWAS

Why John Howard Yoder Was Not a Pacifist

The souls of the organizers of this conference are in deep trouble. If Protestant evangelicals had anyone to whom they could confess, they would need to seek out such people, because they certainly have sinned. Their sin is to have put me in a situation that tempts me to sin, that is, they have put this weak soul, as the Catholics say, "in the near occasion of sin." I have been so placed because events have conspired to make it necessary for me to give my paper knowing that my paper will be followed by a paper by John Milbank. Which means Milbank has to listen to me tell him why I am right and he is wrong about most things but more importantly why he should be an advocate of Christian nonviolence. This is an occasion of sin, at least for a pacifist, just to the extent I am tempted to use this favorable, but coercive, turn of events to frame the issues in a manner favorable to me before Milbank gets to speak. If this is but the outworking of metaphysical violence, I intend to make the most of it.

It may seem odd for me to use this occasion to pick a fight with Milbank. I suspect many people assume that John and I are more or less on the same side. That assumption, I think, given the cultural options of the day, is correct. However, as Michael Hanby, my former student who now studies with John, has observed, "That people think Hauerwas and Milbank are on the same side is only an indication of how dumb a time it is in which we live. In another cultural situation Hauerwas and Milbank would be sworn enemies." Hanby, I think, may well be right—which means in another time Milbank might make the case why my kind should be burned at the stake. After all, I represent the anarchical Anabaptist whom the orthodox, whether they be radical or not, usually think threatens the presumptive unity claimed by Christendom. From the orthodox point of view, pacifist readings of Scripture cannot help but appear heretical, and heretics are rightly regarded as the worst sort of criminals. If you are serious, and Milbank is serious, you ought to be willing to kill people like me.

I am, of course, having fun, but I begin this way to illustrate the argument I want to make. My argument quite simply, and it is a simple point, is that pacifists cannot let their understanding of Christian nonviolence be determined by what we are against. We do not know what violence is or may be if we do not know violence against the background of a more profound peaceableness. Accordingly, I cannot let Milbank determine what I need to say about Christian nonviolence. But it is not easy for pacifists to display peaceableness because violence seems to be far more interesting and entertaining. For example, any attempt to develop a defense of "Christian nonviolence" merely reproduces the problem I am trying to avoid. The very phrase "Christian nonviolence" cannot help but suggest that peace is "not violence." Yet a peace that is no more than "not violence" surely cannot be the peace that is ours in Christ.

This is not just a terminological problem. It is an ontological and moral problem that makes clear why the modern attempt to separate ontological and ethical questions could not but distort the character of our lives. In the Christian tradition Augustine, rightly I think, maintained that sin is literally nothing. Just as the lie parasitically lives off the truth, so violence cannot be named or identified unless our lives are constituted by more determinative practices of peace.[1] I hesitate to acknowledge the ontological questions at the heart of any attempt to develop and/or defend Christian pacifism because Milbank is a much more adept metaphysician than I can even pretend to be. I will never understand Deleuze, much less be able to argue as Milbank does with him. Yet I think I have said enough to make clear why I think it would be a mistake to try to convince anyone, even Milbank, to become a pacifist by pretending to know what violence is to be avoided.

This is one of the reasons I have always felt something of a fraud when I claim to be a pacifist. My sense of being fraudulent is not simply because—Texan that I am—I am a violent person. That I do not know how to be nonviolent is, of course, a problem, but even more troubling is my sense that I do not know what I am claiming when I claim to be a pacifist. I assume, however, that my declaration at least means I create expectations in others who can and should call me to account for living in a manner that belies my conviction that if I am to live a truthful life I must be nonviolent. In other words, nonviolence at least is a declaration that should make us vulnerable to others in a manner that hopefully can put us on the way to being at peace in a world of violence.

If peace is ontologically the character of our existence, then I think it is a mistake to describe John Howard Yoder as a pacifist. He could not be a pacifist because, as he never failed to emphasize, "there is no such thing as a single position called pacifism, to which one clear definition can be given and which is held by all pacifists."[2] What made, and continues to make, Yoder's work so significant for me was his refusal to make "pacifism" a position, an implication, derived from more determinative theological claims. You simply cannot find in Yoder any account of "pacifism" that can be abstracted from his Christology, eschatology, ecclesiology, or understanding of the Christian life. Yoder did not find it necessary to provide an ontological account of his understanding of Christian nonviolence, but I think the way he worked exhibits why peace is metaphysically more determinative than violence. Yoder's understanding of Christian nonviolence is constitutive of his understanding of God and how God has, through the work of the Holy Spirit, made us participants in God's salvation.

After surveying other forms of pacifism in *Nevertheless,* Yoder identified his own position as "The Pacifism of the Messianic Community."[3] This is a stance of nonviolence that is unintelligible without the confession that Jesus is the Christ and that Jesus Christ is Lord. "In the person and work of Jesus, in his teachings and his passion, this kind of pacifism finds its rootage, and in his resurrection it finds its enablement."[4] Christian nonviolence can, therefore, not be a position about violence abstracted from discipleship to this One as God's anointed. Discipleship, moreover, is not a heroic endeavor of individuals, but rather the way of life of a community that finds in its shared life a foretaste of God's kingdom.

Christian nonviolence, therefore, for Yoder does not name a position or even a principled stance that works from a predetermined understanding of what counts as violence or nonviolence. Rather, Christian nonviolence names the present reality of a community that refuses to be determined by the very "world" it creates by its own existence. In his extraordinary but never published book, *Christian Attitudes to War, Peace, and Revolution: A Companion to Bainton,*[5] Yoder does not even discuss what he takes to be the most defensible account of Christian pacifism until the end of the book. He rightly, I think, understood that our Christian forebears were not pacifist if we mean by that a position they could identify in distinction from their understanding of what it means to worship and be disciples of Jesus Christ.

Yoder, therefore, has no reason to deny that in the early centuries some Christians were in the Roman army or that the reason other Christians did not serve had more to do with idolatry than the avoidance of violence. In Yoder's words, "pacifism did not stand by itself." Christians found themselves in tension with the authority structure of the day for numerous reasons. The objection to the shedding of blood was just one part of a polar whole. Accordingly the question "Did the early Christians reject the state *as such*?" cannot be answered. It cannot be answered because there was no "state as such."[6] Therefore, where it was possible for early Christians, at some times and places, to qualify their polarization with authority structures, they did so without feeling any unfaithfulness. For example, "by the end of the second century Christians could and did use the civil courts to define property law, e.g. to protect the legal status of a Christian cemetery. Christians didn't feel that such 'involvement' was a moral sell-out."[7]

That Christians could use the legal structure to protect the graves of their dead was not a problem for Christians because it was clear that law did not constitute their lives—the church did that. In similar fashion Christians in the fourth century could find themselves in the Roman army even though they still did not think they could kill or swear oaths of loyalty to Caesar. They could do so, Yoder observes, because the Roman soldiers were often simply bureaucrats. They carried the mail, administered the roads, enforced the laws and the prison system. In short, they were not violent at all, "except in the global sense that they were 'part of the system,' or in the political sense that such a person has the status of an officer. Yet he doesn't kill anybody, he doesn't persecute anybody, he doesn't throw anybody to the lions. He probably even is dispensed from the oath and the ceremonies."[8] So grew what Yoder calls "creeping empire loyalty." Such loyalty clearly results in "Constantinianism," which Yoder, I think, rightly deplores. But it is crucial to see that he does so for reasons that are not that different from Augustine—namely, with Constantinianism the true church becomes invisible because now it is assumed that God is governing the world through Constantine. As a result, peace is turned into an ideal rather than a practice constitutive of the church.[9] Correlatively, Christians now look for sources of moral knowledge other than the Scriptures and, in particular, the teachings of Jesus. Christians begin to think the primary moral question is "What would happen if everyone acted like that?" no longer remembering that Christians should ask, "How must we act as disciples of Christ?"

I cannot pretend that this is an adequate account of Yoder's pacifism, but I hope I have at least convinced you that Yoder's pacifism does not name a position separable from his overall theological stance. For Yoder, pacifism is what he takes to be "the politics of Jesus," that is, the church. In Yoder's words:

> The cross was the effect of the fact that his new regime was a *kingdom:* he talked about it in political terms, in connection with righteousness, decision making, money and power and offenders and all the other things that politics deals with. Yet it was non-coercive. So the way he lived it was to die for it, and he told his disciples that they would have to do the same. But if the new order in its newness is characterized by non-coerciveness, then the community which is the bearer of this order will have to be a voluntary community. That means in turn

that the community that bears this new order will have to be for the time being a minority community. This option is what came later to be called "church." The word *ecclesia* in the Greek of the time was not a religious term. It means town meeting, assembly, a group of people gathered to do business of public concern. That's what Jesus created; directly by gathering people around him during his earthly ministry, indirectly by the fact that his message after the resurrection and pentecost produced that new kind of body within society.[10]

So Yoder is not a pacifist if by that you mean someone who assumes that pacifists know in advance what may and may not be violence. Of course Yoder assumes that Christians do not kill, but that is only to state what it means to be a pacifist in the most minimal fashion. The practice of peace among Christians requires constant care of our lives together, through which we discover the violence that grips our lives and compromises our witness to the world. If the church is not peace, then the world does not have an alternative to violence. But if the church is not such an alternative, then what we believe as Christians is clearly false. For when all is said and done, the question of peace is the question of truth and why the truth that is ours in Christ makes possible a joyfulness otherwise unobtainable.

Why Milbank Should Declare He Is a Pacifist

Now that I have convinced you that Yoder is not a pacifist, I want to argue that Milbank should be forced to declare that he is a pacifist. At least he is a pacifist just to the degree that Yoder is not a pacifist. Put in the terms made immortal by that preeminent American politician, George Wallace, I hope to show when all is said and done there is not a dime's worth of difference between Yoder and Milbank on matters that matter about peace. In what difference there is, moreover, Yoder is right and Milbank is wrong. In more friendly terms: it is not that Milbank is wrong, but rather an indication that sometimes Milbank does ontology when he ought to be listening to Jesus.

Milbank is, of course, rightly famous for his contention that in contrast to the mythos that shapes modernity, a mythos that assumes "in the beginning there was chaos and violence," Christianity

recognizes no original violence. It construes the infinite not as chaos, but as a harmonic peace which is yet beyond the circumscribing power of any totalizing reason. Peace no longer depends upon the reduction to the self-identical, but is the *sociality* of harmonious difference. Violence, by contrast, is always a secondary willed intrusion upon this possible infinite order (which is actual for God). Such a Christian logic is *not* deconstructible by modern secular reason; rather, it is Christianity which exposes the non-necessity of supposing, like the

Nietzscheans, that difference, non-totalization and indeterminacy of meaning *necessarily* imply arbitrariness and violence. To suppose that they do is merely to subscribe to a particular encoding of reality. Christianity, by contrast, is the coding of transcendental difference as peace.[11]

Milbank supports these claims by providing a rich account of the Trinity that I think has yet to be appreciated for its quite extraordinary power.[12] As interesting as Milbank's trinitarian reflections are, however, more important—at least for the subject before us—is his account of Augustine's two cities in the last chapter of *Theology and Social Theory*. His account of Augustine is important exactly because Milbank uses an account of Augustine to help us see why the ontological presumption of "In the beginning there was peace" does not entail pacifism. Augustine is crucial for Milbank because Augustine rightly saw why Christian theology entails the presumption of the ontological priority of peace over conflict; a presumption, moreover, anchored not in universal reason, but in a narrative, a practice, and a dogmatic faith.[13] That is why, finally, Christians cannot defeat narratives of violence in principle. Finally, we can only out-narrate them.[14]

Milbank interrupts his account of Augustine in order to provide an analysis of the work of René Girard. Milbank does so, I think, because his criticism of Girard allows him to challenge not just Girard's account of atonement, but all accounts of the atonement that offer an "explanation of violence." Milbank thinks Girard is right to stress Jesus' refusal of violence, but he does not provide a sufficient account of the concrete "form" taken by Jesus' nonviolent practice. Girard's (and Anselm's) "satisfaction theory of the atonement" makes sense only to the extent "they remind us that Jesus is significant *as* the way, the kingdom, *autobasileia*. One can rescue Girard's argument for Jesus' finality and divinity if one links it with the idea that the exemplary narratives of Jesus show us the 'shape,' and the concrete possibility of a non-violent practice."[15] Accordingly, an abstract attachment to nonviolence is not sufficient to be nonviolent. We need to practice nonviolence as a skill, a skill honed through the idiom of the Bible, which reaches its consummation in Jesus and the church.

I call attention to Milbank's criticisms of Girard because they sound very much like what Yoder might well say. Yet I hope to show that Milbank's own account of the necessity of violence comes very close to making the same mistake he finds in Girard. In other words, Milbank's ontology of violence leads him to believe he knows more about violence than he should if Christology precedes ontology.

Milbank quite rightly, and again in a manner similar to Yoder, objects to any interpretation of *The City of God* that thinks Augustine is providing a theory of the state to which the church must then be related. Augustine criticizes the Roman commonwealth exactly because it is not a polity, but rather grounded in the individualism of antique ethics and politics. In contrast the church is a *polis,* a political reality, extended through time.[16] The bonds between the church and whatever may pass as the state are, therefore, best kept "hazy." For the church is to make *usus* of the peace of the world, that is, of slavery, "excessive" coercion, and competing economic interests, but the church can never try to derive these things from her own life. Therefore a "Christian" ruler must use the earthly peace by subordinating such a peace to the ecclesial purpose of charity. In short, after Christ the "Christian emperor" is just only to the extent he or she understands the ruler's function to be an exercise of pastoral care.[17]

For Augustine, and for many others in the early church, the division between coercion and noncoercion was the crucial criterion for "separating the political from the ecclesial." Augustine came to see, however, that the church as well as the *imperium* must of necessity "use coercive methods" whose justification depends on the purpose "that coercion has in mind." The purpose of ecclesial coercion can only be peace, which can ultimately be attained only by "non-coercive persuasion" because the free consent of the will is necessary for peace to be achieved. However, according to Milbank, and this is the crucial move, Augustine correctly saw

> the need for some measures of coercion, in some circumstances, because free-dom of the will in itself is not the goal, and sometimes people can be temporarily blind and will only be prevented from permanent self-damage when they are forced into some course of action, or prevented from another. Such coercive action remains in itself dangerous, as it risks promoting resentment, but this risk is offset by the possibility that the recipient can later come to understand and retrospectively consent to the means taken. Such action may not be "peaceable," yet can still be "redeemed" by retrospective acceptance, and so contribute to the final goal of peace. And Christianity has traditionally seen peace as the com-prehensive eschatological goal, and *not* as the name of a virtue.[18]

According to Milbank, however, the earthly city's coercion does not have true peace in view but rather seeks no more than the compromise of wills, which cannot help but become an end in itself. Insofar as the *imperium* lies outside *ecclesia* it remains a *tragic* reality, disciplining sin, in which the punishment itself is nearer to sin than the peace of God. Augustine's fundamental mistake, therefore, in legitimating the coercion of the Donatist was in the realm of ontology.[19] His account of nonsinful, "pedagogic" coercion tried to justify a positive account of punishment, which was inconsistent with his best onto-logical presumptions. It was so "because in any coercion, however mild and benignly motivated, there is still present a moment of 'pure' violence, exter-nally and arbitrarily related to the end one has in mind, just as the school-master's beating with canes has no intrinsic connection with the lesson he seeks to teach."[20]

All punishment cannot help but be a tragic risk because punishment by its very nature has a privative relationship to Being and, therefore, cannot escape the taint of sin. That is why God cannot be said to punish. We are not punished for our sin, but rather sin is our punishment. At the most basic level punishment is self-inflicted. The church must seek to reduce the sphere of the operation of punishment while recognizing the tragic "necessity" of "alien" punishment. To be sure the trial and crucifixion of Jesus calls into question all forms of alien discipline, which means the church must be an *asylum,* a refuge, in which forgiving and restitutionary practice is possible.[21] But we cannot hope for this practice to be extended into the state because the state, "by its very nature," can only be committed to the formal goals of *dominium.*

I confess it is not at all clear to me why Milbank wants to begin talking about the "very nature" of the state or, more importantly, describing that nature in terms reminiscent of Max Weber and Reinhold Niebuhr. Milbank, in a review of my book *Against the Nations,* quite rightly called me to account for underwriting a "residual Niebuhrianism" in my defense of pacifism.[22] Yet I cannot help but hear Niebuhrian themes in his account of the unavoidability of violence. More important, it is by no means clear to me why Milbank's account of punishment—even if we accept his view that punishment always entails an "alien moment"—does not in fact commit him, particularly given the state formation characteristic of modernity, to what amounts to a pacifist position. After all, it is hard to see how the liberal state has the legitimacy necessary to punish. Moreover, if Milbank is trying to argue that violence is unavoidable because we cannot avoid the necessity of punishment, it is by no means clear how he can move from his defense of punishment to, for example, a defense of war.

As far as I know Milbank addresses how war might be understood and/or justified in only one brief paragraph in *Theology and Social Theory.* Drawing on Rowan Williams, Milbank characterizes Augustine's view that a war in defense of the state, or any form of excessive coercion, can be justified only when what is being defended against is "fundamentally unjust."[23] I am not at all sure what point Milbank is making, but I take him to mean that the punishment "war" names cannot even retrospectively be consented to by those who suffer such violence. But then I must ask, Does Milbank thereby think that attempts to limit war in the name of justice are impossible? Moreover, if he does so, then why should we not think he is a pacifist?

Of course, Milbank may want to argue it is by no means clear we know what "war" is. As I have argued elsewhere, too often those who would appeal to a "just war" assume they know what a war is and then ask if this or that war conforms or not to just war criteria. Such a view fails to understand that the just war "theory" at its best is the attempt to discipline the violence of the state in a manner that only certain forms of that violence can bear the honorific description of war.[24] If the violence just war practices seek to discipline comes only after the so-called war has begun, then it is too late for the war to be "just." At this point I am simply asking Milbank how he understands attempts to discipline war in the name of justice.[25] I assume he would argue that war must be fought to secure justice; but it is not clear what account of justice he assumes can justify war.

Milbank also owes us a richer account of violence than the ontological moves he makes provide. I am not sure what to make of the claim that every form of coercion and punishment involves a moment of "pure violence," that is, an arbitrary association of pain with a particular lesson. Is this an ontological or empirical claim? If it is the latter, it is clearly not sustainable.[26] Indeed it seems to me the very concept of a moment of "pure violence" is the kind of abstraction Milbank found doubtful in Girard. *Violence* is an analogical term that depends on paradigmatic narratives if we are to understand the different kinds of violence that enable us to make meaningful distinctions. That process is never-ending, particularly when the narrative that determines our discernment of violence is the life and death of Jesus. Attempts to find the one feature that makes violence violence, that shortcuts the process of analogical reasoning, must be resisted as a premature—if not violent—attempt to get a handle on history.

Yoder does not pretend that Christians can be free of the violence that comes from being "part of the system." To be so involved, however, does not mean that we cannot make distinctions between violence and coercion as well as various kinds of violence that tempt us to live less than nonviolent lives. Indeed I assume that is why Christians rightly declare that our worship as well as our desire to follow Jesus requires, as well as makes possible, nonviolence. Such a declaration is a promissory note that Christians must always be ready to discover how our lives may be implicated in violence that we have failed to notice.

That is why the nonviolent have such a stake in truthful speech. For we often learn that our failure to acknowledge the violence we do to one another as well to ourselves is the result of our inability to name our engagements. Christians committed to nonviolence, therefore, can never assume we know we are nonviolent. Rather, our nonviolence is a declaration that renders our lives vulnerable to challenges that may reveal we are implicated in forms of violence we have not recognized or have chosen to ignore. By discovering the violence in our lives we hope we may witness to those who do not follow Christ the violence that may grip all our lives.

A Word on My Behalf

I want to end by saying a word on my behalf. Put differently, I want to make candid some of the presuppositions that have shaped the way I have tried to provide an account of Christian nonviolence. I have, of course, never pretended that I have anything to say about nonviolence that Yoder has not said and said better than any of my efforts. I have, however, attempted to develop some conceptual machinery that I hope may be of some use for helping us, as the original title of the paper for this conference promised, "live peacefully in a violent society." For I continue to think that Christian nonviolence is necessary not because it promises us a world free of war, but because in a world of war as faithful followers of Christ we cannot be anything other than nonviolent.

I mean I simply think Milbank is wrong when he observes that "Christianity has traditionally seen peace as the comprehensive eschatological goal, and *not* as the name of a virtue."[27] To be sure, Milbank's judgment that peace is not a virtue is supported by Aquinas. Aquinas, quoting Augustine, observed that virtue is not of the last end because virtue is the way to the end. Therefore peace cannot be a virtue because peace is of the last end.[28] Yet the matter is more complex (which is almost always the case in Aquinas) because peace is the work of charity, which no one denies is a virtue. Peace is not a virtue only in the sense that it is encompassed in charity—which is at once a virtue and an activity— through which we love God and our neighbor. And we must remember that in Aquinas charity is nothing less than our friendship with God.

Peace and friendship, moreover, share similar characteristics to the extent they are interdependent virtues. They are odd virtues because they first qualify a relationship rather than a passion. Years ago I wrote an essay called "Peacemaking: The Virtue of the Church" in which I tried to develop, on the basis of Matthew 18:15–22, how peacemaking names an activity intrinsic to the church that requires a community of people capable of telling one another the truth.[29] I have no intention of boring you by rehearsing the argument I tried to make in that essay, but I call attention to it because that essay exemplifies my conviction that peacemaking, just as friendship was for Aristotle and Aquinas, is necessary for any account of the Christian virtues. Indeed peacemaking is, as Aristotle observes at the beginning of Book Eight of the *Nicomachean Ethics* in regard to friendship, "some sort of excellence or virtue, or involves virtue, and it is, moreover, most indispensable for life."[30]

I raise the question of whether peace can be considered to be a virtue only because I think exploration of this issue helps us understand why Christian nonviolence cannot be determined or justified if we think all that is required is for us to be "not violent." This is the same point with which I began this essay, but I hope the importance of this suggestion has become clearer in the light of the questions raised by Milbank about nonviolence. Advocates of Christian nonviolence betray the very activity about which we care when we direct attention primarily to what we are against. Such a strategy cannot help but give the impression that most of our life is gripped by violence from which we must try to rescue some small shards of peace. But I believe that our existence is one constituted by peace, God's peace, and that violence is the exception. That is why it is so important for those of us committed to Christian nonviolence to work to name for ourselves and our neighbors the peace, the friendships, which we cannot live without.

I believe the best essay I have written on peace is called "Taking Time for Peace: The Moral Significance of the Trivial."[31] It is a modest little essay in which I tried to counter the survivalism associated with the work of Jonathan

Schell and Gordon Kaufman by calling attention to peaceable activities such as raising lemurs, sustaining universities, having children, and, of course, playing baseball. To be sure, in the face of alleged nuclear destruction these appear trivial or inconsequential activities; but I believe without them and many other such examples, we have no hold on what it means to be nonviolent. If we are as Christians to survive the violent societies that threaten to engulf us, we will do so just to the extent we discover such worthwhile activities through which we learn not just to be at peace but that we love peace. That is why, contrary to the title of this essay, nonviolence cannot be explained. It can only be shown by the attractiveness of the friendships that constitute our lives.

TWELVE

VIOLENCE

Double Passivity

JOHN MILBANK[1]

I

Is the question of evil the same as the question of violence? It might seem so, since all violence is evil—even justified violence is the justification of a lesser evil. But is all evil violence? For the theory of radical evil, the answer might be no: evil does not remove or destroy; instead it sets up its own dark kingdom. This view is incoherent.[2] For the theory of evil as privative, by contrast, evil always removes and destroys. The depriving of good is perforce also a disturbing of the peace. Inversely, if peace is a harmonious plenitude, when it is disturbed there is always an instance of noisy distortion, which impairs just distribution.

So evil is violence, violence is evil. But why are there then two words for the same thing? Pure synonymity? Not exactly. Were evil simply violence, then one might take it that peace was simply an absence of conflict. But for privation theory peace is also positive justice, harmony, and affinity. Peace is also the Good and the True and the Beautiful. It is rather the theory of radical evil that tends to view peace as mere absence of disturbance, as the nonviolation of "the other" by a will that respects freedom. So even if this perspective interprets the will to evil as a positive volition, it still defines its action as a formal invasion of freedom rather than a destruction of substance or a turning from a *telos*. If evil is radical, then it only disturbs the peace, and does not also conceal the good. Evil here is like a club: as a weapon it is positive and neutral; but in its effect it is simply negative, illegitimate invasion. Here there are two supposedly indisputable visibilities: one of the positive willing agent, the other of manifest violence.

Privation theory, however, denies all this obviousness. It questions the evidence of both visibilities. First of all, violence is never merely witnessed; it must also be judged. Is the outstretched arm a push, an assault, or a stay? Is the crack of the whip a spur, a rebuke, or a caress? It is clear that apparent violence may not after all be violence. Second, and inversely, the asserting will may in reality be negative, as I have argued elsewhere. In this case apparently nonviolent and neutral assertion is, after all, privation and therefore violence.

For in terms of the effect of evil, the theory of radical evil focuses *too much* upon violence. Life, after all, is one invasion after another: if invasion as such is violence, goodness is the Rousseauian secreted glade. But if, rather, we must discriminate among invasions, then violence is violence only when it ruins an essence (how something should be) or diverts from a goal (how something should develop). In this case, violence is violence when it is also evil.

On the other hand, the theory of radical evil also disguises an invisible violence. For privation theory, evil is not simply the psychopathic will to violence. The theory of radical evil, when deconstructed, logically asserts that the moral will is also the psychopathic will, and even that the psychopathic impulse must be allowed play in order *both* to stimulate and train, *and* to provoke in reaction, the moral impulse (this is J. G. Ballard's Nietzscheanism without French polish). Privation theory is able to overcome this diagnosis of human nature only by insisting upon the ontological contingency of pathology as original sin—*even if* this be rooted also in our biology. It asserts that originally and more properly, human nature has a self-transcending character, which orientates it toward the supernatural. Hence our reality is not measured by our apparent capacity, but by our aspiration.[3] Against the given, one appeals to the lost and renewed gift of grace, and the fact that our given perversity is *unsoundable:* the most searching psychoanalysis is forced to speak of death drives, fundamental sadisms, and so forth. Privation theory rightly reflects that the minimum of sense that can be made here concerns a deluded pursuit of more substantive and abiding pleasures.

But most crucially of all, privation theory *levels* the moral will with the psychopathic will. The theory of radical evil thinks through an ethics of immanence rooted in the human will and not the event of grace (to which even the atheist Badiou must appeal, in opposing this theory).[4] It logically concludes to a premoral undecidability between the sublime and the psychopathic. Privation theory releases us from this abyss of horror only by fully owning up to the leveling of "the moral" and "the immoral" indicated by the theory of radical evil. It points out that the "good" will to freedom in its unteleological neutrality is bound to be as evil as it is good. Hence the positive assertion of private autonomy is judged to be *just as* evil as its evidently evil and perverse enjoyment of heteronomous interferences (the Sadeian reality of the Kantian subject).

Such autonomy is exposed by privation theory as deprivation of our participation in being as gift: in this way privation theory attacks as evil not just exterior and visible destruction, but also interior and invisible self-assertion. The latter is here diagnosed *as also* evil; but this means as also secretly violent: a violence against Being, an attempted and illusory violence against God.

In the end, for privation theory there is a perfect convertibility of evil with violence. The evil will is as violent as the evil act, because both are equally *deficient* in character. For the theory of radical evil, by contrast, only the act and not the will is violent. Yet this theory also construes the act, as we have seen, too much merely as violent and not also as the evil distortion of the good. Privation theory sees disturbing of the peace also as inhibition of the good, and is only able to diagnose the evil will as *occult violence* because it interprets it also as an inhibition of a participation in infinite plenitudinous goodness.

II

What follows in this essay is an attempt to read violence in terms of the above theory that evil and violence are convertible but not identical: exactly like a couple of malign transcendentals. The same relation pertains, of course, between evil and falsity, evil and disunity, evil and nullity, evil and ugliness— all of which antitranscendentals play some sort of latent role in my account. That "violence" is also an antitranscendental naturally implies that peace is a transcendental: a position implicitly affirmed by Dionysius, Augustine, Aquinas, and Cusanus.[5]

I have already tried to show the main consequences of this theory: first of all, if evil converts with violence, then evil is never positive. Second, if violence converts with evil, then violence is never simply *evident,* because we have to *judge* whether a substantive good has been impaired. Thus a kind of "phenomenological pacifism," which shies away rigidly from "apparent" violence, is here ruled out. Instead, violence has always to be diagnosed, and in a double fashion. Much apparent violence may be exonerated, while much occulted violence must be disinterred. What we are mainly concerned with, therefore, is the question of violence and spectatorship.

In three different ways, it seems to me, those in the wealthy middle-class West today have become characteristically *onlookers* of violence, rather than (at least for now) participants in enactments of violence. We no longer carry daggers in our belts and whip them out at the slightest provocation, like, for example, the young J. S. Bach when faced with a recalcitrant viola de gamba player. Instead, we watch endless scenes of violence in filmed recordings—scenes of violence in wild nature, human violence in remote places, or else of simulated, fictional violence.

This is the first and most obvious way in which we have become primarily onlookers of violence. Later in this chapter I will address the debate about the relative dangers or else innocuousness of watching violence, especially fictional violence. These reflections will lead to the paradoxical conclusion that looking at violence is actually *more violent* than participating in violence—that to be violent *is* actually to survey in a detached, uninvolved fashion a scene of suffering. The *most* violence lies in an occulted violence. Clearly this conclusion will tend to undercut any assumption that because we are primarily the watchers of violence, we are removed from it and live in an essentially postviolent society.

This conclusion has implications for the other two ways in which we have become onlookers of violence. The second way concerns our gaze upon the past: history has been regarded increasingly ever since the eighteenth century as the place where savage acts took place on the basis of superstition and confessional prejudice; and where such acts persist, as for example in the Balkans or the Near East, this is seen today as a kind of historical hangover, affecting only the margins of our modern world. But the question here is, If we experience a sense of moral superiority when we gaze, passively, at a violent past wherein active intervention is now, by definition, forever impossible (because of the irreversibility of time), are we, in fact, analogically or even literally *doing violence* to the past?

The third way concerns the increasing recommendation in modern times of refraining from actual physical violence as the exercise of a supreme good; for example, in the sphere of punishment.[6] Frequently this pacifism has been associated with the setting up of quasi-utopian communities in a removed wilderness, or else with groups, like the Quakers, committed primarily to international and commercial rather than national and political activities and often the promoters of penal reform. The pacifist outlook seems to assume that where one is presented with acts of violence in real life—either toward others or to oneself—then to retain the stance of *onlooker* is morally superior to undertaking a defensive counterviolence. The pacifist elects to *gaze at violence,* and he maintains this stance even if he turns his face away from a violent spectacle, since it persists in his memory. But in fact, this question of averting one's gaze also points toward the issue to which I will return later concerning the counterintuitive character of the pacifist outlook; and one can note here that the very notion of the counterintuitive has metaphorical links with "averting one's gaze." For if the pacifist is confronted with an act of violence against the innocent, which he is not going to meet with counterviolence—shall we say, a posse of marauding Apaches about to assault pioneering women and children, or else a bunch of gung-ho American pilots about to bomb into submission "subversives" in the Third World—then does he stay and watch, or does he shrink quietly away to his prayers? If he does the latter, if he averts his gaze, then how will not the innocent, catching this act out of the corner of their terrified eyes, not perceive here the signifiers of indifference or embarrassment? On the other hand, if he stays to watch, how will they not discern in his gaze of pious sorrow a trace of the nonintervening voyeur? Pacifism, then, is counterintuitive down two possible forks; it is aphoretic, and therefore impossible for human-ity as ordinarily understood.

Moreover, the implication of these reflections is that the refusal of physical counterviolence itself cannot avoid the taint of malice, or the communication of a violent intention. Failure to see this itself derives from a failure sufficiently to look, to the second power, at the scene of violence plus onlookers: failure, then, of a sufficiently explored, sufficiently involved and sympathetic rather than detached, intention. Failure, in other words, of an adequate phenomenology of the scene of violence, which nevertheless judges as much as it discerns.

But if this is the case, then it is not simply that pacifism as nonviolence is less moral than the defensive use of physical violence. It is also that pacifism, as looking at violence, is at least as violent, and probably more absolutely vio-lent, than actual physically violent interventions. This then will confirm my more general conclusion, which I have yet to argue—that gazing at violence is the most violence, indeed the very essence of violence.

It is this conclusion which I now wish to establish, in relation to the first site of spectatorship—namely the watching of recorded violence, real or feigned.

III

The question of taking pleasure in violent spectacle has been with us at least since eighteenth-century discussions of the aesthetics of the sublime.

Edmund Burke was by no means alone in this period in raising the specter of a perverse pleasure in the horrific and repellent. John Dennis already linked the experience of the sublime to "enthusiastic terror," and James Beattie noted, some-what uneasily, the "gloomy satisfaction" that we take in shipwrecks and other catastrophes held within a secure, distancing frame.[7] The distinguishing of the experience of the sublime from both the experience of beauty and the commit-ment to virtue raised for the first time in modernity a theme that helps to define it, namely, the claimed recognition of an aesthetic realm indifferent to the ethi-cal—that garden of delights which nurtures the *fleurs du mal.* (Although in the end the tortured and Kabbalistic Baudelaire was seeking to release a beauty trapped by modern urban evil—like the affection of a prostitute, or the glance of a lost stranger—that is also an alienated goodness which the plenitude of the *Kalon,* beauty and goodness itself, requires in order to be itself.)

One may conjecture that in ages when horror pressed in upon people from all sides, it was less easily rendered a spectacle, and that with the rise of the pos-sibility of safe tourism to threatening places, and equally the increased likeli-hood of urban encounter with horrors that merely "pass one by," the possibil-ity of gazing with impunity at the fascinatingly catastrophic was vastly increased. However, this social circumstance is surely not what was decisive, for antiq-uity and the Middle Ages were dimly aware of such psychological possibilities. In *The Republic,* Plato tells of Leontion, who, noticing some executed corpses lying outside the north wall of Athens, experienced an almost irresistible desire, warring with his disgust, to go up and look at them. And in the *Confessions,* Augustine notes that we may often attend the theater because we enjoy being made sad by "tragical passages" we could not ourselves "endure to suffer"; this theatrical drug is for him no true medicine, since it achieves no catharsis, but rather induces addiction.[8] Yet neither Plato nor Augustine saw in these phenomena a dreadful possibility, reality's dark blooms. Instead, for both they are to do with a fascination for nothingness, which is a false fascination, always predatory on the reality it gradually erodes.

To modernity this interpretation, which reduces the perverse urges to banality, seems implausible: is not the lure to enjoy destruction *as lure* something intensely positive? But the clue to the truth of the diminished intensity of this lure, compared with the urges to create and enjoy life, lies in the circumstance of spectatorship. As Augustine notes, my enjoyable commiseration with the sufferings on stage is linked with the impossibility of my intervening to alleviate them (for they are feigned); hence the whole experience depends upon an absolute bar against reciprocal participation sealed by a double passivity: the scene exhibited is only there at all to be watched, but since watching is all the watchers can do, they are themselves confined to a *telos* of mere reception. Neither the players nor the audience may actively intervene in the other sphere, and each sphere—stage and audience—is only there for the other one. Naturally, life as a whole could not be like this, because then nothing would ever happen: we would all remain stuck in the final tableau of a masque, or confined to our seats as a perpetual audience. Therefore, the whole point of every spectacle is that it must end, and indeed what the audience has come to see is how it will end, or in other words the manner of its death.

So it ceases to be the case that the problem is one of certain spectacles of death, which arouse intense enjoyment. Instead, the point is that every staged "scene" is a scene of horror, a spectacle of termination, and that it is so because the artificial creation of the situation of pure spectacle is a recreational relaxation precisely because it is a diminution of life, or its real interactive excitements, its real consummations and overwhelmings by power (which is not violence, if the power be really power—that is a manifestation of the actual). It follows that the circumstance of spectacle is a deintensification of being, and that in itself it *is* the spectacle of destruction—a drama that to be justified must be reintegrated as ritual through its staged gestures of return and resurrection. It further follows that just as only the Eucharist renders the gaze at the crucified God nonperverse, the purest spectacles of pure destruction represent the lowest degree of intensity, the most drugged and frozen tableau. Here one is either a pure sadist, or a pure masochist, but in either case utterly passive, and indeed relieved of the degree of activity that informs every reception in order for it to be *a response* or mode of interpretation or intervention. Without the middle between active and passive—which is more properly an entirely "active reception" or nonidentical repetition of activity[9]—passivity itself vanishes down the gulf of its last gaze upon the *nihil* of achieved destruction, or the last presentation of that destruction.

But then why, (post)modernity will ask, are artistic scenes of violence able to reawaken us from our complacent bourgeois slumbers and remind us of our framing by natural death and violence? The answer is that this slumbering is itself a nihilistic embrace of death in disguise: it has already relaxed life by restricting the dangers of unexpected death precisely through the increase of deathlike petrified spectacle everywhere: of routine securities guaranteed by the acting out of the same scripts, and the witnessing of these actings out by the various policing agents, such that neither performance nor judgments of the performance (following the rule book) can interfere with each other's prescribed operations.[10] Contemporary bourgeois life, which is now in the main a sterile, uncreative, and proletarianized reproduction of "information" (as the insurgents of May 1968 already diagnosed), is therefore already theater, and therefore (given the conclusions above) already the theater of cruelty, and all that is lacking in the bourgeois is not knowing this to be the case.

Art and the theater only wake it up to this fact, and offer in addition that increased intensity which comes "at the last gasp," when the secret seeker of death, faced with death's arrival, at last recoils from it, as well as recognizing and explicitly embracing the object of his desire. But by the same token, the theater of cruelty, like all merely sublime art, only realizes to the full the bourgeois urge to diminution of the real. The fact that at last it reveals and exposes that tiny degree-almost-zero of remaining intensity, which persists even in the least intense of all lives, disguises from view that its spectacle of horror is the least intense thing imaginable. A breezy day in Peckham, a bus ride to Upminster, would be less suburban.

But there again, modernity asks, and has asked ever since the eighteenth century, were not primitive times, the times of invention, danger, uncertainty, adventure, and closeness to nature, also the times of exhibitions of ritual violence? Rituals in which all participated, which were therefore not mere theater. And is it not precisely such ritual, such active, engaged, participatory art, with no active and passive, no artists versus spectators of art, which the modern avant-garde seeks to reclaim?

But to this one must answer, resolutely, that while indeed "ritual" was no mere domain for "primitive" societies over against the everyday (as Talal Asad has rightly insisted),[11] yet even so, just to the degree that this ritual incorporated experiences of ritual violence, which means framed violence you can *safely* watch, boundaries had to be established and zones of noninterference set up between performers and spectators. That is to say, ritual violence, violent sacrifice, and violent initiation must *already* constitute to a degree a realm of theater, and the continuous reinvocation of primitive ritual by theatrical modernity should therefore cease to surprise us.

By contrast, the purest urge to nontheatrical ritual, to a ritual coincident with life, and without performers and spectators, is surely not to be located in "the primitive." Rather, one might look for it, first of all, in Plato's vision in the *Laws* of a city with a festival for every day of the year which offered itself to the gods through its conversion of every procedure into dance and music;[12] second, in the monotheistic faiths, which tend to view the highest sacrifice as praise offered harmoniously by all, in such a fashion that all sing and all hear, while all transpire upwards with their song into the secret heavenly sanctuary, and all expect to return, for a while, to the flow of temporary life. Here, therefore, violent (later nonviolent) sacrifice establishes no partitions between the killed who departs and the living who remain, or between the licensed killers and an audience watching from a safe distance (even monotheistic sacrificial procedures are approximated to the purely liturgical, nontheatrical pattern).[13]

The above considerations suggest, therefore, that a modern "society of the spectacle" retreats from the pure liturgy of monotheism to a pagan theatricality. And like paganism, it invests its hopes in a controllable economy of violence: where this much and no more blood was once shed to appease the gods, now this much and no more simulated violence, or rather as much *simulated* violence as you like, will appease our "aggressive urge"; and the absence of real wars to watch (from a safe distance) ensures that, indeed, no more real wars or mass oppressions ever again occur. From the horrors of the Second World War and of Auschwitz has been reborn, again, such a would-be atoning art, which seeks to face up to, present, and repeat symbolically and so prophylactically the unimaginable, the sublimely inconceivable atrocity. We cannot run away from this, it is implied (by Hermann Nitsch, Damien Hirst, J. G. Ballard, and so forth), for now that it has occurred, we have to admit the unlimited degree of our thrilling at such spectacle, and art alone, art with a boldness of rupture to match that of Auschwitz, can now purge away our complicity and take upon itself the future salvific prevention of equivalent or worse real calamities in the future.

In this way modern art, which is increasingly only an art of the sublime—of shock and rupture without attraction—recycles the disturbance of a Baudelairean aesthetic diabolism (and removes its saving ambiguity) as the ultimate Aristotelian catharsis; the true pagan, priestly virtue. But two things are overlooked here; the one theoretical, the other historical. The first, theoretical point is that all violence is, in a sense, simulated: to be successfully violent we must shield ourselves from the effects of violence; to enjoy violence we must switch off our capacities for sympathy. In short, we must, in this instance uniquely, be spectators of the deeds we perform. And here intervention in the plot, as in an interactive computer game, does *not at all* cancel the boundary between performer and spectator, but only perfects it: the player on stage I can apparently kill from my seat in the audience is all the more a player watched by me or whom I simply watch; even the players manipulated by me in a virtual reality without upshot for my love are all the more under the control of my gaze, all the more reduced to the realization of my preexistent fantasies. By comparison, a play I did not write *may* alter my life, and to that degree does not so purely happen only on stage as the fantasy I can "interactively" control.

But the best spectacle of all is the most apparently real and yet controlled. In fact it *is* the real, it is the real terrified individual, who can truly relay to me a pure passivity, which I therefore can most enjoy according to the perverse canons of enjoyment of the same pure passivity (meaning the degree zero of activity just before death). That is to say, the only purgation that will satisfy is the real killing, the real sacrifice: artists have begun to kill and rearrange animals and the organic world in order to intensify (as they think) sublime rupture, just as their increasingly indistinguishable allies in iniquity, a majority of "scientists," are also rearranging reality in the name of the "beautiful," or our endless increasing needs for more food, more variety, more prolonged "life," more "normal" life and increasingly more choice, more strangeness (at this point they join hands with the artists, the technicians of sublimity). But if the degree of shock is never quite enough, if the stakes of catharsis forever rise, and if, also, the most perfectly simulated violence is actual violence (as has just been demonstrated), then the demand to purge horror by horror is the demand for . . . horror.

This is the point aptly described by J. G. Ballard in his great visionary novel *Super-Cannes* as the "stepping through Alice's looking glass"—the point at which we live actually in the world of simulation and, for example, kill real people with real bombs, yet without real risk or loss of life to one's own side, as in the Gulf and Afghanistan wars. Or else again, the point at which we propose to put on trial, torture, and execute real people, but in secret, in a virtual legality outside normal legitimacy: but nonetheless permit "the victim" to watch. Here occurs no reversion to public execution, which displayed the objectivity of the law, since not all can now be spectators. Instead it is the purest and most unprecedentedly barbaric indulgence by the state of psychopathic impulses to private vengeance. Perhaps soon, indeed, as Ballard envisages, "therapeutic" suspensions of legitimacy permitting the enactment of perverse crimes in secret by the privileged few will be covertly allowed.[14] Since September 11, 2001, we have clearly stepped through the looking glass.

Therefore it turns out that the stringent crudities of Plato and Augustine are more perceptive than the subtleties of Aristotle: the drug of violence is no dialectical *pharmakon,* but merely addictive. Tragedy offers no catharsis as the purely tragic, and if hope remains, it must rather reside in the possibility that there *are* no innate "aggressive urges," or rather that they are a naturally and culturally contingent historical legacy.

Here one can ask, Just how would one locate them, given that almost every known instance of aggression can be linked with some occasion of aggression, or actual aggression that precedes it? If this fact of a chain of aggressive acts brings us up against "pointless aggression," and if such radical aggression can again erupt *de novo* in any given instance, then its pointlessness is an absolute mystery and we *do not know* how to understand it *or* express it or perform it in terms of recognizable reasons or pleasures or delights. (Even in animal nature aggressivity far exceeds function.) To point to "exercise of power" will not do here, since power over something still involves "a point" that resides in a measure of pleasure in, and appreciation of, the thing or person controlled by power; *absolute* power for its own sake without these interactive dimensions would kill the thing or person controlled, and in thereby losing its power become once more pointless, without assignable reason or pleasure. At this juncture the celebration of the purely sublime has to take refuge in sheer *mystique*. One can note here the double thrust of privation theory: evil is "explicable" as the pursuit of the lesser good, yet a diminished pursuit is ultimately nihilistic, and so not explicable at all. This is not, however, positive radical evil, but a radical negativity.

It follows that neither in terms of the privated pursuit of peace, nor as a surd mode of mysterious anti-action, which "is" not, since it denies actuality, is one justified in envisaging aggressivity as innate. Rather it is fiction, theater, and contaminated mythology, which itself trades upon this invented tragic scenario.

Plato was therefore right: acceptable poetry is liturgical praise of the divine and heroic, but mimesis within a fictional frame is to be eschewed—or received only, we may qualify, if integrated back into a liturgical frame by its own self-negating gestures within that frame: as Milton achieves in *Paradise Lost*. If drama involves *only* negative capability, and no subtly insinuated act of real subjective commitment by the author to his words, then it becomes nihilistic. This was Wittgenstein's suspicion concerning Shakespeare; that he was no true hymnic *dichter*. Yet it was surely a misreading. Shakespeare's villains and anti-heroes are precisely captured by the abyss of pure drama, and this *tragic delusion* is clearly condemned by framing liturgical gestures of resurrection, which increasingly punctuated and closed his plays. In this way, as Keats discerned, negative capability encourages a sublime gesture of faith rather than one of gnosis or autobiographical self-absorption.[15]

But without such liturgical recouping of negative capability, the theatrical and fictional inherently tend to the spectacle of violence that *is* real violence. Is it not, after all, clear that if violence is culpable as denying (ending) some reality, then it is culpable for *pretending* something; while conversely, what fictionalizes is violent unless it doubles this irony by another irony intended to reinforce a real already threatened by pretense (in this way Socratic irony was a counterfiction)?[16] Thus Plato's refusal of epic and theatrical fictions about the gods, which are intended—unlike hymns and instructive myths of origins— merely to divert us or to reflect our given humanity, is *exactly the same gesture* as his refusal of violence within the divine realm.[17]

The second, historical point is that in our recent past, science and art have always first mimed the horrors to come. Unteleological evolutionism (the Darwinian variety; now scientifically in eclipse) more or less demands eugenicizing, since if we are outcomes of chance, we require redesigning. It sought to shore up liberalism with a greater "beauty" of convenience, but engendered only a greater means of totalitarian, expert control over an ignorant, submissive populace. Likewise, avant-garde art of the kind that sought either to relieve the monotony of modern life (Salvador Dalí, for example) or else to augment and make palpable its speed for the sake of ensuring our deepest passionate satisfaction (Italian futurism) in fact encouraged the yet more sublime vision of the imposition of unimaginable force and horror by a few political artists upon their many willing admirers. (Other instances of the modernist avant-garde, however, constituted a genuine protest.) So what may the far more shocking interventions of 1990s art and science (engendered precisely by the liberal response to a horror it seeks to prevent from happening again) betoken for the present century?

We are all too soon beginning to see. . . .

IV

At this point it is time to revert to the two other issues concerning violence and spectacle. First of all, our gaze upon the past.

If we merely look upon the violent past in judgment, do we not reproduce the scene of double passivity? Do we not assume that the conflict and illusions of the past are over and no longer inflect the course of events today? Inversely, do we not assume that the past, since it is finished with, cannot in any sense be resumed and redeemed?

We get in this position of double passivity vis-à-vis the past where we imagine that violence is essentially over, and so framable by our gaze. We then do violence to the past, because we render it *too* different from our present and fail to sympathize with its dilemmas.

Violence is far from over, and if anything has been increased by being abstracted and generalized. Today, violence is like the regularity of breathing, which goes on all the time and is a fire so slow (fire, since it is oxidization) that we do not notice that it is fire. Likewise, we do not today see brutality—especially the exclusion and elimination of those who fail in the competition of the marketplace. Now that knowledge is also subject to the market, and the quest for truth has consequently been abandoned in favor of the sloshing about of "information," we do not notice that since information is a valuable product—inhibiting random chaos and threatened by the entropy of out-of-dateness—it assumes that many will lack information and will be socially defined *as* the uninformed or else the deficient in personal data (according to entirely standardized criteria).

Truth, by contrast, is not like this, since it does not stand in contrast to chaos as an island of arbitrary systems, and cannot become out-of-date. Because of its consequent nonvanity, truth is marked by plenitude and democratic availability: it is Augustine's sunlight.

Computers, though, insofar as they impose the reign of information, are the enemies of truth and democracy. Our gaze at their screens is the constitution through watching and receiving of inherently violent transactions, which, in the end, when we step through their looking glass, always involve real physical violence.

Online, therefore, we are clubbing each other to death, but invisibly, very very gradually, and at a huge remove. When this process does appear, then we finally see what we collectively do, but assume that it has nothing to do with us, individually. But just as breathing is the most massive combustion, so also this slowed-down and distributed violence is actually increased violence, like a torture that is all the more torture through being long drawn out.

Likewise, it is increased as a *trade* in violence, or in abstract, purposeless power: power for *its own sake*, which is another definition of what constitutes violence. Modern economics and politics have discovered how to instill a kind of order from the systematization of the random, the pursuit of disorder, the battle of all with all. There is nonetheless a dialectic at work here, because the increasing pursuit of power through simulations of the real— the competitions for signs, images, logos, genes, and *patents* for all these things—potentially places in the hands of random individuals extraordinary capacities for violent interactions (which in the end are brutally physical)— computer network subversions, chemical and biological mutations. Soon we might all be Gollums, scrabbling for a binding ring of power that every individual may in theory wield. The only antidote to this logical extension of capitalist freedom is a terroristic policing of "terrorism," such as is now being put into place.

By contrast, the violence of the past, though more physical, was more measured. In the era of the great world faiths it resulted, accidentally, in a sense, from the pursuit of peace—from their visions of peace, or a reality that enabled peaceableness to be attained, and therefore from an envisioned ontological peaceableness (this is especially the case, I would argue, for the monotheistic faiths). By contrast, modernity has tended to despair of this vision and to espouse instead theses of ontological conflict, which suggest—often with increasing despair—that *violence* can only be tempered, not eradicated.

Hence we have no reason to patronize or despise the past. Of course the major religions were violent in practice, and in certain ways they were justified in being so—even if they also resorted, in their human fallibility, often to excessive and unjustifiable violence. Since they believed that they possessed keys to the harmonization of human life in accord with reality, they inevitably at times deployed coercion when faced with those who opposed this reality in various ways. And sometimes they *should* have done just this; it was a matter of proper self-belief. The liberal enlightenment also pursued a vision of universal peace and also defended it coercively. The only difference is that the liberal vision is less generous (less "liberal" in fact), and is in a sense equally a vision of universalized violence. Hence its coercive defense of its peace often seems indistinguishable from a defense of the arbitrary—law from criminality. By contrast, violence enacted in the name of a substantive *telos* can more plausibly pose as essentially educational, as a self-denying coercive ordinance.

The real point here is that although Christianity, for example, certainly requires in the end *free consent* to the truth, it does not fetishize this freedom merely as a correct mode of approach: truth is what most matters, and moreover a *collective* commitment to the truth, since truth itself is the shareable and the harmonious. Thus in certain circumstances, the young, the deluded, those relatively lacking in vision require to be coerced as gently as possible. Anyone professing to be shocked by this is, I submit, naïvely unreflective about what in reality he already accepts (for example in the secular schooling of the young) and is thinking in overindividualistic and overvoluntaristic terms that are ontologically impossible.

There is also one specific consideration that applies to Christianity alone, which should be taken into account: Christianity is the religion that risks subordinating the law, since the formal generality of the law, while it may inhibit violence, is itself a mode of counterviolence. Instead, Christianity looks for salvation and an entire realized peace to the infinite and unpredictable variety in occurrence of the good: a radically unleashed *phronesis,* which is also the attentive but unroutinized self-giving of charity. But to subordinate the barriers and taboos of the law is also to take a terrible risk—the risk of the advent of a totally unleashed violence, instead of the *eschaton* of peace. Here, perhaps, lies the most acute Jewish critique of Christianity—namely that, like the Norse Loki, it has unchained the hound of *danger*—allowed it, in Franz Steiner's phrase, to march into the heart of civilization in a fashion that I have already described.[18] The Christian, though, can only abide by his or her commitment to all or nothing.

In a sense then, yes, Christianity has led to violence: first, because it is a universalizing religion; second, because it aims so high. The best is always likely to turn out to be also the worst. But why, then, should we patronize our ancestors and the unimaginably complex and perilous situations in which they found themselves, by apologizing on their behalf? In a word, we cannot as human beings suppose that violence is entirely unavoidable, insofar as it runs the educative risks of redemption.

And this leads me back to the third issue of violence and spectacle, namely pacifism. Here the main point has already been made: pacifism is aporetic because both gazing at and averting one's gaze from violence are intuitively complicit with its instance. Christian pacifism, then, has to erect itself as a counterintuitive doctrine. But then why (as Stanley Hauerwas asks) should not theology challenge intuitions that may be embedded in our fallen nature? Well, it seems to me that the intuitions violated here are not fallen ones, but created ones. For the impulse to protect the innocent is rooted in our animality, embodiment, and finitude.

There is an analogy here to Bernard Williams's insistence that ethics should not be so counterintuitive or counternaturalistic as to challenge our natural impulse always to save our own nearest and dearest first in the event of a common catastrophe.[19] To take any other position is again to deny our finitude, and our limited range of intense capacity for affection and attention. One can see this by asking the question: Suppose the neglected nearest and dearest survive, despite our neglect? With the best intentions or respect for our altruism, how will they, as warm-blooded animals, really *read* our pious neutrality? Will not the whole future of our relations with them be colored by our choice? Not surprisingly, perhaps, most Christians have so confused Kant and Comte with the Gospels that they do not realize that Aquinas would have been in essential agreement with Williams here, and that the entire Christian tradition at least up to the time of the Angelic Doctor interpreted *agape* as "neighbor love" to mean precisely a preferential love for those nearest to us, those with the most inherited, realized, and developed affinity with us, as well as those strangers with whom suddenly we are bonded whether we like it or not, by instances of distress, shared experience, or preferred comfort.[20] The Samaritan is also the neighbor, and Jesus is clearly *not* here teaching us to respect or help strangers only as strangers. Nevertheless, one should interpret the parable to mean, in addition and inversely, that the daily neighbor is also the arriving stranger through time,[21] and this reading duly qualifies, without canceling, the main point that has just been made.

This specificity of given proximity, which is yet also the endlessly surprising gift of renewed contingent arrival, is *our only* creaturely way to participate in God's equal love for all. The latter, then, can only be implemented on earth, collectively and socially as a vast web of interlocking affinities within a common but sufficiently accommodating and varied culture. Without this theological view, one collapses into overprecious aporias about the treatment of some being also the neglect of others.

Somewhat similar considerations apply to our relation to the innocent, or relatively innocent. We are not, and should not aspire to be, angels, equally close to all. On the contrary, we are naturally closer to the endangered, or to those we interpret as such, or to those whose cause we sympathize with. We *should* defend—even sometimes with violence—what we believe in, though with the knowledge that we may well be mistaken. Otherwise we are not risking some sort of conjecture as to the nature of the Good—and if we fail to do this, then the Good itself will fade into unreality, since we are both finite and fallen, and do not enjoy a beatified immediate intuition of goodness in all its plenitudinous immediacy.

This, I think, is the key to what Charles Péguy called "the mysterious charity" of Jeanne d'Arc: even in a situation of very complex and often sordid human passions she had to seek to elect the relative good, and even physically to fight for it, given that otherwise it would be destroyed.[22]

Of course, as Augustine implied, any good you have to fight for is not the absolute good. The very reason for fighting for something is that it is threatened, and obviously the real absolute good is never threatened in this kind of way. But since we have only weak intimations of the absolute good and only enjoy these in theory when conjoined with some practical attempt to enact it in fragile finite structures, pacifism is like a kind of overapophatic iconoclasm, which despises the necessary fragility of these realized intimations. It seeks to have a kind of cheap and easy participation in the eternal. It tries to leap out of our finitude, embodiment, and fragility. In this way, pacifism strangely colludes with its seeming opposite, the Machiavellian and pagan republican error of seeking to immortalize and maintain forever what is fragile, and bound, in the end, to pass away. Equally to underrate or to overrate the fragile is a terrible mistake, and interrupts the economy of the participation of time in eternity.

A reading of Péguy's verse play, *La Mystère de la Charité de Jeanne d'Arc,* gives rise to several reflections which are relevant to the issues that I am trying to resolve here. For one thing, Jeanne's lay status is crucial. There is something about the absolute demonization of all war and conflict that smacks of a clerical despising of the laity from within the walls of a monastery or a presbytery, wherein the need to oppose, to deceive, etc., may at least *appear* not to arise with the same exigency.[23] Even if Dostoyevsky's monasticization of all society is, in a sense, a correct aim (if this means trying to bring about a liturgical society), one can nevertheless see that the monasticization of the whole of society is much more difficult than the monasticization of a celibate few. For this general attempt to produce a liturgical society has to reckon with both sex and conflict. And the placing of sex outside the purview of the sacred is in a way highly parallel to the absolute condemnation of warfare. In both cases, one has to do with a kind of despising of the lay Christian, and an inability really to think of a way in which a lay Christian can be a Christian at all.

In the Middle Ages, the elaboration of the notion of chivalry was, in a sense, an attempt to elaborate a lay theology in a way that I think very few people now understand. This lay theology resisted an unintelligent clerical squeamishness about sex: as the *Roman de la Rose* asks, if clerical chastity is the "highest" path and yet grace is offered to all, how is this consistent with God's approval of nature and generation? Only the Olympian gods, the authors of this work argue, were jealous of the human physical bliss of the Golden Age; such an attitude is alien to the God of creation and grace, and therefore sexual puritanism is pagan and not Christian.

Chivalric theology also resisted an unintelligent clerical preciosity concerning conflict: Wolfram von Eschenbach in his *Parzival* points out through the mouth of his protagonist that if clerical nonviolence is "the highest," then fighting a just war would imperil one's salvation, at least to some degree.[24] If some wars are just, they lie therefore within the scope of providence, and such impairment therefore seems inconsistent with divine justice and grace. (One should nonetheless accept that this point is in tension with another equally valid point: namely that *some* people—clerical and lay—should exhibit already the eschatological life of peace. Sexual abstinence, however—if sexuality is a good—cannot really parallel this. The celibate path is rather a matter of remaining in childish innocence as a reminder of the danger of fallen sexuality, with its reduction of human to animal passions, which for humans, unlike animals, are evil and violent.)

Now Péguy in many ways revived these lay concerns, and not surprisingly, and not of course without terrible ambiguities, he adhered to a renewed cultus of the female warrior Jeanne d'Arc. But his strange drama exhibits other features that allow us to make further and surprising connections. Throughout its course he meditates in a more or less Jewish fashion on the fact that it seems that the atonement has not worked and that in the end Christ, and the church, have been refused. This also raises the issue of the *contingency* of the incarnation and crucifixion. Jeanne d'Arc says repeatedly: yes, Jesus was refused and executed in his time, but the peasants of France would not have refused him. Equally, though, and with seeming contradiction, she suggests that Christ's message could have been preserved *only* because it arrived to the exceptional people of Israel at an exceptional moment.

Her extreme naïveté has a sophisticated point—how can we entirely know that elsewhere Jesus' appeal would not have worked or else would have utterly failed? This then links up to the further point that if the atonement is to be effective, if it is really to be an atonement at all, then it must be verbal in order to be nominal, received in order to be precedent. That is to say, received in some degree (first of all by Mary), though only through the hypostatic presence amongst us of the Holy Spirit, which is the church. In this way a more pneumatological approach to atonement recovers also a Jewish perspective, while inversely the christological dimension provides the language and presence of a finality of atonement lacking within Judaism.

For atonement to be ontologically actual, Christ's appeal must still after all work within history: there must really in some sense exist the *ecclesia*. His example must somewhere and somehow be followed, and this *mimesis* must clearly involve further acts of mutual atoning that realizes the hypostatic presence of the Holy Spirit.

So one can say that a certain Jewish dimension seems for Péguy, the *Dreyfusarde,* to supervene upon the Christian: first of all, in terms of the need for continued atonement, and for a collective redemption that requires the "right positioning" of all in relation to all in space and time through mutual exchange (the Jewish mystical gathering up and reweaving together of the lost "divine sparks": this should not of course be interpreted as betokening any sort of catastrophe in the eternal; only the aporetic loss of divine glory in the world through the fall, which God immediately corrects, although our own realization of this correcting must be gradual).

Second, in terms of a renewed apocalyptic. Yes, Péguy seems to say, the road to redemption lies through suffering evil, rather than betraying truth, and yet even in order to suffer evil and thereby defeat it, evil must be not *only* undergone but also *opposed*. Otherwise, there is a sense in which atonement has failed. This insight comprehends why the New Testament ends in a renewed Jewish fashion: with apocalypse. For even metaphoric war, or opposing, is still nevertheless war, and in suffering evil we do not only in a sense accept it, but only suffer it precisely because we also oppose it, and therefore are at war with the demonic.

To be sure, evil as ultimately nothing need not be opposed, yet evil as predatory upon the positive—as confining the positive to an "enclave" where its nature as relative good is threatened because it no longer communicates with the supreme good (like Baudelaire's *fleurs du mal*) —must be opposed, must be *refused,* else it is simply accepted. Even if one says, "I oppose all violence," the word "oppose" gives the game away: violence has tragically sucked even you, the pacifist, into its *agon*. Standing aloof, not intervening when you might—this mere gaze—is *also* an act: it *opposes* the violent person by violently leaving him to his violence and not trying to stop him in his tracks. Contrariwise, it *is* important actively and chivalrously to oppose violence: for example, to stop someone from going as far as murder, even if one thereby kills him, for soon (now or hereafter) he may come to repent of his intentions, whereas it is far more difficult to repent of the actual deed. Not to see this is to underrate the importance of act and to fall prey to a Kantian privileging of motivation.

It is because we can be good only collectively that we cannot exercise pure peaceableness alone. Once there is violence, we are all inevitably violent. And violence can be eradicated only collectively, by a strange apocalyptic counterviolence, which is in the end a divine prerogative, yet is also obscurely anticipated within time. This is why, for St. Paul, although every Christian is a farmer, he is also a soldier "who should never get entangled in civilian pursuits" (2 Tim. 2:4). Christians do, indeed, believe perfect peace to be the ultimate ontological reality and so to be attainable. But in that case, peace names the eschaton, the final goal; if there is peaceableness on the way to this goal, then this is a peculiarly intersubjective virtue. I rather doubt whether individual exercise of "peaceableness" has very much meaning. For now, we must rather try together to be peaceable. In the penultimate, which both peace and conflict now sometimes anticipate, there will be fought the unthinkable and for us aporetic "conflict against conflict." However, in the ultimate beyond the last battle, even the refusal of evil will be redundant: then there will be only peace.

Because "peaceableness" was never exactly seen as an individual virtue, I suspect that there were no real "pacifisms" in premodernity, and that pacifism is profoundly linked with individualism. Likewise, it is linked with an overvaluation of freedom, since it assumes that forcing a person's will is the worst thing possible; even though in subtle ways, we of course do this all the time.

We therefore should not and even cannot be pacifists. Instead, prior to the ultimate, we are always partially already in the apocalyptic situation of "opposing force," if by force one means the attempt to disturb, for egoistic reasons, the harmony of reality. In opposing force, we are always tragically deploying the enemy's means. We are like Frodo Baggins's servant Samwise, putting on the ring of evil force in order to remain invisible and escape the orcs, so that his master may ultimately destroy this symbol of abstracted power for its own sake—which, like the ring of Gyges in Plato's *Republic,* notably confers invisibility on the wearer. In *The Lord of the Rings,* there is a complex blend of double risk: renunciation of absolute power—the *copied* and *stolen* master ring that is not, like the lesser originally wrought rings, a *gift*—combined with occasional trickery of that power leads to a victory that nonetheless appears to be a lucky accident, or else the work of providence.[25] Likewise, we can only try to force force with reserve and with hopeful risks that distorted realities will come to repent. This is the best we can do; our scenario is apocalyptic, not utopian.

If the above considerations are sound, then we can see that the spectator of sublime artistic violence, the Christian apologist for the Christian past, and the Christian pacifist idealist all actually enact different versions of the same scenario of double passivity that constitutes any "fictional" spectacle. In this way, the past is distorted into fiction, and present situations that demand our risky response are likewise distorted. But we have also seen that watching fictional violence does not just lead to violence, nor is it just a variant of violence. Rather, it is violence itself: the "safe" gaze into the looking glass of narcissistic perversity. This gaze always invites an actual step behind the looking glass into the world where now, as always (and yet now more than ever before), violence is real because it is always only virtual, just as nonliturgical virtuality is always violence.

And the virtuality of violence converts diabolically with the negativity of evil, revealing pure virtuality to be violence, just as lack of being is evil. Or virtuality is evil, just as negation is violence. This is the cross, the antichiasmus.

ADDENDUM

Testing Pacifism: Questions for John Milbank

First Questioner: Professor Milbank, if I could take issue with your characterization of pacifists. It seems to me that you fall into something of a false dichotomy in describing the options available to pacifists. You see them as having the option of either observing or ignoring violence. It seems to me that the actual witness of pacifists through the ages is that of actually placing ourselves between the violent oppressor and the innocent victim. For instance, in the story from the Gospels in which rocks are thrown at the adulteress, the pacifists, perhaps, would place themselves between those rocks and that woman. That would seem to me not an easy witness, but a costly one. It is one that does not collude with violence; it opposes violence, and also is not necessarily anti-communitarian.

Milbank: I don't really have a problem with that in a sense. It doesn't seem to me that that is any special privilege of pacifists at all. I don't think there is anything particularly pacifist about the mode of action you have just described. On the contrary, it is the responsibility of everybody to oppose violence with minimal violence. And getting in the way of the rocks is infinitely preferable to chucking a rock back at the person doing it. Nonetheless, it is probably *not* the right response—assuming that you are not a pacifist—because this person is going to go on throwing rocks, is going to dodge around, you are going to miss some of his missiles, so you really need to aim a rock to his head, which you hope will knock him unconscious, rather than actually kill him. And it is when it comes to that kind of decision, which one can't really evade, that actually the alternatives do become exactly what I have said.

Second Questioner: Would you consider Martin Luther King Jr., and Mahatma Gandhi to be pacifists? Or would you consider their approach to be simply nonviolent? Are these identical or separate practices?

Milbank: No, I do not think the use of nonviolent direct action is necessarily pacifist at all. For one thing, it nearly always does involve some measure of coercion. You are trying to force someone to do something. But I think such modes of action are admirable if they can be effective. It is absolutely an imperative to adopt the least violence possible. But not only that, also such modes of action, while being slower, can be more effective, because people can be impressed by what you are doing. A kind of weak degree of coercion is often more liable to win over the person that you are opposing. And so certainly if it takes longer, it may in the end produce a much more effective result. It may produce what you want without the same kind of legacy of rancor. So I really have the utmost admiration for the people who have developed these kinds of techniques, and nothing that I have said would be intended to gainsay that in any way whatsoever.

Third Questioner: You mentioned artists who do actual violence to animals. Then you mentioned their partners in iniquity, the scientists. Is it a correct interpretation of your argument to say that these people do violence to nature by their changing it to satisfy human needs?

Milbank: No, that is not correct, because that would rule out almost everything, wouldn't it? It is more a question of doing it in relation to unexamined human needs—that some of them might not necessarily bear a lot of examining. I think, more generally though, it's a sort of random production of an abstract ability to do almost anything. That can be extremely dangerous if done without any foresight about what are the possible or likely applications of certain processes—as if just any extension of power, in itself, is simply a good to be pursued. And it seems to me it is likely that that kind of exercise of power is likely simply to encourage the idea that we should extend free choices as far as possible—that people should have unlimited ability to kind of redesign their bodies and their very nature. I am not trying to give a blanket disapproval to altering things. It is much more a question of alteration with total disregard for any questions of what a true human *telos* or flourishing might be.

Fourth Questioner: One can consider a broad spectrum of actions as violent. Would you clarify what you mean by violence, and what counts as violence as distinct from opposition? I wouldn't normally consider opposition as necessarily violent.

Milbank: I tried to give several different definitions of violence. But I guess opposition implies some sort of violence because it suggests that you are opposed to something that is not likely to agree with you and you are going to go on meeting that in a forceful fashion. Opposition, it is true, is a type of persuasive discourse that hovers somewhere in the middle between peace and violence, because you are hoping the person will repent and agree. But oppositional discourse would go on trying to force itself into an arena in the absence of capitulation.

Fourth Questioner: Would oppositional discourse that doesn't include violence still be a form of violence? Is disagreeing a form of violence at some level?

Milbank: I think it is. I think it is a low-key form of violence.

Fourth Questioner: So it seems that to a certain degree, to be honest with your definition of violence, we are enacting some kind of violence through opposition.

Milbank: Yes.

Fifth Questioner: I would like to congratulate you on escaping Hegel, at least somewhat, by stepping back into Platonism—somewhat. *Theology and Social Theory* is a monumental piece of work, but I get to the last chapter and it seems that your musical ontology blows apart. I don't understand how you can maintain absolute difference at the same time that you incorporate violence into that symphonic movement or that melody. It seems that in attempting to escape that you are actually falling back into the same pagan mythos that you critique Nietzsche for. What we have done here is to make violence fundamental, inescapable, and ontologically real. But it seems like from the beginning we have to have this notion of absolute peace that we risk everything on. Otherwise, I think, we fall back into Nietzsche's mythos of violence.

Milbank: Well, I agree about that, but I don't think it conflicts with believing that creation means there is absolute peace at the origins. This has been subverted, disturbed. Yet we have faith that this will be once again restored, because the created order is founded in peaceable and harmonious difference—which is the life of the Trinity. I think you can believe that without necessarily being a pacifist. Because the issue about pacifism seems to be more about the following. Given that there is a violent interruption within time of ontological peace, is there any way not to be at all complicit with this violence, not to resort to counterviolence? And it is there that I have tried to set out the arguments for why I don't think it is the case that at least individuals by themselves can take this kind of pacifist stance, and I am very skeptical even about what this would really mean.

Fifth Questioner: Could we phronetically take the risk, and could that be an alternative? That the good that we see at this source of reality could actually arise by taking the risk of nonviolence?

Milbank: I am sure a lot of the time that something like that is what we should be doing, when I am talking about minimum violence. Indeed, a lot of us are now increasingly living in such dangerous circumstances that we almost have no option but to go that way. I think that is another reason, though, why we shouldn't sort of patronize the people in the past, living in very different kinds of circumstances. When it comes to the issue of violence, I am not, of course, saying that all power is violence, or that power exercised in a persuasive way is violence. What violence is, originally, is the refusal of peace. And as peace and justice are inseparable, it's also the refusal of justice and of the true harmonious order. It is a refusal, if you like, of teleology. So there is a sense in which if you are committed to the right teleology, even if you have to resort to some kind of force, then, as it were, inside that mailed fist, there is some kind of persuasion really. So much is that the case in fact, that if the punished or forced person sees that, the force ceases to be violence. But it is like a kind of hinge, and like a kind of risk, and in *Theology and Social Theory* I did say that I don't think that Augustine had enough sense of the risk and ambiguity of punishment. Although I think now even more strongly that he was right to see that as inescapable. You can tell that I have had children since I wrote *Theology and Social Theory.* [laughter]

Sixth Questioner: You have said many intriguing and challenging things, and I was particularly interested in the idea of doing violence to history—and perhaps I should say to begin with that I live in Gary, Indiana, which is said to be the murder capital of the United States just now. I am not sure that quantification is central, but the matter of doing violence to history I thought was a very important point—except then I was baffled by the way you treated it. Are you saying that the old times were more violent, or are you saying that the twentieth century may be the most violent of all?

Milbank: In a way, I am arguing more the latter, that violence is now more subtle and concealed, but more pervasive, so we shouldn't patronize the past. Although our violence has become more concealed and subtle, it is still in continuity, in many ways, with the violences and conflicts that we've inherited from the past. We shouldn't look at the past and say, "Why did Christianity do these absolutely terrible things in the past?" as if it was all completely different.

Seventh Questioner: I am intrigued by your critique of narrative representations of violence because such representations have often been very important tools of people committed to nonviolent social change. I am thinking of the writings of Elie Wiesel, or a novel like *Uncle Tom's Cabin* being used to challenge the violence of slavery, and I wonder, to take the rock-throwing example again, if we live in a society where there is a lot of rock throwing going around, isn't it better to tell the story of Jesus and the woman accused of adultery than to throw rocks at the rock throwers?

Milbank: Yes, I'm not really wanting to quarrel with that. What I was trying to talk about was the pure logic of fiction as such, if you are, as it were, celebrating something like fiction for the sake of fiction, or seeing it as a distraction or a drug, a *pharmakon* in some way. So, I was criticizing in a way the catharsis view, but I was not at all wanting to deny that fiction can have what I would call liturgical purposes—in other words, when it leads one back into life via an essential detour. You know, because it is making things strange, it is getting you to look at things in a different way—it is posing different possibilities, and all that sort of thing. I wasn't trying to criticize that at all. I was, rather, criticizing a particular way of reading art for which the repetition of horrific spectacle seems to be seen as the only answer to spectacles so terrible that there is really nothing to be said of them. And I think the danger of that is that it precisely starts to create the cultural conditions for another such repetition, in actuality. That was much more the thing I was trying to get at. Inci-

dentally, I am not quite sure about *Uncle Tom's Cabin* being completely innocent of spectatorship. Harriet Beecher Stowe had never visited the South.

Seventh Questioner: Certainly, I would agree with you that it is in the kind
of odd transition from sentimental and sensationalist literature.

Milbank: And as we know, a lot of the Northern intervention against slavery was hysterically millenarian at times, and self-serving in a way that was very
ambiguous.

Seventh Questioner: Well, right, I would just insist that it was ambiguous
and not as wholly to be repudiated as modern nihilism.

Milbank: No, I was just trying to indicate the ambiguities about fiction in
some of the cases you have cited, that is all.

Eighth Questioner: I have a question about the gaze upon violence as a
means of formation of Christian character in community. A preeminent book
that has shaped the folk in the Anabaptist tradition, perhaps especially the
Amish, second only to the Bible, is the *Martyrs' Mirror,* which intriguingly has
"A Bloody Theater" as a subtitle. The book, and especially the etchings and
illustrations of the martyrdoms, show killing as spectacle. The killings are often
done on high platforms. The martyrs are lifted up to the gaze of everyone. The
first in the sequence, in the *Martyrs' Mirror,* is Jesus, of course, and he is similarly lifted up to the gaze of the spectators. One can distinguish, I believe, four
groups of spectators here. There are the village folk who came to watch the
spectacle when it happened. There are the killers themselves, the executioners,
and the magistrates who made the decision to do so. Third, there are the martyrs themselves, who have contemplated and gazed upon their own deaths in
prison and see it approaching. And then, closer to us, there are these humble
Amish and Mennonite families who gaze upon the image and have their Christian character and piety formed in community. In a way, I was almost thinking that you were saying that these fourth ones are the most violent of all. Of
these four, are those who are gazing upon the pictures in the *Martyrs' Mirror*
now the most violent of all?

Milbank: No, I am not trying to say that at all. That would only arise if they
were in a situation of gazing for the sake of gazing, of a kind of gloating. All I
was trying to argue was that in carrying out a violent deed, you are sort of detach-
ing yourself from your deed. You are not going with it. You are simply looking
at what you have done and removing yourself and enjoying what you have done
as a spectacle—a spectacle that you have got a kind of absolute control over, but
which can't hurt you. So you are absolutely safe. There is an analogy here to
watching a scene of fictional horror, because there you are absolutely safe: it cannot affect you, and you have the sense of control. It would be a perverse enjoyment of this Anabaptist manual that I would be talking about in which it was
just a matter of gazing and nothing else. That is really what I am getting at.

Ninth Questioner: In this conference, at least in the sessions I have attended,
I'm not aware that we have addressed the very specific issue of investing, and

what we are doing with paychecks. You brought up the violence in the middle class and the important observation that violence continues to become less visible; our involvement seems to be more and more removed from this violence. Certainly, it strikes me that the matter of investments and mutual funds involves questions of environmental stewardship, where we don't know what a company's money is being invested into, and what it is producing. I would be delighted to hear some of your thoughts on that.

Milbank: I would absolutely agree. That is another illustration of the way in which we are all involved in anonymous violence. And the question I suppose is "How do you respond to that?" One answer would be "Well, withdraw from everything iniquitous," and then someone else would come back and say, "Well, where are you going to stop—actually?" That is the point of Shaw's play *Major Barbara,* of course.

Ninth Questioner: It seems that one possibility would be to say, "Well, it seems like a Christian approach to this would be to not invest in the market." That is an option.

Milbank: What I was going to say was that I thought, in spite of that sense of where would you possibly stop, there still can be a case for trying to avoid the most gratuitously awful things. It is never an argument to say, "Well, everything is bad." But as to the issue of wholesale withdrawal, I am very uneasy about that, because it seems to be a kind of sectarian option, a going off into the wilderness option, which leaves most people sunk in the general situation. It is so difficult to detach yourself and will become increasingly more difficult really not to turn to instituted things, social services, health services, that kind of thing. All of which are ultimately bound up in the market system. Or do you somehow remain with it and try to modify it in small ways, and keep alive the discussion of alternative possibilities? I mean, if there is ever going to be a revolution and a move toward better economic practices directed toward the common good, the people who are going to have to carry it out are, probably, businessmen—you see what I mean? You know, there is more hope, in a sense, in remaining with those people and trying to get them to reflect on things, however unlikely that might seem.

This question/answer session with John Milbank occurred following his presentation at the Christianity and Violence conference. He has edited his responses for this volume.

THIRTEEN

CHRISTIAN PEACE

*A Conversation between Stanley Hauerwas
and John Milbank*

Alan Jacobs: In his paper, John Milbank invoked Charles Péguy and his verse drama, *The Mystery of the Charity of Joan of Arc*. The question is whether such actions as Joan of Arc engaged in, whether a military program of the kind that she followed, can indeed be compatible with charity. Is it possible for one to act violently and thereby do Christian charity? Stanley, what do you think?

Stanley Hauerwas: Well, as John knows, I agree with him that one of the deepest prejudices I dislike in modernity is the presumption that there is absolutely nothing for which it is worth dying, and the corollary that we should only kill people out of extreme necessity. So, insofar as charity names a set of practices that indicate that violence can be put to use in service to the neighbor, I think that that is a possible reading. What is interesting about that, I think, is how you would actually read historical circumstances in which Joan of Arc lived in terms of whether she thought she had any other alternatives. Again, I agree with John; I dislike intensely the pacifist reading of history that wants to lay deep judgment and blame against those Christians who used violence.

Earlier in my talk, John, I said the reason I think that Christians so often have been such enthusiastic killers is because we have been such enthusiastic die-ers. As a result, you get a kind of reverse logic in Christianity. That is the reason I think one of the most important challenges before those of us who are pacifists is to give an account of the conscientious participation of Christians in war. People are to be honored if it was conscientious participation, because so often it is not conscientious. Pacifists must claim our brothers and sisters who conscientiously participate in war as at least akin to those of us who refrain from war. So John's further suggestions about Joan of Arc working out a lay theology against clerical prejudice against sex and war is a project pacifists can readily join.

John Milbank: Not specifically Joan of Arc!

Hauerwas: I always loved sex. [laughter] John has put together a nice alternative there, but I have some suspicion about it. But let me turn it. John takes the Augustinian move that Paul Ramsey made the heart of his account of just war. Augustine said, "We do not use violence in our own defense—better to die than do an evil—but we do use violence in defense of an innocent neighbor." And all innocence means here is that they did not deserve the attack; not that they are, for example, babies. Jesus may have asked us to turn our cheek, but he did not ask us to turn our neighbor's cheek. Since that is the case, then Christians must be ready to defend with violence those who share goods with us as neighbor regard. The phrase "should defend with violence those who share goods with us" raises the question for me—it is not unrelated to Joan of Arc—of whether Christians ought to have standing armies integral to the church itself. Because I share with John the general distaste for liberal regimes, I cannot imagine, therefore, John would think any of them are capable of conducting a just war. But does that mean that given Milbank's position one of the most important things we can do as Christians is to develop standing armies as part of the church organization itself? [laughter]

Milbank: However much this probably appeals to Stanley, I am afraid I have to say, "No." [laughter] It has always been clear that the church was a community trying to go beyond justice, at least in a restricted sense, toward the rule of reconciliation. Indeed the church *has* always had its own equivalents to secular law: it has always had its own system of rules and penances, and so on. But clearly it is has understood itself as aiming beyond law and punishment, toward reconciliation. If repentance is what matters, then forcing people is simply hopeless. If some measure of coercion is allowed by the church, and Augustine is one instance, but there are others, it is extremely minimal. It involves things like exclusions and excommunication ultimately seen as educative. These are devices clearly distinguished from the more drastic laws exercised by the state for the sake of order. But I don't think the Augustinian outlook is simply a two-kingdoms outlook either. I think there is a desire to minimize the more drastic coercion and indeed, as far as possible, to approximate even the rule of the state to a kind of pastoral model of rule, in which there is direct concern for the welfare of each individual. This pastoral model of rule seems to derive from the Orient and from Israel, rather than from Greece, and I think it is a very interesting aspect of our political legacy. So no, I certainly don't, obviously don't, think the church can have standing armies, and you always have to mark this point. The more things really matter, the more they are goods, then the less they need to be, or can be, defended (a point I learned from Rowan Williams). My only point was an attempt to nuance that a little by suggesting that we usually don't have direct access to those goods. The permanent abiding goods are often mediated by more fragile goods, and the two are thoroughly mixed up, if you like. This is why I don't think it is enough just to say the fragile goods don't matter, but nor is it good enough to overevaluate them in terms of trying to render immortal what is intrinsically not immortal. This is why I invoke Machiavelli at that point. But not to think that there are finite, fragile goods that sometimes might have to be defended with force, because otherwise they will disappear, seems to me to underrate the degree to which the Good itself is only going to be mediated and shown to us in those fragile goods. That is why I made a parallel between pacifism on one hand, and iconoclasm on the other. For to me it would not be an accident that pacifism tends to be espoused by churches that don't have very much to do with images.

Just a quick note on the just war: I still think that the liberal state might wage a just war against a totalitarian one. I think the Second World War was a just war.

Hauerwas: How you would evaluate World War II as a just war depends a lot on how you understand the relationship between noncombatant immunity and proportionality.

Milbank: Aspects of it clearly were not just. I'd agree with Bishop Bell's stance on saturation bombings, without question.

Hauerwas: If I may, let me summarize the strategy of my paper. Attempts like yours [Milbank's] to provide a kind of phenomenology of violence that begins from some presumption that we can make a clear distinction between violence and nonviolence is not where we pacifists begin. Some pacifists begin that way, but it is not where christological pacifism begins.

Milbank: That is what I thought. So you were not a direct target.

Hauerwas: But I want to be. [laughter]

Jacobs: You are trying to maneuver yourself into the line of fire. [laughter]

Hauerwas: But the idea would be that you can never close off the presumption as a pacifist that you may be involved in violence that you hadn't recognized. And so the pacifist must be committed to constant renegotiation about violence. The kind of analysis you give is part of the kind of consideration any pacifist would have to take quite seriously. In particular, the lovely way that you helped us see the spectatorial gaze can be as implicated, if not *more* implicated, in a violence than the actual enactment of violence. Though if I were the subject of a spectatorial gaze as opposed to an active gaze, I would prefer the spectatorial gaze, or at least living under such a gaze. So it depends on what perspective you are going to take on at that point.

Milbank: I wouldn't want to deny that. It is more that the spectatorial gaze, in order to fulfil itself as spectatorial, is going to demand actual violence in the end. That was the point.

Hauerwas: I quite understand that and the pacifist would have to take that very seriously. Pacifists make a mistake when they think that their primary job is to be not-violent. Peaceableness is a practice that must be more determinative than not-violence, because analogically you won't even know what violence is unless you are already experiencing the kinds of peaceableness that will allow you to name a violence that has seized you that otherwise you wouldn't have known. So I do not want to resist that analysis, but rather to ask, in terms of the spectatorial gaze, about this issue. We are in Lent, and our gaze is now being directed to the cross. How, if you are right, do we avoid being spectators? And was God—God's self—a spectator to the extent that the cross was a violence that Jesus had to accept? I am anxious to hear how the theological work can be done in terms of the actual gospel idiom in light of the analysis you gave.

Milbank: That is a very interesting question. I am resistant to the kind of trinitarian theologies that involve the Father gazing at the Son on the cross, and the Son gazing back at the Father. Because that seems to underrate the extent to which the Father is absolutely involved with what is happening on the cross, such that he is not really a spectator.

Hauerwas: Are we?

Milbank: Are we spectators? Not if we partake of the Eucharist. Isn't that the answer?

Hauerwas: That would be an answer I would give, I think. But if I am saved from being a spectator of the crucifixion by my participation in the Eucharist, and the Eucharist is where I am included graciously in God's very sacrifice for the world—God's sacrifice for the world surely is about freeing the world from the world's violence—then how can you ever get up from the eucharistic celebration and do violence? This seems to me to be on the outer limits. Because otherwise, as Richard Neuhaus once said to me as I was trying to kill him . . . [laughter]

Milbank: Stanley does *need* pacifism! You must always bear this in mind. [laughter]

Hauerwas: . . . there is nothing incompatible in Sandinistas and government forces getting up from the Eucharist, going to the side of the chapel, picking up their mutual AK-47s, and trying to blow one another away! Now I assume you don't want to be on Neuhaus's side on this.

Milbank: This is mean! Neuhaus supported guerrillas in Nicaragua? I can't quite believe that anyway.

Hauerwas: No, he was for the government.

Milbank: Oh, I see. No, it is completely wrong to get up from the Eucharist and go and shoot Sandinistas. You should be Sandinistas getting up and shooting the government! [laughter]

Jacobs: Now we are getting someplace.

Hauerwas: So there *are* good guys and bad guys! But does that in any way invalidate the peace of Christ that they have exchanged as part of the reconciliation, that is intrinsic to the eucharistic celebration itself? What will the world know? How will the world understand what the peace of Christ is?

Milbank: There are so many things to say here. Couldn't there be a certain danger of idolizing the peace of Christ, if you took it as identical with a particular mode of human behavior, which you could somehow define in a formalistic kind of fashion? In other words, you know, follow these procedures but not those other procedures. Presumably, the peace of Christ primarily is eschatological. It derives from God, from God's absolute power, and for certain it is saying, "Yes, absolute power is utterly peaceful," because it is in no way divided against itself.

Hauerwas: If you make that move, it seems to me *eschatology* is just another word for *ideal,* and as a result, the kingdom really isn't present.

Milbank: No, that can't be the case, because obviously, the church is in some measure an anticipation of the eschaton. Therefore, the church, certainly in itself, has to in some way embody peace. However, although I have said that you can call the ultimate good peace, and, inversely, you can call evil violence—because evil is negativity and therefore the very essence of violence is destruction—nonetheless when I talk about harmony, this presupposes that peace is also justice; this presupposes that everything is in its proper place, given its proper due. So I would worry if one used the word *peace* too often and never uttered the word *justice,* just as I would worry if one uttered the word *violence* too often and never uttered the word *injustice,* because again it belongs to the essence of violence, i.e., that it is injustice, that it is taking away from how things should be and therefore it is taking away from giving things their due. I think one ought to remember that once one is in the situation where the peace is being disturbed, there is also injustice, and obviously one wants neither of them. Nonetheless, one of the effects of evil is to create tensions between different aspects of the good. This is the dilemma. Indeed, the body of Christ, the peace of Christ is here shattered in this specific fashion. And the question of how you reconstitute it is full of difficulties, and I don't really understand why somebody who is going out to fight for justice—and is saying, "I have to, in these extreme circumstances, fight the people removing the conditions under which real peace would be possible"—is violating the exchange of peace in the Eucharist. I'm not sure I even see the point.

Hauerwas: One of the points would be that maybe you ought not to have the Eucharist at all in those contexts. Let the pope put them under interdiction and say that this society is so rent by hatreds and division that as long as these Christians are committed to killing one another, they should not be able to participate in the Eucharist.

Milbank: Well, yeah, but it seems as if you are somehow simply putting, shall we say, the Sandinistas and their opposers, the corrupt upholders of oligarchy in Nicaragua (and I am not trying to say that when the Sandinistas got to power they proved innocent, of course), on the same level and saying there is no more and less involved here. I understand the point you are making, but what about situations where Christians are involved in extreme injustice, which, as I say, is like a kind of slower violence, sometimes? Are we going to say the same thing then?

Hauerwas: Yes, absolutely, yes. But I do take comfort from 1 Corinthians 11. I assume that they eat and drink to their own damnation, which might be a reason to have the Eucharist. [laughter] I think it is clear that God is killing us in America because of our wealth, and that is coming directly from our Eucharist celebration. I mean, it is not a bad way to go. [laughter]

Milbank: Interdictions in the past have often been, as you know, exercised as instruments of power. And I think I'd probably lean more in the direction of suggesting that you never withhold the means of grace. It seems to me there could be a danger in this sort of reflection of imagining that—well, either that Eucharist exists to the way the community is, or else there could be a danger of saying, "Well, these people are misusing the Eucharist," as though the Eucharist was a worldly thing that could be misused . . .

Hauerwas: Right.

Milbank: . . . or could really be affected. Again, I think I would err much more in the direction of saying everybody should be given the Eucharist because you don't know what effects this would have. What would be the justification for withholding the Eucharist from some Nicaraguan old lady whose own narrative and biography matters just as much to God as do the foes in Nicaragua?

Hauerwas: The issue I am trying to press is really the eschatological nature of peace.

Milbank: Yes.

Hauerwas: And we believe that God has really made peace present. We have it and we wait for it exactly because we have received it.

Milbank: Yes.

Hauerwas: Now, and in that sense, that is the reason why again I say that I think you make a mistake when you say that peace is always of the end and not a virtue. I understand, and I have said, that you have Aquinas seemingly on your side on this, but I think that peace is a virtue, intrinsic to charity, and certainly, charity is a virtue.

Milbank: Yes.

Hauerwas: And since charity is a virtue, that embodies the peace we now receive. And this is the eschatological issue. Then it surely seems right to me for you to say, "Look, whatever the phenomenology of violence I have given here, Christians are rightly understood to be in their fundamental life peaceful." And that means, therefore, that we simply refuse to accept certain kinds of necessities of "What would you do if . . . ?"—where the "What would you do if . . . ?" presupposes that a people formed by peace does not exist in the world. They do exist; they are the church. That means that world is different in terms of not accepting the alternatives between violence and nonviolence just as a given.

Milbank: I didn't exactly say that peaceableness was not a virtue at all. I said that if it was, I thought it was perhaps a peculiarly collective virtue.

Hauerwas: Yes, I say that too.

Milbank: I didn't think you'd really disagree with that.

Hauerwas: As friendship is a virtue so friendship and peaceableness are mutually implicated. They are peculiarly communal virtues that are secondarily qualifications of passions. They are first and foremost activities. That means the very discovery of what violence may be does not lead to the further implication that I may sometimes have to use violence.

Milbank: I don't think I have any sort of problem with that. I would obviously affirm this notion that Christians are peaceable people, and they are trained in a different set of expectations so that, for example, the first response to a person trying to stab someone would be to get him to desist by saying the key persuasive thing. Which is exactly what Jesus did; he knew, somehow, how to say the right thing to make people desist. So that charity, if you like, is a great skill.

Hauerwas: Absolutely. Exactly right.

Milbank: And I would certainly want to look at it that way, and I think that the only difference between us is to do with the point where that kind of thing doesn't work and where you are faced with some kind of choice. I am trying to say that, in subtle ways, little ways, there are all kinds of resorts to violence that we might not even quite call by that name. I guess what you are saying in response to that is, "Well, yes, the pacifist knows that, but is always trying to get beyond that."

Hauerwas: Right, by being a part of a certain kind of community.

Milbank: Yes, and again, obviously I would want to endorse that, that you are trying to get beyond even mitigated violence. But at the same time, I would want to say that there can be situations where a resort to violence is not necessarily wrong. I mean, there is a sense in which violence in itself is always wrong, but there can be situations where one can feel that refraining from violence would be equally wrong or very likely actually more wrong.

Hauerwas: I don't know why I would want to imagine that. Why would I want, as someone schooled into the peaceableness of God's church, to invite that kind of imagination? Because just at the time I invite that kind of imagination, I become less than what God has made us to be in terms of forcing alternatives on me. I mean, pacifism is to force an alternative on me that I really probably don't like very much. And that is what I think salvation is. Salvation is always doing what I don't like very much. [laughter]

Milbank: Doesn't sound very eudaemonistic.

Hauerwas: Oh, no, you discover, retrospectively, you are happy, John. [laughter]

Milbank: Sounds a little like a cold bath! [laughter]

Jacobs: I want to take us in a particular direction. One of the things that complicates, for instance, our discussion of the Sandinistas, is that when they partake of the Eucharist they are participating in the life of the church. When they go pick up their rifles, then they are involved in the state in some way, and there are these overlapping commitments. I wonder if we could focus this issue to a certain degree by narrowing it to questions about the life of the church? I am thinking of a topic that has come up a couple of times in this conference: the need that parents have to exercise a kind of coercion over children, with the hope that at some point my son will realize that there was a good reason for me to insist that he wear his coat when it is thirty degrees outside. And that he will no longer see that as an act of cruelty or violence. And I think of a particular historical moment in which this was an issue in the church: in fifth-century North Africa when Augustine was confronted by the Donatists. He decides after a time that he must suppress the Donatists by the use of coercion, violence. And he says to the Donatists whom he is coercing, "Someday you will understand why I am doing this, and you will realize that this is not an act of cruelty or viciousness, but is, in fact, an act of charity that I am exhibiting toward you." So I would like to ask you, gentlemen, are there any circumstances in which you could say that Augustine was right to do this?

Milbank: Sure, I think there probably was. I think it is very hard for us to envisage these kinds of situations because we tend to think of them in terms of the contemporary church, faced with some kind of breakaway group, and it clearly would be unjustifiable today to make this sort of intervention. But I think that in Augustine's situation in Africa at the time, the church was much more the very focus of social order altogether and the kinds of questions at issue were completely different. Given those different circumstances, I doubt if it is for me to say that he was wrong. It is extremely difficult to discern this sort of thing. I mean, I am trying in a way to see what the actual nub of the issue here is. The classic example about children's education is to me very important, because I think it does raise the issue of something to do with living in time in the sense that we have certain people, like children for example, or other grownups, who are groping toward something, but they haven't quite got there yet. And I think in those situations, we do exert all kinds of subtle modes of coercion. Teachers do it. People put barriers and goads in people's way because there is something they cannot yet quite see, but which you know they are going to see. Of course, all this stuff is incredibly dangerous, but it also seems to me that it is in some way inevitable. And I am just not quite sure what Stanley is talking about, when he talks about being trained in the life of peaceableness and so on. What Christian tradition is he referring to? I usually think in terms of the mainline, creedal traditions, probably also in terms of churches that have the threefold order of ministry and churches that uphold the decisions of the ecumenical councils. That's my normative reference point.

Hauerwas: Lutherans and Catholics always agreed you ought to kill the Anabaptists.

Milbank: But the Lutherans don't have the threefold order of ministry.

Hauerwas: They only killed them unjustly. [laughter]

Milbank: Those are my normative points of reference if I am talking about Christian tradition. There has been inculcation of peaceableness, of charity, and justice, and mercy, and all these virtues, but this allowance for some measure of coercion has always been in the picture. I myself have tried to underline that this is much more of a tragic risk than the tradition has sometimes allowed. And I think that you have to see that this tragic risk is required because immature humanity was in some way being misled. So certainly, it is required only in a fallen world. But I just want to reiterate that I think one of the facts of fallenness and of evil is that it does tend to set up a conflict between different goods, different aspects of the Christian good, which really of course, all belong together. So written in that kind of situation, it does seem to me that you can still be pursuing peace and doing violence, because you may be trying to defend justice. And justice is just as *important* an aspect of peace as what one might describe as formally peaceful behavior.

And there is something in what Stanley says that I cannot quite get into clear focus. It is something to do with a kind of overrating of process and method that I somehow feel is after all modern.

Hauerwas: I have criticized John Yoder because sometimes I think John's language of the voluntary is overdetermined in modernity exactly because it puts too much stress on process separate from the material convictions that you want the process to serve. Oscar Wilde would say the problem with socialism and the Mennonites is too many meetings. And, of course, that is a kind of coercion in itself—too many meetings, that is. [laughter] But what I think is worrisome, John, about starting with an issue that begins by saying "If you don't wear your jacket, you don't get to go outside, because it is twenty degrees" is that before long you are saying, "We have to defend the Western world." Among people who want to use the kind of phenomenology of violence that you are insisting upon there has been that kind of slide. The reason why you need a community that will allow you to make the kinds of discriminations for which I am calling is so that the purposiveness is never lost. Of course, there are certain kinds of force and power being used, but power is not violent in and of itself.

Milbank: That is true.

Hauerwas: Therefore, if you make those kinds of discriminations, it seems to me that you are not going to be able to say, "On the whole, I am for peaceableness." That is like saying, "I promise to keep my wedding vows," with my fingers crossed. The problem with the fingers crossed is it invites me to look for exceptions down the road.

Jacobs: You have set up a kind of test there, which needs to be met. Do you think, for instance, that Augustine's behavior toward the Donatists met that test of keeping the purposiveness in mind?

Hauerwas: Actually, I think it does. What Augustine actually did—if Garry Wills is right in the lovely little biography that he did of Augustine—Augustine really went to extraordinary lengths to find reconciliation with the Donatists to avoid the violence. I did, John, in my talk, defend the Inquisition, because, of course, heresy is a worse sin than violence. And if you are concerned about the social order, and you want to love your brother and sister, you want them to be worshiping the right God. So if, as a matter of fact, heresy is the destruction of our salvation, then it is a very serious sin, which should be repressed if you can.

Jacobs: Worse than murder, he says.

Milbank: I am very confused now. [laughter]

Hauerwas: I was doing this as a thought experiment, John, which is a way to say that most of what Augustine did to the Donatists was done as Christians should do it. I think the calling forward—and I am going to be very careful here and not use the phrase "the state" because I don't think there was a "state"—that calling forward the officials to punish the Donatists in a manner that was extraecclesial was wrong. I think that was a mistake exactly because then you lost the call that you were making to the Donatists to come in. I defended, John, just as you did, excommunication and the ban, as the fundamental form of Christian punishment, because what excommunication names is really a call of hospitality. Excommunication says you are already out, so let us give you the conditions for coming home. Therefore, I think, excommunication of the Donatists would have been just what one would have wanted in terms of Augustine's behavior in that regard.

Let me move in a little different direction, John, to press another point that you made, with which I think I agree. John quite rightly indicated that charity has an order. And since we cannot love everyone charitably, Aquinas quite rightly saw that there was an order of charity that presupposed that you were to love those nearest to you, i.e., kin. He gave very specific accounts of that order—for example, if you as a son saw your family threatened, your first obligation was to save your father, because it was from your father that you had received life. Then you could save the mother, and then down the list you could save your children. Whether you agree or disagree with this kind of casuistical reflection, you need to do that kind of work to see what kinds of ways you need to think about protection. But it seems to me, then, the move you made is that we would normally protect our children rather than our father . . .

Milbank: And we have a duty to protect ourselves. Here I am worse than Ramsey. You must protect yourself, absolutely. Aquinas would say that.

Hauerwas: You must protect yourself insofar as the self names a role in a community of service that the community would be less without. So it is not a self-centered claim.

Milbank: No, it is not self-centered. I'm very worried about a complete over-riding of the animal instinct which ensures that if someone attacks you, you naturally defend yourself. Because nobody can look after you better than you, there is a sense in which you have first responsibility toward this little bit of being. It is not self-centered.

Hauerwas: I understand. But, John, I want to come back to my main point. I am a little worried about this move that you are making where you use the language of creation. Because it seems—God save me from accusing you of being a Calvinist . . . [laughter]

Milbank: Stanley always has some neat tricks!

Hauerwas: But the Calvinists always say to me and about Yoder, "Well, you guys just don't have an adequate doctrine of creation." By an adequate doctrine of creation, they mean that there have to be moral norms and moral responses that can be known *simpliciter,* separate from redemption. And if creation also is an eschatological concept that gains its intelligibility from God's eschatological rule from the beginning, there is no way then, it seems to me, that you can appeal to creation in terms that would separate the disciplining of our desires for survival from what we have learned through the cross and the resurrection. So, the appeal to those kinds of desires as having overriding status seems to me to be a problem for Christians, because such desires have been put under a different economy. Besides, you don't want to really agree with Bernard Williams.

Milbank: No, that was really just agreement at one point for the sake of a comparison. But there are points where the Christian may be happier with a sort of Nietzschean naturalism than with a kind of Kantianism. And you would go along with that as well.

Hauerwas: Absolutely.

Milbank: Nevertheless, I think your criticism may be partially right; but I certainly shouldn't give any account of created impulses outside of the context of how these are regarded in the light of cross and resurrection. But what the cross and resurrection do is exactly to restore the true created order (even if the christological instance exceeds this order).

Hauerwas: Right, right.

Milbank: Given that Adam in Paradise received grace and was directed toward the beatific vision and all that. But yes, I think I agree with you up to a certain point. I think it would be a good idea to insert some account of the way this orientation works in relation to the Gospels. Yet the Gospel injunctions do not obliterate the natural law of self-protection that we share with animals, even if for us what is to be protected is an animality directed toward a supernatural end, such that in certain circumstances the very meaning of "protection" is thereby drastically revised.

Hauerwas: Let me come back to the other point I was going to make. To be sure, I ought to protect my children as the order of charity, and I should do everything I can to save them from unjust death. But what if it is the case that saving them involved me in actions of violence that belied what I thought the child should live for? Is it not better for them to die than for me to engage in actions that would betray what I think they ought to live for?

Milbank: Well, for example, if you killed another child or caused another child's life to be taken instead of your own, it would be better for your child to die.

Hauerwas: Right. I could even give the idea that finally life is a matter of being protected from violence. I mean there are a lot worse things than death, John, even the death of our children.

Milbank: Yes, one can accept that. But usually, shall we say, killing the person who is taking an interesting life is probably going to be an accidental result of trying to stop it happening—that is to say, of pursing justice. This is an important point. I can't quite see why this sort of defensive action implicitly says, "Life can only be protected by violence." I mean, this is an anomalous action in an anomalous circumstance.

Hauerwas: The example is very persuasive. All I am trying to do is to thicken the example in a way that shows there is more at stake in any of these examples than just dying or living.

Milbank: I agree. If you are saying there are circumstances where it can be better to let the innocent die because life on earth is not the be-all or end-all of everything, then I completely agree. But at the same time, since the time we have on earth is the time of redemption—the time in which we can come to be redeemed—it is clearly not simply trivial and unimportant. The important thing in the end, of course, is going to be enjoyment of the beatific vision. But clearly we are led toward that through life on earth, and the destruction of life on earth is therefore not trivial.

Hauerwas: The object of the Christian is always to survive. I quite agree. We have an obligation to live. And the Christian is never willing to die too readily if for no other reason than that we don't want those who would kill us to bear that sin. So, it is a matter of charity to resist. There have to be forms of resistance. The question is, then, what *are* the forms of that resistance? Obviously, one of the forms of resistance was, for example, among the Anabaptists, to become farmers and to become part of Constantinian folk culture that gave their children protection. But as John Yoder always argued, just to the extent that you became that, you betrayed your witness to the world. And so you have to be in the world even if that means endangering your children. That must be the case if Christians are to be the kind of nonviolent witnesses that the world wants and needs.

Milbank: I agree with all that.

Hauerwas: I thought you would.

Jacobs: I want to ask one last question, and then we'll have a few minutes for questions. So if anybody wants to start lining up now, it would be a good time. This morning in Stanley's talk, he said that he was a little concerned that John was doing ontology when he should be thinking about following Jesus. And I am wondering whether we do have a clear distinction between doing ontology and following Jesus, or whether doing ontology can be one of the ways to follow Jesus. It was too provocative a comment for me not to ask John to say something about it, and then, I think, maybe Stanley will be able to qualify his statement.

Milbank: Yes, I am not sure whether this is an issue about emphasis or an issue about substance. If it is an issue about emphasis, then Stanley might be quite correct that I haven't said enough about following Jesus or haven't dealt enough with the narrative level of the Gospels or something along those lines. That might very well be true. These things are partly accidents of what one has come to write about and for what reasons. I would certainly be resistant—but you know, I think Stanley would agree—to the idea that one can have a purely narrative theology or a theology purely focused toward practice, which doesn't engage in any reflection on the, as it were, the "scene" within which the narrative is happening. The narratives were always asking questions about the context in which a narrative is situated.

Hauerwas: Right.

Milbank: I was thinking about *The Lord of the Rings* earlier. Tolkien engages to the point of madness in writing endless appendices about the world in which the story of his narratives is set. Of course, it goes on and on forever. But you know, there is a way in which you have to. There is going to be an issue about an ontology, and I suppose I have been concerned with the way in which the biblical legacy might modify Greek ontology. That is really the focus of my concern. Although it is true that I have been led, simply for empirical reasons, to think that sometimes we have almost exaggerated in recent years the gulf between the Bible and Platonism, or the Hebrew and the Hellenic legacy, and that the church fathers were actually more right about this than we may imagine. But that is just a kind of empirical matter. I am still concerned with producing an ontology that is thoroughly consonant with the Bible. Sometimes looking around when I am in America, I find lurking here an issue about whether one puts the weight on practice or on theory in some sense. You know, there is a sort of an American, possibly pragmatist bias, which supposes that if you want to ask about the truth of things you see what it leads to, you look toward the outcome.

Hauerwas: Which is a misunderstanding of pragmatism.

Milbank: It probably is. Certainly of Peirce it is a misunderstanding.

Hauerwas: And of James.

Milbank: Maybe even of James, I don't know. But all I would want to say, at that point, is that it seems to me that vision and practice are absolutely indissociable, because we don't fully understand what people are doing until we find out something about their vision. But nor do we fully understand people's vision until we find out what they are doing. You can't put the emphasis on one thing rather than the other. So, if I have gone on about ontology, it is not because I think it is the whole story.

Hauerwas: My point was only the same point you made against Girard. For you say Girard's satisfaction theory of the atonement—I guess it is debatable whether he had one—"only makes sense if they remind us that Jesus is significant *as* the way, the kingdom, *autobasileia.* One can rescue Girard's argument for Jesus' finality and divinity if one links it with the idea that the exemplary narratives of Jesus show us the 'shape,' and the concrete possibility, of nonviolent practice."[1]

Milbank: I see.

Hauerwas: Accordingly, "An abstract attachment to non-violence is therefore not enough—we need to practice this as a skill, and to learn its idiom. The idiom is built up in the Bible, and reaches its consummation in Jesus and the emergence of the Church."[2] That is a quote from you. And what I am saying is that I don't see you carrying that forward.

Milbank: Okay, so you want more reflection about concrete existence?

Hauerwas: Yeah. I just think if you are starting with phenomenology, you are going to end up by imposing an alternative on Christians that doesn't begin within the idiom of the Bible itself.

Milbank: I don't think I have said anything that would suggest that you wouldn't be beginning with the Bible and the tradition of reflection on the Bible. I certainly don't mean to have done that. I agree that there are more concrete exegetical tasks. Maybe they are better carried out by other people, I just don't know. But when I speak of "idiom," I mainly mean that it is "ineffable" and can *only* be performed in practice. (The honest unabashed theoretician is better than the writer about practice who *displaces actual* practice.)

Hauerwas: We are not going to read a *Politics of Jesus* from Milbank, in other words. Right?

Milbank: I guess not, but it is not to say that I don't think that it should be done. But I will say one thing, and that is that I do reflect a lot on the question of the relationship between ontology and time, and whether in any sense there can be something like an ontological revision, at least of finite structures of existence. And you will find that in my joint book with Catherine Pickstock about Aquinas [*Truth in Aquinas* (London and New York: Routledge, 2001)], we argue that Aquinas *does* think the incarnation brought about certain kinds of ontological revision.

Hauerwas: Absolutely.

Jacobs: I think at this time we need to deal with the concrete existence of people standing at the microphones.

First Questioner: I have a question concerning your [Hauerwas's] concept of community in relationship to pacifism. I basically agree with what you were saying, except the one little piece that bothers me, and that is the possibility of sainthood that does involve individual or personal witness within the community and one that should be imitated. So, if you could comment a little bit about that possibility, I would appreciate it. But second, on the issue of community and formation of Christians and discipleship, it seems to me that if Christians are going to engage in violence, to sort of go back to this Christian standing army issue that Stanley suggested as a thought experiment, then we have to be good enough at it in order to not do more damage and harm than the possible good that we would do. Which means we have to train in violence in order to use it effectively as a matter of Christian discipleship. Now I cannot in my own imagination understand how that can be compatible with Christ, with the life of discipleship, with the life of the Eucharist, Christian life. So those two questions.

Hauerwas: Christian tae kwon do. [laughter]

Milbank: Well, I've already dismissed your Christian standing army. But as to Christians training for war, do you have the same problem with Christian capitalists? Isn't it a bit strange that a lot of people are saying this sort of thing now when probably most people are not going to get anywhere near war, or there won't be any pressure on them to be a soldier? Wow, suddenly you're discovering this is wrong. And you are not looking at certain moral ambiguities much closer to home, it seems to me.

First Questioner: There certainly are all sorts of ambiguities. I think it is impossible to avoid participation in violence in the larger way that you are talking about it. But the issue becomes, do we actively and intentionally use violence to attempt to achieve certain kinds of ends?

Milbank: Certainly not. Because it would be difficult for me to think how one could train someone intentionally to be a Christian capitalist as well.

Hauerwas: But there is an important distinction, as Yoder thinks, between the police function and the war function; it might be possible to train police in a way that they do not have to carry guns to do their job well within our communities. They would be trained to intervene in violence.

Milbank: There is a funny little island that has been doing that for a long time. [laughter]

Hauerwas: I know. Less and less.

Milbank: I'm afraid so. But even so, most policemen on the beat don't have guns.

Jacobs: Let's take a second question here.

Second Questioner: Thank you both. This is a related question. I was troubled a bit by your response to the example of the stoning of the woman caught in adultery. Some years ago, Clint Eastwood was described by someone as playing in his films the American ideal of the male: he will be patient with you and even polite up to a point, but if you push him too far, he will blow your head off. It sounded to me an awful lot like that was what you were advocating in summation. And I want to know if Christians are called to a different way than that American ideal. What does it look like?

Milbank: Yes, they are. They are not called to reach for their guns as the first move. Clearly, if we are following Jesus, the first response is somehow to hit on the right word that is going to stop this person doing it. But, if you are not a pacifist, then I was asking what do you do when this man is really crazed and really persisting, really is throwing stones at this woman. You probably don't even think, actually. And the fact that you don't even think but try to put him out of action is significant. A kind of training that is going to somehow root out that human animality from us, I am suspicious of, really.

Third Questioner: John, it seemed like the decisive argument against pacifism in your presentation was that the pacifist aphoretic was essentially counterintuitive. And as you said, those intuitions are not fallen but correct. Now Stanley has already addressed that a bit, because it sounds like that was a sort of naturalizing of the supernatural. My question is twofold: One, now that you have seemed to have conceded that point to Stanley, would you take that back at this point and say pacifism is not counterintuitive? And if not, doesn't that make Jesus' response to Peter in the garden—which I think we have to repeat at some point, at least Tertullian told us we did when he said, "No more of this"—doesn't that make Jesus' actions immoral and shouldn't Jesus have said to Peter, "Save me first, and if you can save the other twelve disciples, do that. I am making a run for it"?

Milbank: No.

Third Questioner: I am just wondering if you are willing to concede that pacifism is in fact only counterintuitive if you have some kind of grace-perfects-nature account where nature is self-evident.

Milbank: I never intended originally to separate off nature from grace, or a natural from a supernatural end. It is simply that I don't think that grace operates by canceling out animality; it doesn't operate by turning us into angels, into purely spiritual beings: "In my flesh will I see God." And so my concession to Stanley was merely saying I needed to configure this more explicitly in terms of the gospel. But, I didn't mean by that, to say that I thought it would change my substantive position, which was something to do with this demeanor of pacifism being in the "turning away" versus "looking at" situation. It is not so clear to me what examples there are in the Gospel accounts on which all this could actually turn, because we don't have presented there precisely these sorts of situations. Yes, Peter reacts aggressively, and is rebuked by Jesus, and told not to carry on. Maybe because Peter hasn't read the situation properly, whereas Jesus knows what the situation is. Reading off from these kind of stories general injunctions to nonviolence seems to me often to overlook their very specific kind of situatedness that Jesus is seeing correctly: He has to make a stand in Jerusalem for the truth; resistance is not what is required here. We know there is a point in the Gospels where he tells the disciples to take up swords; there are certain times where one response is right, and others where another response is right (more so, I think, than we sometimes like to imagine). It is clearly the case, however, that in general Jesus is suggesting a "turn the other cheek" strategy, and I suppose one way of looking at this is to say that he is asking us to augment that part of our nature that is naturally generous. Although, certainly, that does involve suspending one's reaction of irritation, and it certainly also suggests a kind of deflating of the action of the person assaulting us; I do think there are very difficult issues of interpretation here. You do have to point out, yes, it is this specific example of somebody taking your cloak. Jesus never says, "If somebody stabs you with a sword, expose yourself even more." Again, building a general rule on something like a parable or a short phrase is extremely perilous. These things clearly have to be interpreted, and the interpretation of them is not going to be all that easy. And I can't see that there is, at least to begin with, any real tradition of an actually decisively pacifist understanding of these things. Indeed, the point for me, I suppose, would be that the responses involved in the Gospel examples—like giving another your cloak as well, etc.—are not *passive,* they do involve actually doing something. They don't involve either just gazing or just turning away.

AFTERWORD

ALAN JACOBS

1.

One of the consequences of the events of September 11, 2001, has been the renewal of an old set of arguments about the relationship between religion and violence. Since the perpetrators of the terrorist acts were Muslims, one might think that Christianity would not enter directly into these conversations, but in fact Christianity has often been implicated in the events by those who see a similar underlying logic to the two faiths. The claim that "religion," or some particular religion, is somehow the cause, or at least the chief provocation, of grossly violent acts is not a new one; indeed, each of the chief versions of this claim has a long ancestry. For those Christians who wish to understand why their beliefs have come under such criticism, and to evaluate the justice of the complaints against them, it might be useful to delineate these chief versions, as they have reemerged in the aftermath of September 11.

A. Islam in particular is a religion that endorses violence. This has been heard little in recent months except from some conservative Christians. I take the absence of this argument to stem from a refusal to generalize about a faith held by millions because of the actions of a very few; it is interesting and to me rather touching that arguments about whether Islam is intrinsically violent have been far less visible in the aftermath of 9/11 than they were when Islam first came to the attention of the whole American public, when Iran took its hostages in the American embassy in Tehran in November 1979. It's in keeping with the mood and concerns of that time that a popular guide, Thomas W. Lippman's *Understanding Islam* (the first edition of which appeared in 1982), raises the question of whether Islam is intrinsically violent on the first page of its introduction. Lippman says that "the belief that Islam promotes violence" is "at best a half-truth."[1] It's not likely that he would go even that far today, in our more culturally sensitive age.

Though such "cultural sensitivity," it should be noted, is not the invention of the late twentieth century. In the eighteenth century Edward Gibbon, that vigorous opponent of Christianity, saw Islam as a far more attractive alternative. This was so in theory: "More pure than the system of Zoroaster, more liberal than the law of Moses, the religion of Mahomet might seem less inconsistent with reason than the creed of mystery and superstition which, in the seventh century, disgraced the simplicity of the gospel." And also in practice: "The wars of the Moslems were sanctified by the prophet; but, among the various precepts and examples of his life, the caliphs selected the lessons of toleration that might tend to disarm the resistance of the unbelievers."[2]

B. The "Abrahamic religions" (a phrase that in the aftermath of 9/11 zoomed from obscurity to near-ubiquity) are *all* intrinsically violent, violent from their origins. After all, do we not associate Abraham himself most vividly with his willingness, at least, to perform the ultimate act of violence upon his own son, at God's command? And are we not moved to wonder at a God who would ask such a thing of Abraham—and perhaps wonder even more at a God who would but *appear* to ask such a thing, who would trick Abraham in that way? In *Fear and Trembling,* Kierkegaard famously raised the key problems about God that arise from this situation. He first asks, "Is there such a thing as the teleological suspension of the ethical?"—by which he means, can we ever be justified in performing an act that seems to be thoroughly immoral if we do so because we believe some greater end *(telos)* to be at stake? But in considering this question, we might try to understand what *telos* could possibly outweigh the moral prohibition against killing one's child; which leads Kierkegaard to his next question: "Is there such a thing as an absolute duty toward God?"[3]

That the God of Abraham would *demand* "absolute" obedience is for many precisely the stumbling block. One of the more noteworthy recent attempts to identify and describe this problem is Regina Schwartz's much-praised *The Curse of Cain.*[4] For Schwartz, the frightening absolutism of the God of Israel's demands is evident almost from the beginning of the biblical narrative, when his refusal to accept Cain's sacrifice leads to Cain's murder of his brother. For Schwartz, God's inexplicable rigor—inexplicable to her, at any rate[5]—*produces* a violent act, one that God responds to, in the curse pronounced upon Cain and his descendants, with a different kind of violence: the violence of banishment, exclusion. What Freud might call the primal scene of violence, here at the beginning of the Bible, generates, by a kind of inexorable logic, future violences performed in the name of monotheistic fidelity. Given such an origin, the "Abrahamic religions" cannot help being violent; they are initiated and circumscribed by acts of coercive force. Thus the reply of the journalist Christopher Hitchens when a reader of the *Independent* of London asked him, "What do you consider to be the 'axis of evil'?": "Christianity, Judaism, Islam—the three leading monotheisms."[6]

Of course, many will argue that other religions are as violent as, or more violent than, the Abrahamic ones. In *People of the Book*, for instance, David Lyle Jeffrey provides a brief but harrowing survey of certain cultural practices of pre-Christian Northern Europe, in order to show the kinds of violence that

Christianity delivered many cultures from.[7] But such arguments are uncompelling to some scholars: to take but one example, Rosemary Radford Ruether, in a recent article, wants to distinguish between kinds of religious violence, the "tragic violence" of Aztec human sacrifice versus the "righteous violence" common in the Christian church and best exemplified by the Spanish Inquisition. Radford Ruether admits that Aztec religion involved "the cutting of the breast of the victim to offer the palpitating heart to the gods, the flaying of victims so priests could ceremonially don their skin"; on the other hand, she points out, "the root of this spirituality was a sense of human life and the life of the cosmos as fragile, vulnerable and sustained only through an exchange of life forces between humans and the gods." Plus, "the sacrificed ones of Aztec society were seen by the Aztecs as ascending to the heavens, becoming gods." (It is not clear whether Radford Ruether thinks that it would be less painful to have your heart ripped from your chest and held still beating before your eyes if you had previously been told that you were soon going to ascend to the heavens and assume divine status.) Finally, "Mesoamerican culture was not without ambivalence toward human sacrifice." In all these ways, Radford Ruether implies, "the spirituality of giving life to sustain the life of the world" is to be contrasted with the Spanish Christians' "spirituality of punishing evil to vindicate God." She ends her article with a pair of questions—"Which [of these two spiritualities] is finally more dangerous? Which is finally more 'redeemable'?"—because the answers to them are, to her, so obvious.[8]

C. Religious belief in general, because of the universality of its claims and its insistence on the ultimate consequentiality of belief or unbelief, tends to make its believers feel threatened by alternative beliefs or nonbeliefs, and people respond to such perceived threats with violence. (Presumably such critics would be unmoved by Radford Ruether's distinctions between kinds of violence.) In its twentieth-century form, this argument tends to treat powerful political or social commitments, like those associated with communism or Germany's national socialism, as in effect religious. A modern *locus classicus* for this position is E. M. Forster's essay "What I Believe," which begins in this way:

> I do not believe in Belief. But this is an age of faith, and there are so many militant creeds that, in self-defence, one has to formulate a creed of one's own. . . . Faith, to my mind, is a stiffening process, a sort of mental starch, which ought to be applied as sparingly as possible. I dislike the stuff. I do not believe in it, for its own sake at all. Herein I probably differ from most people, who believe in Belief, and are only sorry they cannot swallow even more than they do. My law-givers are Erasmus and Montaigne, not Moses and St. Paul. . . . My motto is: "Lord, I disbelieve—help thou my unbelief."
>
> I have, however, to live in an Age of Faith—the sort of epoch I used to hear praised when I was a boy. It is extremely unpleasant really. It is bloody in every sense of the word.[9]

Forster begins the last paragraph of his essay by writing, "So that is what I feel about force and violence"—thus cementing the link between belief and "force and violence."

Many prominent thinkers today (Richard Rorty is notable among them) hold to some version of Forster's position. Indeed, this seems to be Regina Schwartz's actual position, as opposed to the antimonotheistic one she articulates in *The Curse of Cain*. In an interview posted on the Web site of her publisher, the University of Chicago Press, Schwartz modifies the argument of her book in interesting ways. To an inevitable question—"But isn't there violence in cultures that are not monotheistic?"—Schwartz replies, "The issue I am focusing on is the price of imagining collective identity under one principle and banishing the rest—it doesn't have to be one god, it can be one nation, one kinship group, one territory. . . . The issue, to be precise, is not one versus many gods, but one defining principle versus many principles."[10] As far as I can see, this is indistinguishable from Forster's position, or Rorty's, which is that a kind of ad hoc pluralism is more humane and less dangerous than the commitment to any person or principle or institution that requires "absolute duty"; but, if this represents Schwartz's true thinking, then the subtitle of her book (and indeed the whole book itself) is rather misleading, for the problem is not "the violent legacy of monotheism," but rather "the violent legacy of any absolute principle," or "the violent legacy of belief."

In any case, the general theme itself is clear: one person's, or one culture's, absolute commitment to one source of authority endangers people and societies who do not share that commitment. On this account, violence is the natural outgrowth of passionate conviction.

D. Religions that promise life after death "devalue human life" and make people more willing to inflict and to suffer deadly violence. This is the argument made by Richard Dawkins just a few days after the September 11th disasters.[11] (One would like to believe that Dawkins was writing intemperately because he was moved by what he himself calls "deep grief and fierce anger," but his comments are perfectly consistent with what he has written about religious belief for years and years.) Dawkins's key claim is that "religion" is "a ready-made system of mind-control which has been honed over centuries, handed down through generations"; its teaching about the afterlife is the perfect technique for convincing young men to die, and kill others, for a cause:

> If death is final, a rational agent can be expected to value his life highly and be reluctant to risk it. This makes the world a safer place, just as a plane is safer if its hijacker wants to survive. At the other extreme, if a significant number of people convince themselves, or are convinced by their priests, that a martyr's death is equivalent to pressing the hyperspace button and zooming through a wormhole to another universe, it can make the world a very dangerous place. Especially if they also believe that that other universe is a paradisiacal escape from the tribulations of the real world.

In brief, "Religion teaches the dangerous nonsense that death is not the end." Dawkins is immensely frustrated that so obvious a point would not gain universal, or at least widespread, recognition: "I am trying to call attention to the elephant in the room that everybody is too polite—or too devout—to notice: religion, and specifically the devaluing effect that religion has on human life. . . . To fill a world with religion, or religions of the Abrahamic kind, is like littering the streets with loaded guns. Do not be surprised if they are used."

E. All of the above problems are linked to, or exacerbated by, the "irrational" character of religious belief. Again and again commentators have suggested that people who *believe* irrational things will also *perform* irrational acts. This is a commonplace of the critique of religion at least as far back as Voltaire, in whose *Candide* (for example) the people who hold rational beliefs—and, even more important, have developed the capacity to see when the evidence is lacking for well-founded beliefs, and therefore maintain a healthy skepticism toward comprehensive explanatory structures—are the most peaceable and most generally virtuous. No highbrow quotation has been bandied about more in the months since 9/11 than Voltaire's aphorism: "Those who can make us believe absurdities can make us commit atrocities."[12]

2.

It is tempting to respond to such claims—all of them have logical holes in them large enough to drive the proverbial truck through—and indeed in describing them I have not been able to refrain from pointing to some of those chasms. But the claims and counterclaims have been going on for several centuries now, and it's not clear to me that another round of exchanges would be useful, at least not in this context. Instead, I wish to focus on two issues; first, what people mean by "causation" in this matter—for instance, when they say that religion "causes" violence or is the "source" of violence—and why the search for a cause has historically been so important; and second, what "violence" *is*—or, more specifically, what it has become in the aftermath of Michel Foucault's work—and why in this intellectual climate it seems impossible to have a nuanced and useful discussion about it.

Causation, then. It is interesting in this context to note that Richard Dawkins has no hesitation about saying that "Religion is . . . , of course, the underlying source of the divisiveness in the Middle East which motivated the use of this deadly weapon in the first place." Not *a* source, not even the *major* source, but, simply, *the* source of the Middle East's problems. The kind of crudely universal explanatory tool that Voltaire heaps scorn on is precisely what Dawkins uses here. To respond to the great Lisbon earthquake by saying that "all is for the best in this best of all possible worlds," or to say that this amorphous entity called "religion" is "the underlying source of the divisiveness in the Middle East"—really, what is the difference? Both statements are equally vague, equally coarse, and equally useless. It is impossible even to tell what Dawkins *means* by "religion." Which raises the question, Why does someone as intelligent as Dawkins make such ready recourse to so obviously limited an instrument of understanding? Similarly, does Regina Schwartz really believe that, were the Hebrew Scriptures to say that God thought Cain's sacrifice was perfectly acceptable, and that the children of Esau were heirs of the promise as much as those of Jacob, ethnic and cultural competition for land and natural resources in the Middle East would have been eclipsed by a spirit of cooperation?

One force at work here, especially in the thought of scholars in the humanities, like Schwartz, is a belief in the linguistic malleability of the world: in the social and political powers of redescription. It is the belief that ideology is a greater force than nature, and that if the foundational texts of an ideological sphere could be revised or replaced, the whole world would be changed. (Most people who hold this view do not think that such redescriptive tasks are simple or could produce immediate results; but they do believe that in the long run redescription *works* to change our world.) Here again Rorty is a key figure: the idea that intellectual change is brought about not by defeating one's opponents through the use of clearly defined and universally accepted dialectical methods, but rather by "changing the subject," by redescribing (in a literary and rhetorical way) the situation, is probably his most important and influential idea. In a debate with Umberto Eco, Rorty went so far as to suggest that we are perfectly free to "redescribe" a screwdriver not only as (say) a tool for opening a parcel but even as an ear-scratching implement. Eco's reply is both very funny and very much to the point:

> A screwdriver can serve also to open a parcel (given that it is an instrument with a cutting point, easy to use in order to exert force on something resistant); but it is inadvisable to use it for rummaging about in your ear precisely because it is sharp and too long to allow the hand to control the action required for such a delicate operation; and so it would be better to use not a screwdriver but a light stick with a wad of cotton at its tip.

Therefore, Eco concludes, "there is something in the conformation both of my body and the screwdriver that prevents me from interpreting the latter at my whim."[13]

My point is simply that a belief in the "redescriptibility" of the world can generate the sequent belief that even so universally conspicuous a problem as violence is the product of inadequate description, and can be made to disappear, or at least can be greatly mitigated, through rhetorical adjustment. In this account of the prevalence of violence, neither what Christians call "fallen human nature," nor the Darwinian argument that violent tendencies have been selected by nature for their adaptive qualities, nor such mundane concerns as scarcity of desirable resources need be invoked. Indeed, Schwartz critiques at length the *language* of scarcity of resources in the Bible, without ever asking whether— in what is after all one of the less richly hospitable environments in which humans live—scarcity might sometimes be a *fact of life.* For people like Schwartz, religion is primarily a set of *words,* words that produce ideological convictions that in turn produce behavior; if the words are changed, then so too will change the convictions, and in the end the (violent) behavior. Causation, in this model, is a function of language.

It would seem highly unlikely, if not impossible, that Richard Dawkins should make a case for the power of religion to generate violence that at all resembled Schwartz's. After all, Dawkins is one of the more famous proponents of the view that natural selection is the overwhelmingly dominant explanation for the genetic makeup of all currently existing organisms: he is what Niles Eldredge calls an "ultra-Darwinian," or, in Stephen Jay Gould's more overtly contemptuous phrase, a "Darwinian fundamentalist."[14] His writings, along with those of the philosopher Daniel Dennett, have been key intellectual supports for the movement generally known as "evolutionary psychology" (and its immediate ancestor sociobiology, of which Dawkins has long declared himself an adherent). Surely Dawkins would be bound to offer an explanation for both religion and violence that linked their prevalence in some way to natural selection.

Yet Dawkins's argument is essentially identical to Schwartz's: violence is the product of religious ideology:

> Could we get some otherwise normal humans and somehow persuade them that they are not going to die as a consequence of flying a plane smack into a skyscraper? If only! Nobody is that stupid, but how about this—it's a long shot, but it just might work. Given that they are certainly going to die, couldn't we sucker them into believing that they are going to come to life again afterwards? Don't be daft! No, listen, it might work. Offer them a fast track to a Great Oasis in the Sky, cooled by everlasting fountains. Harps and wings wouldn't appeal to the sort of young men we need, so tell them there's a special martyr's reward of 72 virgin brides, guaranteed eager and exclusive.
>
> Would they fall for it? Yes, testosterone-sodden young men too unattractive to get a woman in this world might be desperate enough to go for 72 private virgins in the next.
>
> It's a tall story, but worth a try. You'd have to get them young, though. Feed them a complete and self-consistent background mythology to make the big lie sound plausible when it comes. Give them a holy book and make them learn it by heart.

This is Dawkins the village atheist talking, not Dawkins the scientist. Perhaps this particular passage can be excused by Dawkins's understandable anger and grief over the destruction of human life, but he offers no other explanation. In the end, Dawkins can but *assert* that religion is the sole cause of this violence; and, to the obvious question of why religion itself is so prevalent—he admits that "most people fall for it"—he can but mournfully hope that "one day we may understand" the reasons for this strange phenomenon. (His usual speculation—and here he is in agreement with his frequent rival, Gould—is that we find the contemplation of *pattern* irresistible, and can't resist imbuing pattern with meaning.)[15]

There are scientists (mostly in the sociobiological or evolutionary-psychology tradition) who have sought to offer accounts of religious belief that would explain *why* nature might select for faith, but Dawkins isn't one of them.[16] Following Dawkins's own habit of speculating on why people believe what they believe, I would guess that his reluctance to offer evolutionary explanations for religious faith is that such explanations make the project of eliminating religious faith highly improbable; indeed, if possible at all, only possible in the very long term (especially given Dawkins's commitment to evolutionary gradualism). This is a conclusion no one would willingly come to who believes that religious belief is destructive and wishes to see it eliminated. For Dawkins, therefore, it is more hopeful to treat religion as an ideology than as an evolutionary adaptation: otherwise there is no foreseeable end to the violence we perpetrate on one another.

Indeed, the whole notion of religion as the cause or source of violence is, I believe, a function of the desire to believe that violence is eliminable. Redescription is a hell of a lot faster than evolution, and is wholly within human control. It is highly uncomfortable even for committed Darwinians to see human violence in the same way they see violence elsewhere in nature. About the "macabre habits" of digger wasps Dawkins can be quite stern:

> This sounds savagely cruel but . . . nature is not cruel, only piteously indifferent. This is one of the hardest lessons for humans to learn. We cannot admit that things might be neither good nor evil, neither cruel nor kind, but simply callous—indifferent to all suffering, lacking all purpose.[17]

But he doesn't sound this note when contemplating the twisted, smoldering wreckage of the World Trade Center. Dawkins, like all reasonably decent people, has a great investment in believing that human violence is remediable. It is a pity, then, that his most deeply held convictions give him no warrant whatsoever for thinking that such a remedy is possible.

3.

The kind of violence that Dawkins writes about is straightforwardly physical: it is the infliction of pain and damage upon bodies. Schwartz too writes of physical violence, but throughout her book suggests that forms of ideological or psychological violence are perhaps equally dangerous and lamentable. This extension of the term "violence" to cover a wide range of deplorable acts is a relatively recent phenomenon, I believe, and one that deserves serious consideration from Christians: for Christianity—more than either of the other two "Abrahamic" faiths and, I believe, more than any of the world's major religions—is susceptible to the charge that it is intrinsically violent in certain non-physical ways.

In his extraordinarily useful book *Keywords* Raymond Williams outlines seven historically important meanings for the word "violence":

1. "physical assault"
2. "the use of physical force, including the distant use of weapons or bombs"
3. "as in 'violence on television,' which can include the reporting of violent physical events but indicates mainly the dramatic portrayal of such events"
4. "violence as threat"
5. "violence as unruly behavior"
6. "as in 'violently in love'"
7. "to be done violence to—to be wrenched from its meaning or significance"[18]

But in 1975—the year before the first edition of *Keywords* was published—a book appeared in France that would ultimately have a transformative influence on the American academy's discourse about violence: Michel Foucault's *Surveiller et Punir,* translated two years later as *Discipline and Punish.*[19] Gerald Graff tells a wonderful anecdote that encapsulates the logic of Foucault's book and its difference from the set of meanings Williams identifies:

> A friend of mine once remarked that on reading the opening pages of *Discipline and Punish,* an account of a hideous feudal-style drawing-and-quartering, he almost threw up. "Then I read further," he said, "and realized that for Foucault those had been the *good old days.*"[20]

Why were they the good old days? Because in the medieval world, argues Foucault, the techniques of discipline and social control were so rudimentary that they could but inflict pain on those who had already violated the social codes, rules, and laws. Subsequent centuries would achieve increasingly sophisticated techniques of *discipline*—discipline that would *train* bodies to behave in ways so thoroughly controlled that no after-the-fact punishments would be necessary; and in the twentieth century would come techniques (chiefly deriving from modern psychological therapy) that would make people *self*-disciplining and *self*-policing. This internalization of discipline is, for Foucault, deeply insidious. The medieval methods of punishment were straightforwardly coercive; their violence could not be hidden; but contemporary disciplinary structures have people controlling themselves under the illusion of self-help and self-empowerment. This constitutes *secret* violence, a violence that can be experienced unwittingly—something rather different from any of the meanings Williams managed to identify.

On this read of things, the essence of violence is coercion and control; and physical destructiveness stands to such coercion in something like an inverse relationship. One's will is most thoroughly coerced and one's body most completely controlled when one "voluntarily" participates in a social practice or organization. The strictest construction of Foucault's argument would suggest, then, that the Inquisition's *auto-da-fé* is *less* coercive than the contemporary American "seeker service." For some approving readers of Foucault, such a conclusion constitutes a reductio ad absurdum of his argument; for others, it's the illuminating culmination of Foucault's historical logic. But even if one takes the less stringent view, and opines that inviting people to attend a seeker service is rather less coercive than burning them at the stake, it is easy to see how Foucault's argument lends itself to a thorough critique of a proselytizing religion like Christianity. *Persuasion* is at the heart of Christian evangelism, especially, and Foucault's work in *Discipline and Punish* has the effect of blurring the lines between persuasion and coercion.

And it is not only Foucault who accomplishes this blurring: there are homegrown American traditions that have the same effect. In one of his legal essays, for instance, Stanley Fish lists a series of ways in which political disputes can be resolved, concluding with this item: "or by the intervention of an armed force." Reflecting on this list, Fish notes that

> only the last is usually given the name "force," but . . . the other actions are but softened versions of the last, instances of what [Oliver Wendell] Holmes refers to as the mitigation of "good manners." . . . Force, in short, comes in hard and soft versions.[21]

Similarly, in an earlier essay Fish had responded to certain legal theorists' emphasis on the importance of following procedure—on the grounds that a common commitment to procedure helps societies avoid recourse to violence—with a series of pointed questions:

> Could it not be said that procedure rather than doing away with force merely masks it by attenuating it, by placing it behind a screen or series of screens? After all, the crucial question . . . still has to be asked: Who gets to make the rules? And once that question is answered, another question (it is really the same) waits behind it, who gets to say who gets to make the rules? If the answer to these questions turns out to be something like "whoever seizes the opportunity and makes it stick," [and for Fish this always *is* the answer] then there is finally little to distinguish the rule-centered legal system from the actions of the gunman: this gunman is merely better camouflaged. . . . [Indeed,] here is a forceful capture even more sinister than that performed by the gunman because it wears the face of legitimate authority.[22]

This claim about the "camouflaged gunman" of liberal procedural rationality is simply a wittier version of Foucault's argument in *Discipline and Punish,* and, like Foucault's argument, if accepted it is bad news for Christianity. To anyone persuaded by this account of the hidden force of persuasion, Christianity certainly is intrinsically violent, and in its apparently gentle and peaceful modern forms more dangerous to the unwary unbeliever than the flames of the Inquisition were to the bold heretic: after all, the *auto-da-fé* only burns the body, while the stratagems of evangelism capture the will.

In my view (of course) the argument is deeply flawed, and in at least two ways. First of all, we know that people routinely refuse invitations to church and turn away unmoved from televised evangelistic crusades—just as all sorts of people manage to refrain from ordering Big Macs or purchasing large-screen TVs; conversely, *no one* walks away unharmed from being drawn and quartered or burned at the stake. (It's odd to have to say this, but the current situation apparently requires it.) Persuasion simply is *not* force, and this can be clearly illustrated by the frequency with which people resist it. That is, after all, what makes force force, violence violence: irresistibility. We do not increase our understanding of the world by doing away with the distinction between irresistible acts of force and eminently resistible words of suasion.

If the argument is therefore empirically flawed, it is also conceptually deficient, because it singles out certain powers in the world and identifies them as exerting coercive pressure on the human will while ignoring many other powers that act in the same way. The *effect* of Foucault's and Fish's arguments is to treat the human will as though it would be free were it not for the lamentable violences of law or religion or what Foucault calls "the Norm" (though neither Foucault nor Fish would, I presume, accept such an idea if it were put to them directly). In fact, *many* ideologically driven forces act upon us every day, seeking our approval, our investment, our obedience. What makes our lives complicated, in this regard, is that these forces are not unanimous: they pull us in different directions. A person who ends up at church on Sunday may have come very close to spending the morning with the *New York Times* and a latte from Starbucks—or spending it in a pornography shop. Each of these social institutions holds as an implicit motto the words of Jesus: "Compel people to come in" (Luke 14:23). But because their suasive powers are resistible, and because they represent mutually exclusive opportunities, at least at any given time, they fail of actual compulsive force. (The "brainwashing" techniques of many religious cults derive from a shrewd recognition of this problem: cults win and keep converts by eliminating from a prospective candidate's intellectual, perceptual, and moral world all the influences that might counter the influence of the cult itself.) The critic who lumps together violence and persuasion in one undifferentiated mass leaves himself or herself unable even to *begin* the task of understanding why different people are "compelled" by different opportunities, why options that some people find themselves helpless to reject are wholly unattractive to others, why some people are highly vulnerable to persuasive strategies that positively repel others.

In this light we can see how the argument that proselytizing religions are intrinsically violent resembles the argument that religion is the cause or source of violence. Both emerge from the scramble to offer simple solutions to immense and apparently intractable problems. They are deeply *reductive* arguments, and reductive arguments, I believe, tend to result from impatience or fear. The pervasiveness of violence in our world prompts both: impatience to "solve" the "problem," to put an end to violence; and fear lest we are unable to find a solution, so that violence persists or even escalates and spreads. If we can convince ourselves that religion not only causes physical violence but is also intrinsically coercive, even when it appears most peaceable, then we have both an explanation and a mandate: an explanation of the mess that our world is in, and a mandate to fix it by eliminating the cause. On just these grounds Voltaire formulated his motto: "Écrasez l'Infâme!"—crush the infamous one, the "infamous one" being Christianity. The essays in this book constitute a refutation of Voltaire—not, let me hasten to add, a refutation of the charge that Christians have often, and in the name of their faith, been culpably and shamefully violent. Rather, these essays collectively repudiate any simplistic explanation of violence and, at the same time, deny the legitimacy of the mandate to "crush" Christianity. It would be a good thing if some of our Voltaires would pay attention.

CONTRIBUTORS

Victoria Barnett, M.Div., is a scholar on the history of the churches during the Holocaust. She has been a consultant to the Church Relations Department of the United States Holocaust Memorial Museum in Washington, D.C., since 1994, and is associate editor of the Dietrich Bonhoeffer Works translation series (Fortress Press).

Kenneth R. Chase, Ph.D., is Associate Professor of Communication and Director of the Center for Applied Christian Ethics at Wheaton College (Illinois).

David P. Gushee, Ph.D., is Graves Professor of Moral Philosophy and Senior Fellow of the Center for Christian Leadership at Union University, Jackson, Tennessee.

Stanley Hauerwas, Ph.D., is Gilbert T. Rowe Professor of Theological Ethics at the Divinity School of Duke University.

Alan Jacobs, Ph.D., is Professor of English and Coordinator of the Faith and Learning Program at Wheaton College (Illinois).

James C. Juhnke, Ph.D., is Codirector of the Oral History Institute and Professor Emeritus of History at Bethel College, North Newton, Kansas.

Joseph H. Lynch, Ph.D., is Distinguished University Professor and Engle Professor of the History of Chrishanity at at Ohio State University.

Dan McKanan, Ph.D., is Assistant Professor teaching church history at St. John's University and the College of Saint Benedict, Collegeville, Minnesota.

John Milbank, Ph.D., is Francis Ball Professor of Philosophical Theology in the Religious Studies Department at the University of Virginia.

Richard J. Mouw, Ph.D., is President and Professor of Christian Philosophy at Fuller Theological Seminary, Pasadena, California.

Mark A. Noll, Ph.D., is McManus Professor of Christian Thought and Senior Director of the Institute for the Study of American Evangelicals (ISAE) at Wheaton College (Illinois).

Luis N. Rivera-Pagán, Ph.D., is Henry Winters Luce Professor of Ecumenics and Mission at Princeton Theological Seminary.

Glen Stassen, Ph.D., is Lewis B. Smedes Professor of Christian Ethics at Fuller Theological Seminary, Pasadena, California.

NOTES

Introduction: The Ethical Challenge

1. I take both these terms from argumentation theory. Ch. Perelman and L. Olbrechts-Tyteca define a pragmatic argument as that "which allows a thing to be judged in terms of its present or its future consequences." See *The New Rhetoric: A Treatise on Argumentation,* trans. John Wilkinson and Purcell Weaver (Notre Dame, Ind.: University of Notre Dame Press, 1969), 267. An inherency argument is traditionally understood within debate theory as pinpointing the underlying causes, or essential characteristics, of an undesirable policy.

2. See François Houtart, "The Cult of Violence in the Name of Religion: A Panorama," trans. John Bowden, in *Religion as a Source of Violence,* ed. William Benken and Karl-Josef Kuschel (London: SCM Press, 1997), 1–9.

3. See Houtart, 1–2.

4. See Edward Schillebeeckx, "Documentation: Religion and Violence," trans. John Bowden, in *Religion as a Source of Violence,* ed. William Benken and Karl-Josef Kuschel (London: SCM Press, 1997), 129–42.

5. For a full exposition of her argument, see Regina Schwartz, *The Curse of Cain* (Chicago: University of Chicago Press, 1997).

6. For an overview of the historical debate within Christianity, see Charles Villa-Vicencio, "Introduction," in *Theology and Violence: The South African Debate,* Charles Villa-Vicencio, ed. (Grand Rapids: Eerdmans, 1988), 1–10. Originally published in Africa in 1987.

7. For this and more revealing comments on the shift away from nonviolence, see Desmund Tutu, "Freedom Fighters or Terrorists?" in Charles Villa-Vicencio, ed., *Theology and Violence,* 71–78, esp. 77.

Chapter 1: The First Crusade: Some Theological and Historical Context

1. Biblical quotations are taken from the New Revised Standard Version as printed in *The New Oxford Annotated Bible with the Apocryphal/Deuterocanonical Books,* ed. Bruce M. Metzger and Roland E. Murphy (New York: Oxford University Press, 1994).

2. The bibliography on the Crusades is immense. See *A History of the Crusades,* 6 vols., ed. Kenneth Setton (Philadelphia: University of Pennsylvania Press, 1955–1959; 2d ed., Madison: University of Wisconsin Press, 1969–1989), which is a magisterial treatment of all aspects of the Crusades; for reliable briefer treatments, see Hans Eberhard Mayer, *The Crusades,* trans. John Gillingham, 2d ed. (Oxford: Oxford University Press, 1986); Jonathan Riley-Smith, *The Oxford Illustrated History of the Crusades* (Oxford: Oxford University Press, 1997), which is beautifully illustrated; and Thomas Madden, *A Concise History of the Crusades* (Lanham, Md.: Rowman and Littlefield, 1999).

3. On the First Crusade, see the relevant sections of *A History of the Crusades,* vol. 1: *The First Hundred Years,* ed. Marshall W. Baldwin (Philadelphia: University of Pennsylvania Press, 1955; 2d ed., Madison: University of Wisconsin Press, 1969); *The First Crusade: Origins and Impact,* ed. Jonathan Phillips (Manchester., U.K., and New York: Manchester University Press, 1997); or Edward Peters, ed., *The First Crusade. The Chronicle of Fulcher of Chartres and Other Source Materials,* 2d ed. (Philadelphia: University of Pennsylvania Press, 1998), which has an excellent collection of sources and interpretations of the First Crusade.

4. Madden, *A Concise History,* 12.

5. Anna Comnena, *The Alexiad,* trans. E. R. A. Sewter (Harmondsworth, U.K.: Penguin, 1969), esp. bk. 10, 308–31.

6. Fulcher of Chartres, *A History of the Expedition to Jerusalem 1095–1127,* trans. Frances Rita Ryan (Knoxville: University of Tennessee Press, 1969); Raymond d'Aguilers, *Historia Francorum qui Ceperunt Iherusalem,* trans. with introduction and notes by John Hugh Hill and Laurita L. Hill, in *Memoirs of the American Philosophical Society,* vol. 71 (Philadelphia: American Philosophical Society, 1968); and Peter of Tudebode, *Historia de Hierosolymitano itinere,* ed. and trans. John Hugh Hill and Laurita L. Hill (Philadelphia: American Philosophical Society, 1977).

7. *Gesta Francorum et aliorum Hierosolimitanorum,* ed. and trans. Rosalind Hill (London: T. Nelson, 1962). I quote the *Gesta Francorum* from the Hill translation.

8. Baudri of Dol, *Historia Hierosolimitana,* cited in Rosalind Hill, ed., *Gesta Francorum,* ix.

9. *Gesta Francorum,* bk. 9, ch. 26, 62.

10. Ibid., bk. 7, ch. 18, 40–42.

11. Ibid., bk. 4, ch. 10, 24, and bk. 5, ch. 12, 29.

12. Ibid., bk. 10, ch. 30, 73.

13. Ibid., bk. 6, ch. 17, 36–37.

14. Ibid., bk. 9, ch. 22, 53.

15. Ibid., bk. 1, ch. 3, 6.

16. Ibid., bk. 2, ch. 6, 13; see William M. Daly, "Christian Fraternity, the Crusaders, and the Security of Constantinople, 1097–1204: The Precarious Survival of an Ideal" (*Mediaeval Studies* 22 [1960]: 43–91).

17. *Gesta Francorum,* bk. 9, ch. 29, 67–68.

18. Ibid., bk. 10, ch. 33, 78–79; for similar religious and liturgical preparations for the siege of Jerusalem, see bk. 10, ch. 38, 90.

19. Ibid., bk. 9, ch. 22, 53–56; I have modified the translation.

20. Ibid., bk. 9, ch. 24, 58: in a vision, Christ says that military failure is due to illicit sexual behavior. Adhemar, bishop of Le Puy and papal representative, criticized the knights' moral behavior in a sermon, reported in bk. 10, ch. 30, 74.

21. Ibid., bk. 2, ch. 8, 17.

22. Ibid., bk. 4, ch. 11, 27; bk. 9, ch. 24, 58; bk. 10, ch. 31, 75; bk. 9, ch. 28, 66.

23. Ibid., bk. 7, ch. 18, 42: Crusaders desecrated the graves of dead Muslims; bk. 10, ch. 33, 79–80: when the crusaders took the city of Marra, their looting was accompanied by indiscriminate slaughter.

24. On the anonymous knight's account of the discovery of the Holy Lance, see Ibid., bk. 9, ch. 25, 59–60. See also Steven Runciman, "The Holy Lance Found at Antioch" (*Analecta Bollandiana* 68 [1950]: 197–209).

25. First Samuel 15:3, "Now go and attack Amalek, and utterly destroy all that they have; do not spare them, but kill both man and woman, child and infant, ox and sheep, camel and donkey." On the ban, see also Deut. 20:1–20. For the anonymous knight's account of the bloody aftermath of the capture of Jerusalem, see *Gesta Francorum,* bk. 10, ch. 38, 90–92.

26. A. von Harnack (*Militia Christi: The Christian Religion and the Military in the First Three Centuries,* trans. David McInnes Gracie [Philadelphia: Fortress, 1981], 35–40) treats Paul's military imagery. In spite of its age (first published in 1903), this is still an essential book on the topic of early Christianity and war.

27. Ibid., 37.

28. Ibid., 49; see the quotation from Origen on 50 n. 28, which allegorizes the wars against the Midianites.

29. Edwin Cyril Blackman, *Marcion and His Influence* (London: SPCK, 1948), 113–24. For a good summary of Marcion's teaching and bibliography, see Hendrick F. Stander, "Marcion (d. ca. 154)," in *Encyclopedia of Early Christianity,* 2d ed., ed. Everett Ferguson (New York and London: Garland, 1997), 2:715–17.

30. Cited in Harnack, *Militia Christi,* 48.

31. J. M. Wallace-Hadrill, *Early Germanic Kingship in England and on the Continent* (Oxford: Clarendon, 1971), 99–100 and 125–29.

32. *The Rule of Saint Benedict in English,* ch. 42, ed. Timothy Frye, O.S.B. (Collegeville, Minn.: Liturgical Press, 1980), 64.

33. Carl Erdmann, *The Origin of the Idea of Crusade,* trans. Marshall Baldwin and Walter Goffart (Princeton: Princeton University Press, 1977), originally *Die Entstehung des Kreuzzugsgedankens* (1935), is a seminal work on the origins of holy war and Christianized knighthood.

34. Harnack, *Militia Christi,* 27–64.

35. For fine, though different, books on Augustine, see Peter Brown, *Augustine of Hippo: A Biography* (Berkeley and Los Angeles: University of California Press, 1967); Gerald Bonner, *St. Augustine of Hippo: Life and Controversies* (London: Canterbury, 1963); and F. Van der Meer, *Augustine the Bishop,* trans. Brian Battershaw and G. R. Lamb (New York: Sheed and Ward, 1961).

36. Frederick H. Russell, *The Just War in the Middle Ages,* Cambridge Studies in Medieval Life and Thought, 3d series, vol. 8 (Cambridge: Cambridge University Press, 1975); see also Herbert Deane, *The Political and Social Ideas of St. Augustine* (New York and London, 1963), ch. 5; and Erdmann, *Origin,* 7–8.

37. Erdmann, *Origin,* 13–20.

38. Jean Dunbabin, "The Maccabees as Exemplars in the Tenth and Eleventh Centuries," in *The Bible in the Medieval World: Essays in Memory of Beryl Smalley,* Studies in Church History, Subsidia 4 (Oxford: Blackwell, 1985), 31–41.

39. On the Peace and Truce of God, see Thomas N. Bisson, "Peace of God, Truce of God," in *Dictionary of the Middle Ages* (New York: Scribner, 1987), 9:473–5; and *The Peace of God: Social Violence and Religious Response in France Around the Year 1000,* ed. Thomas Head and Richard Landes (Ithaca: Cornell University Press, 1992).

40. Quoted in Erdmann, *Origin,* 82.

41. Ibid., 83.

42. Erdmann, *Origin,* 57.

43. Carl Stephenson, *Medieval Feudalism* (Ithaca: Cornell University Press, 1942), 53–55; Marc Bloch, *Feudal Society,* trans. L. A. Manyon (London: Routledge, 1961), 312–16.

44. *Gesta Francorum,* bk. 1, ch. 1, 1–2.

45. *Jerusalem Pilgrims before the Crusades,* ed. and trans. John Wilkinson (Warminster, U.K.: Warminster Press, 1977), contains eighteen precrusade pilgrim accounts; see also Jonathan Sumption, *Pilgrimage: An Image of Mediaeval Religion* (Totowa, N.J.: Rowman and Littlefield, 1976).

45. *Gesta Francorum,* bk. 10, ch. 30, 73.

Chapter 2: Violence of the *Conquistadores* and Prophetic Indignation

1. Cristóbal Colón, *Textos y documentos completos,* ed. Consuelo Varela and Juan Gil, *Nuevas cartas,* (Madrid: Alianza Editorial, 1995), 220.

2. "Letter of Columbus, describing the results of his first voyage," in *The Journal of Christopher Columbus,* tr. Cecil Jane (New York: Clarkson N. Potter, Inc., 1960), 191–202.

3. Ibid., 201.

4. Richard Konetzke, *Colección de documentos para la historia de la formación social de Hispanoamérica,* 3 vols. (Madrid: Consejo Superior de Investigaciones Científicas, 1953–1958), 1:1.

5. Johannes Meier, "La presencia de las órdenes religiosas en el Caribe durante la dominación española" (*Missionalia hispánica,* 43, 124 [1986]: 363–72).

6. Diego Alvarez de Chanca, "Carta al ayuntamiento de Sevilla" (*Revista de la Universidad de La Habana,* 196–197 [1972]: 280–99).

7. Konetzke, *Colección de documentos,* 1:38–57; Rafael Altamira y Crevea, "El texto de las leyes de Burgos de 1512" (*Revista de historia de América* 4 [diciembre 1938]: 5–79).

8. Kirkpatrick Sale, *The Conquest of Paradise: Christopher Columbus and the Columbian Legacy* (New York: Alfred A. Knopf, 1990), 152–83; Felipe Fernández-Armesto, *Columbus* (Oxford: Oxford University Press, 1991), 133–52.

9. *Testamento y codicilio de Isabel la Católica* (Madrid: Dirección General de Relaciones Culturales del Ministerio de Relaciones Exteriores, 1956), 66–67.

10. Lewis U. Hanke, *The Spanish Struggle for Justice in the Conquest of America* (Boston: Little, Brown, 1965; orig. 1949), 26.

11. Konetzke, *Colección de documentos,* 1:89–96.

12. Ibid., 471–78; *Colección de documentos inéditos relativos al descubrimiento, conquista y organización de las antiguas posesiones españolas de América y Oceanía, sacados de los Archivos del Reino y muy especialmente del de Indias,* ed. Joaquín F. Pacheco, Francisco de Cárdenas, and Luis Torres de Mendoza (Madrid: Imp. de Quirós, 1864–1884), 8:489–95.

13. Ibid.

14. Luis N. Rivera-Pagán, *A Violent Evangelism: The Political and Religious Conquest of the Americas* (Louisville: Westminster/John Knox Press, 1992), 42–62.

15. Justo L. González, *Y hasta lo último de la tierra: historia ilustrada del cristianismo,* vol. 7: *La era de los conquistadores* (Miami: Editorial Caribe, 1980).

16. Juan Ginés de Sepúlveda, *Demócrates segundo o de las justas causas de la guerra contra los indios,* ed. and trans. Angel Losada (Madrid: Consejo Superior de Investigaciones Científicas, 1951).

17. Lewis U. Hanke, *Aristotle and the American Indians: A Study in Race Prejudice in the Modern World* (Chicago: Henry Regnery Co., 1959; Bloomington: Indiana University Press, 1970); Bartolomé de las Casas, "Disputa y controversia contra Juan Ginés de Sepúlveda," in *Tratados* (México, D. F.,: Fondo de Cultura Económica, 1965), 1:217–459.

18. Bartolomé de las Casas, "Brevísima relación de la destruición de las Indias," *Tratados,* 1:5–23; Jerónimo de Mendieta, *Historia eclesiástica indiana* (1596) (Mexico City: Editorial Porrúa, 1980), 68–71.

19. Rivera-Pagán, *A Violent Evangelism,* 169–79.

20. *De procuranda Indorum salute: Educación y evangelización* (Madrid: Consejo Superior de Investigaciones Científicas, 1987).

21. Bartolomé de las Casas, *The Only Way,* ed. Helen Rand Parish, trans. Francis Patrick Sullivan (Mahwah, N.J.: Paulist Press, 1992).

22. Hernán Cortés, *Cartas de relación* (Mexico City: Editorial Porrúa, 1985), 11.

23. Hernán Cortés, *Documentos cortesianos, 1518–1528,* ed. José Luis Martínez (Mexico City: Universidad Nacional Autónoma de México—Fondo de Cultura Económica, 1990), 165.

24. Bartolomé de las Casas, "Algunos principios . . . ," *Tratados,* 2:1235–73.

25. "Carta al Papa Alejandro VI (febrero 1502)," in Cristóbal Colón, *Textos y documentos completos,* 479–81.

26. Text in Vicente Murga Sanz, *Historia documental puertorriqueña,* vol. 3, *Cedulario puertorriqueño, tomo I (1505–1517)* (Río Piedras, Puerto Rico: Editorial de la Universidad de Puerto Rico, 1961), 123–27; critique in Bartolomé de las Casas, *Historia de las Indias* (Mexico City: Fondo de Cultura Económica, 1951), l. 3, c. 2, t. 2, 435–38 (henceforth *H.I.*). For their textual and historical analysis, see Luis N. Rivera-Pagán, "Formation of a Hispanic American Theology: The Capitulations of Burgos," in *Hidden Stories: Unveiling the History of the Latino Church,* ed. Daniel Rodríguez-Díaz and David Cortés-Fuentes (Decatur, Ga.: Academia para la Educación Teológica Hispana, 1994), 67–97. It is the English translation of "Las Capitulaciones de Burgos: Paradigma de las paradojas de la cristiandad colonial" (*Apuntes* 13, 1 [spring 1993] 30–48).

27. "The conquest of the Indians began when the conquest of the Moors had ended, in order that Spaniards may always war against the infidels" (Francisco López de Gomara, *Historia general de las indias* [Madrid: Biblioteca de Autores Españoles, Ediciones Atlas, 1946; orig. 1552], t. 22, 156).

28. Christian Duverger, *La conversión de los indios de la Nueva España. Con el texto de los "Coloquios de los Doce" de Bernardino de Sahagún* (Quito, Ecuador: Ediciones Abya Yala, 1990).

29. Américo Castro, *La realidad histórica de España,* 8th ed.(Mexico City: Editorial Porrúa, 1982). On Spanish Muslims and Jews, see Richard Fletcher, *Moorish Spain* (London: Weidenfeld & Nicolson, 1992); and Jane S. Gerber, *The Jews of Spain: A History of the Sephardic Experience* (New York: Free Press, 1992). Our vision of the *Reconquista* is usually one-sided, as it comes basically from Christian sources, which inexorably narrates it as a triumph of the faith against invader infidels. There were, however, other perspectives, other understandings of the event, rooted in the pain and grief of the defeated, who had to suffer affliction, servitude, and exile. A vivid example is the poem by ar-Rundi, a Muslim poet, after a series of Christian military victories, in the twelfth century:

Ask Valencia what became of Murcia,
And where is Játiva, or where is Jaén?
Where is Córdoba, the seat of great learning . . . ?

. . . .
And where is Seville, the home of mirthful gatherings
On its great river, cooling and brimful with water?
These cities were pillars of the country:
Can a building remain when the pillars are missing?
The white wells of ablution are weeping with sorrow,
As a lover does when torn from his beloved:
They weep over the remains of dwellings devoid of Muslims. . . .
. . . .
Those mosques have now been changed into churches,
Where the bells are ringing and crosses are standing.
Even the mihrabs weep, though made of cold stone,
even the minbars sing dirges, though made of wood!
(Cited by Fletcher, *Moorish Spain,* 129–30.)

30. *Religión y estado en la España del siglo XVI* (Mexico City: Fondo de Cultura Económica, 1957), 37: "The central dominating force of the will of the nation was a transcendental idea . . . a religious conception of life, incarnated in the Catholic Church."

31. Bernal Díaz del Castillo, *Historia verdadera de la conquista de la Nueva España* (Mexico City: Editorial Porrúa, 1986), passim.

32. James A. Brundage, *Medieval Canon Law and the Crusader* (Madison: University of Wisconsin Press, 1969).

33. Pedro de Leturia, *Relaciones entre la Santa Sede e Hispanoamérica, 1493–1835* (Caracas: Sociedad Bolivariana de Venezuela; Rome: Universidad Gregoriana, 1959), 1:10.

34. Richard Greenleaf, *The Mexican Inquisition of the Sixteenth Century* (Albuquerque: University of New Mexico Press, 1969).

35. *Historia eclesiástica indiana,* 15–18, 174–77. Mendieta errs in the dates. Luther was born in 1483, Cortés in 1485.

36. Toribio de Benavente (Motolinia), *Historia de los indios de la Nueva España: Relación de los ritos antiguos, idolatrías y sacrificios de los indios de la Nueva España, y de la maravillosa conversión que Dios en ella ha obrado,* ed. Edmundo O'Gorman (Mexico City: Porrúa, 1984). English translation: *History of the Indians of New Spain,* trans. and annotated by Francis Borgia Steck (Washington, D.C.: Academy of American Franciscan History, 1951).

37. Robert Ricard, *The Spiritual Conquest of Mexico: An Essay on the Apostolate and the Evangelizing Methods of the Mendicant Orders in New Spain, 1523–1572,* trans. Lesley Byrd Simpson (Berkeley and Los Angeles: University of California Press, 1966); Pierre Duviols, *La lutte contre les religions autochtones dans le Pérou colonial: l'extirpation de l'idolatrie entre 1532 et 1660* (Paris and Lima: Institut Français d'Études Andines, 1971).

38. *Textos y documentos completos,* 445. On the messianic and providentialist mentality of Columbus, the opus magnum is the magisterial work of Alain Milhou, *Colón y su mentalidad mesiánica en el ambiente franciscanista español* (Valladolid, Mexico: Casa-Museo de Colón/Seminario Americanista de la Universidad de Valladolid, 1983). See also Beatriz Pastor, *Discurso narrativo de la conquista de América* (Premio de ensayo de Casa de las Américas, 1983) (Havana: Casa de las Américas, 1984), 42–46.

39. *Cartas de relación,* 38.

40. In Silvio A Zavala, *Las instituciones jurídicas en la conquista de América,* 2d ed. (Mexico City: Porrúa, 1971), 349.

41. Fidel de Lejarza, "Franciscanismo de Cortés y cortesianismo de los franciscanos" (*Missionalia hispánica* 5 [1948]: 43–136).

42. *Cartas de relación,* 203–4.

43. Ibid., 280.

44. Ibid., 282.

45. Justo L. González, "The Christ of Colonialism" (*Church & Society* 82, 3 [January/February 1992]: 5–36).

46. I have discussed the sixteenth-century Spanish theological debates on the slavery of the native Americans at length in "Debates teológicos sobre la servidumbre indígena en la conquista española del Caribe," in *Diálogos y polifonías: perspectivas y reseñas* (San Juan, Puerto Rico: Seminario Evangélico Puerto Rico, 1999), 17–53.

47. Antonio Ybot León, "Juntas de teólogos asesoras del estado para Indias 1512–1550" (*Anuario de estudios americanos* 5, [1948]: 397–438).

48. Robert Streit, O.M.I., "Zur Vorgeschichte de I. Junta von Burgos, 1512" (*Zeitschrift für Missionswissenschaft* 12, 165–75).

49. *Columbus,* 67.

50. To distinguish it from the also clear, unequivocal, and loud voices from the Native Americans, such as Guarionex, Hatuey, and Aguebaná, whose direct testimonies, however, we are deprived of. The European monopoly of the written word unfortunately distorts every historiographical attempt to reconstruct the voice of the oppressed. See Walter D. Mignolo, *The Darker Side of the Renaissance: Literacy, Territoriality, and Colonization* (Ann Arbor: University of Michigan Press, 1995).

51. For an English translation of the bulls, alongside the Latin originals, see Frances Gardiner Davenport, *European Treaties Bearing on the History of the United States and Its Dependencies to 1648* (Washington, D.C.: Carnegie Institution of Washington, 1917), 56–83.

52. *H.I.,* l. 3, cs. 3–7, t. 2, 438–55.

53. Ibid., 441–42.

54. *Colección de documentos inéditos,* 32:377–378; Diego Venancio Carro, *La teología y los teólogos españoles ante la conquista de América* (Madrid: Escuela de Estudios Hispanoamericanos de Sevilla, 1944), 1:58–61.

55. Ibid., 62–63.

56. Gustavo Gutiérrez, "En busca de los pobres de Jesucristo: evangelización y teología en el siglo xvi," in *Materiales para una historia de la teología en América Latina,* ed. Pablo Richard (VIII Encuentro Latinoamericano de CEHILA, Lima 1980) (San José, Costa Rica: CEHILA DEI, 1981), 137–63.

57. The bull is quoted in Lewis U. Hanke, "Pope Paul III and the American Indians" (*Harvard Theological Review* 30 [1937]: 56–102). Charles V reacted strongly against this and other similar documents of Paul III. The Spanish monarchs considered it essential to control the ecclesiastical affairs in their overseas territories and tried to disallow direct and independent relationships between Rome and the American churches. They claimed the right of *patronato real* (royal patronage) over the colonial religious institutions. See William Eugene Shiels, S.J., *King and Church: The Rise and Fall of the* Patronato Real (Chicago: Loyola University Press, 1961).

58. The las Casas bibliography is immense. Indispensable are two books by Isacio Pérez Fenández, *Inventario documentado de los escritos de Fray Bartolomé de las Casas* (Bayamón, Puerto Rico: CEDOC, 1981); and *Cronología documentada de los viajes, estancias y actuaciones de Fray Bartolomé de las Casas* (Bayamón, Puerto Rico: CEDOC, 1984). See also Gustavo Gutiérrez, *las Casas: In Search of the Poor of Jesus Christ* (Maryknoll, N.Y.: Orbis Books, 1993).

59. David Henige, *In Search of Columbus: The Sources for the First Voyage* (Tucson: University of Arizona Press, 1991).

60. Lewis Hanke, "Bartolomé de las Casas, historiador," in las Casas, *H.I., * ix–lxxxviii.

61. Reproduced as appendix in Bartolomé de las Casas, *De regia potestate o derecho de autodeterminación,* ed. Luciano Pereña et al., vol. 8, *Corpus Hispanorum de Pace* (Madrid: Consejo Superior de Investigaciones Científicas, 1969), 282–83.

62. In Agustín Yañez, ed., *Fray Bartolomé de las Casas: Doctrina* (Mexico City: Universidad Nacional Autónoma, 1941), 161–63.

63. Marcel Bataillon, *Estudios sobre Bartolomé de las Casas* (Barcelona: Península, 1976).

64. José Martí, "El padre Las Casas," in *La edad de oro* (Havana: Editorial Gente Nueva, 1981), 160–70.

65. Simón Bolívar, "Carta de Jamaica (6 de septiembre de 1815)," in *Escritos fundamentales,* ed. Germán Carrera Damas (Caracas: Monte Avila Editores, 1982), 46.

66. Manuel Giménez Fernández, *Bartolomé de las Casas,* vol. 1: *Delegado de Cisneros para la reformación de las Indias (1516–1517)* (Seville, Spain: Escuela de Estudios Hispanoamericanos, 1953; reprint Madrid:

Consejo Superior de Investigaciones Científicas, Escuela de Estudios Hispanoamericanos, 1984); *Bartolomé de las Casas,* vol. 2: *Capellán de Carlos I, poblador de Cumaná (1517–1523)* (Seville, Spain: Escuela de Estudios Hispanoamericanos, 1960; reprint Madrid: Consejo Superior de Investigaciones Científicas, Escuela de Estudios Hispanoamericanos, 1984).

67. Ramón Menéndez Pidal, *El padre Las Casas: su doble personalidad* (Madrid: Espasa Calpe, 1963).

68. *The Revised English Bible, with the Apocrypha* (Oxford and Cambridge: Oxford University Press and Cambridge University Press, 1989), Apocrypha, 122.

69. Las Casas quotes this Latin text, in two slightly different ways in *H.I.,* l. 1, c. 24, t. 1, 130, and *H.I.,* l. 3, c. 79, 7. 3, 92.

70. See Francesca Cantù, "Evoluzione e significato della dottrina della restituzione in Bartolomé de las Casas" (*Critica storica* [1975]: 231–319).

71. Rivera-Pagán, *A Violent Evangelism,* 254–57.

72. Edwin Edward Sylvest, Jr., *Motifs of Franciscan Mission Theory in Sixteenth Century New Spain Province of the Holy Gospel* (Washington, D.C.: Academy of American Franciscan History, 1975).

Chapter 3: Is God Violent? Theological Options in the Antislavery Movement

1. William Ellery Channing, "Likeness to God," in *William Ellery Channing: Selected Writings,* ed. David Robinson (New York: Paulist Press, 1985), 146.

2. David Low Dodge, *War Inconsistent with the Religion of Jesus Christ,* ed. Edwin D. Mead (Boston: Ginn and Company, 1905; orig. 1812).

3. Henry Clarke Wright, *Anthropology; or the Science of Man; in Its Bearing on War and Slavery* (Boston: Bela Marsh, 1850).

4. Frederick Douglass, *My Bondage and My Freedom,* in *Frederick Douglass: Autobiographies,* ed. Henry Louis Gates, Jr. (New York: Library of America, 1994), 177.

5. Ibid., 179.

6. Dodge, *War Inconsistent,* 102, 80, 36.

7. Douglass, *Narrative of the Life of Frederick Douglass, an American Slave,* in *Autobiographies,* 18, 22, 24, 97; and *My Bondage,* 278.

8. Douglass, *My Bondage,* 179.

9. Harriet Beecher Stowe to Frederick Douglass, July 9, 1851, in *The Oxford Harriet Beecher Stowe Reader*, ed. Joan D. Hedrick (New York: Oxford, 1999), 61.

10. Henry Bibb, *Narrative of the Life and Adventures of Henry Bibb, an American Slave. Written by Himself* (Boston: Bela Marsh, 1848), 66.

11. Douglass, *Narrative,* 36; see also *My Bondage,* 213.

12. Douglass, *My Bondage,* 278; and *Narrative,* 58, 65.

13. David Van Leer, "Reading Slavery: The Anxiety of Ethnicity in Douglass's *Narrative,*" in *Frederick Douglass: New Literary and Historical Essays,* ed. Eric J. Sundquist (Cambridge, U.K.: Cambridge University Press, 1990), 126–27; and Ann Kibbey, "Language in Slavery," in *Frederick Douglass's* Narrative of the Life of Frederick Douglass: *Modern Critical Interpretations,* ed. Harold Bloom (New York: Chelsea House, 1988), 149–50.

14. Douglass, *My Bondage,* 350. By suggesting that God and right had been vindicated only in the moment of escape, Douglass implicitly anticipated the controversial thesis of historian Stanley Elkins, who described Southern slavery as a "total institution"—like a Nazi concentration camp—which partly succeeded in dehumanizing its victims. More recent historians have suggested that slave humanity was vindicated not only in escape but also in the autonomy of slave culture, most particularly in the family and the "invisible institution" of slave religion. It is probably significant that Douglass and other fugitive slave narrators had limited exposure to either slave families or the slave church, and may not have appreciated the analogies between these institutions and their own experience of freedom. Still, Elkins is right to insist that research on slave culture not be used to deny the "damage" of slavery. Neither the North, the family, nor the church could provide a refuge capacious enough for everyone whose soul and body were maimed by slavery's violence. See Stanley M. Elkins, *Slavery: A Problem in American Institutional and Intellectual Life,*

3d ed. (Chicago: University of Chicago Press, 1976); and Ann J. Lane, *The Debate Over Slavery: Stanley Elkins and His Critics* (Urbana: University of Illinois Press, 1971).

15. Douglass, *My Bondage,* 286.

16. Garrison, "Preface," in Douglass, *Narrative,* 3–4.

17. Garrison, "Declaration of Sentiments," in *Nonviolence in America: A Documentary History,* ed. Staughton Lynd and Alice Lynd (Maryknoll, N.Y.: Orbis, 1995), 15.

18. Sydney E. Ahlstrom and Jonathan S. Carey, "Introduction," in *An American Reformation: A Documentary History of Unitarian Christianity,* Sydney E. Ahlstrom and Jonathan S. Carey, eds. (Middletown, Conn.: Wesleyan University Press, 1985), 33–34; and Henry F. May, *The Enlightenment in America* (New York: Oxford University Press, 1976), 293.

19. Thomas Jefferson to John Adams, October 14, 1815; cited in May, *Enlightenment,* 296.

20. Garrison, "Address to the American Colonization Society," in *William Lloyd Garrison and the Fight against Slavery: Selections from* The Liberator, ed. William E. Cain (Boston: St. Martin's Press, 1995), 61; *Liberator* (December 29, 1832).

21. Garrison, "Declaration of Sentiments," 14.

22. Ibid., 14–16.

23. *Liberator* (December 16, 1859 and January 8, 1831).

24. *Liberator* (February 5, 1831 and January 1, 1831).

25. Harriet Beecher Stowe, *Uncle Tom's Cabin* (New York: Penguin, 1986), 624, 629.

26. Harriet Beecher Stowe to William Lloyd Garrison, November 1853, in *Oxford Harriet Beecher Stowe Reader,* 77. Garrison's response, depending on one's perspective, was either nuanced or frustratingly evasive. He chided her for failing to identify the "erroneous" views of the *Liberator;* defended his policy of publishing a wide range of opinions, including proslavery opinions; and asked, "If the infernal cruelty of a Legree could not shake [Uncle Tom's] trust in his God and Saviour, do you really think a full discussion of the merits of the Bible, pro and con, might induce him to throw that volume away?" But Garrison avoided stating his own opinion on biblical inspiration, suggesting only that "my reliance for the deliverance of the oppressed universally is upon the nature of man, the inherent wrongfulness of oppression, the power of truth, and the omnipotence of God" (*Liberator* [December 23, 1853]).

27. Harriet Beecher Stowe, *The Minister's Wooing* (New York: AMS Press, 1967), 189.

28. Harriet Beecher Stowe, *Dred: A Tale of the Great Dismal Swamp* (New York: AMS Press, 1967), 2:57–58; and *Uncle Tom's Cabin,* 201, 272, 184.

29. Stowe, *Uncle Tom's Cabin,* 278, 234–35, 333; and *Dred,* 1:263.

30. Stowe, *Uncle Tom's Cabin,* 229.

31. Ibid., 429.

32. Leslie A. Fiedler, *Love and Death in the American Novel,* rev. ed. (New York: Stein and Day, 1966), 266.

33. Stowe, *Uncle Tom's Cabin,* 202.

34. Ibid., 210.

35. Ibid., 504, 523, 553.

36. Ibid., 554. Curiously, Stowe introduces Tom's vision by suggesting a purely naturalistic explanation for it: "When a heavy weight presses the soul to the lowest level at which endurance is possible, there is an instant and desperate effort of every physical and moral nerve to throw off the weight; and hence the heaviest anguish often precedes a return tide of joy and courage." It is not quite clear how she means this to shape our reading of the vision itself, but I would suggest that the effect is one of second naïveté: we know there are all sorts of psychological explanations for Tom's experience, but yet the power still inheres in the experience itself.

37. Ibid., 556.

38. Ibid., 514; and *Dred,* 1:227.

39. Stowe, *Minister's Wooing,* 263.

40. Stowe, *Uncle Tom's Cabin,* 540.

41. Joan Hedrick, *Harriet Beecher Stowe: A Life* (New York: Oxford University Press, 1994), vii.

42. Abraham Lincoln, "Speech at Independence Hall, Philadelphia, Pennsylvania," February 22, 1861, in *Selected Speeches and Writings,* ed. Gore Vidal (New York: Library of America, 1992), 282.

43. Lincoln, "Address at Lewistown, Illinois," August 17, 1858, cited by William J. Wolf, *The Almost Chosen People: A Study of the Religion of Abraham Lincoln* (Garden City, N.Y.: Doubleday, 1959), 96.

44. "Eulogy on Henry Clay," July 6, 1852, in Lincoln, *Selected Speeches,* 87–88.

45. "Handbill," 55; "Eulogy on Henry Clay," 89; and "Address to the New Jersey Senate," 280, all in Lincoln, *Selected Speeches.* See also Melvin B. Endy, Jr., "Abraham Lincoln and American Civil Religion: A Reinterpretation" (*Church History* 44 [June 1975]: 233).

46. "Meditation on the Divine Will," early September 1862, in Lincoln, *Selected Speeches,* 344; and Abraham Lincoln to Eliza P. Gurney, September 4, 1864, in *Selected Speeches,* 432.

47. "Second Inaugural Address," March 4, 1865, in *Selected Speeches,* 450.

48. David Hein, "Lincoln's Theology and Political Ethics," in *Essays on Lincoln's Faith and Politics,* ed. Kenneth W. Thompson (Lanham, Md.: University Press of America, 1983), 134; Alfred Kazin, *God and the American Writer* (New York: Knopf, 1997), 133; and Glen E. Thurow, *Abraham Lincoln and American Political Religion* (Albany: SUNY Press, 1976), 100.

49. Abraham Lincoln to Thurlow Weed, March 15, 1865, in *Selected Speeches,* 451.

50. *Liberator* (February 10, 1865).

51. Kazin, *God and the American Writer,* 136.

52. David B. Chesebrough, *"No Sorrow Like Our Sorrow," Northern Protestant Ministers and the Assassination of Lincoln* (Kent, Ohio: Kent State University Press, 1994), 77, 66, 74–77.

53. "Second Inaugural Address," 450.

Chapter 4: Christians as Rescuers during the Holocaust

1. Arthur Hertzberg, with Aron Hirt-Manheimer, *The Jews* (San Francisco: Harper, 1998), 270.

2. Steven R. Haynes, "Beware Good News: Faith and Fallacy in Post-Holocaust Christianity," in Carol Rittner and John K. Roth, eds., *"Good News" after Auschwitz? Christian Faith within a Post-Holocaust World* (Atlanta: Mercer, 2001), 4.

3. Ibid., 1.

4. This statement is grounded primarily in rescuer and nonrescuer self-reports of religious commitment in Samuel and Pearl Oliner, *The Altruistic Personality* (New York: Free Press, 1988).

5. "Righteous of the Nations," *Encyclopedia Judaica,* vol. 14 (Jerusalem: Keter, 1972), 184.

6. Oliner and Oliner, *Altruistic Personality,* 155 (12 percent); Eva Fogelman, "The Rescuers: A Sociopsychological Study of Altruistic Behavior During the Nazi Era" (Ph.D. diss, City University of New York, 1987) (15 percent); Nechama Tec, *When Light Pierced the Darkness* (New York: Oxford University Press, 1986), 145 (27 percent).

7. David P. Gushee, *The Righteous Gentiles of the Holocaust* (Minneapolis: Fortress, 1994), ch. 6.

8. Oliner and Oliner, *Altruistic Personality,* 154–55, 157.

9. Philip Hallie, *Lest Innocent Blood Be Shed* (New York: Harper & Row, 1979); Pierre Sauvage, producer and director, *Weapons of the Spirit* (Victory Multimedia, 1989).

10. Yehuda Bauer, *The Holocaust in Historical Perspective* (Seattle: University of Washington Press, 1978), 61–62.

11. Philip Friedman, "Righteous Gentiles in the Nazi Era," in *Roads to Extinction,* ed. Ada J. Friedman (Philadelphia: JPS, 1955), 419–20.

12. Pieter DeJong, "Responses of the Churches in the Netherlands to the Nazi Occupation," in *Human Responses to the Holocaust,* ed. Michael D. Ryan (New York: Edwin Mellen Press, 1981), 140–41.

13. Mordecai Paldiel, "Hesed and the Holocaust" (*Journal of Ecumenical Studies* 23, 1 [Winter 1986]: 104–5).

14. Karen Lebacqz, *Justice in an Unjust World* (Minneapolis: Augsburg, 1987).

Chapter 5: Have Christians Done More Harm than Good?

1. Tacitus, *The Annals,* bk. 15, quoted here from *Masterworks of History,* ed. Joseph Reither (New York: McGraw-Hill, 1948), 1:242.

2. New York: Knopf, 1990.

3. Fulcher of Chartres, *Chronicle of the First Crusade,* quoted here from Brian Tierney, ed., *The Middle Ages: Sources of Medieval History* (New York: Knopf, 1970), 132.

4. Michael McGiffert, ed., *God's Plot: The Paradoxes of Puritan Piety, Being the Autobiography and Journal of Thomas Shepard* (Amherst: University of Massachusetts Press, 1972), 67.

5. For their views plus interpretation, see the unsigned editorial, "Did Christianity Cause the Holocaust?" (*Christianity Today* [April 27, 1998]: 12–13).

6. Eugene Genovese, "The Arrogance of History" (*New Republic* [August 13, 1990]: 35).

7. Stéphane Courtois, et al., *The Black Book of Communism: Crimes, Terror, Repression,* Jonathan Murphy and Mark Kramer, trans. (Cambridge: Harvard University Press, 1999).

8. Genovese, "Arrogance of History," 35.

9. Howard Thurman, *Jesus and the Disinherited* (New York: Abingdon-Cokesbury, 1949), 14–15.

10. Ibid., 15, 17, 18.

11. Ibid., 29.

12. Ibid., 7.

13. Ray R. Noll, ed., *100 Roman Documents Concerning the Chinese Rites Controversy (1645–1941)* (San Francisco: Ricci Institute for Chinese-Western Cultural History, 1992), 6.

14. See also the chapter in this book by Luis N. Rivera-Pagán.

15. See especially Lamin Sanneh, *Translating the Message: The Missionary Impact on Culture* (Maryknoll, N.Y.: Orbis, 1989).

16. *New York Times* (March 17, 1998): A10.

17. Matt. 5:3–10, 38–44 (NIV).

Chapter 6: Beyond Complicity: The Challenges for Christianity after the Holocaust

1. Arthur Cohen, *The Tremendum: A Theological Interpretation of the Holocaust* (New York: Crossroad, 1981), 34.

2. For recently published documents regarding this aspect of Nazism, see the Web site for the *Rutgers Journal of Law and Religion,* which has published archival material about the Nazi measures against the churches at www.lawandreligion.com.

3. See Wolfgang Gerlach, *And the Witnesses Were Silent: The Confessing Church and the Jews* (Lincoln: University of Nebraska Press, 2000).

4. See, for example, Nechama Tec, *When Light Pierced Darkness* (New York: Oxford University Press, 1986), 145; and Samuel and Pearl Oliner, *The Altruistic Personality* (New York: Free Press, 1988), 155.

5. See especially David Gushee, *The Righteous Gentiles of the Holocaust: A Christian Interpretation* (Minneapolis: Fortress, 1994), ch. 6.

6. Ibid. See also the chapter by David P. Gushee in this volume.

7. For a study of this group, see Doris L. Bergen, *Twisted Cross: The German Christian Movement in the Third Reich* (Chapel Hill: University of North Carolina Press, 1996).

8. See my discussion of this in Barnett, *For the Soul of the People* (New York: Oxford University Press, 1992), 126–27.

9. Ibid., 35, 57, 156, 159.

10. See the discussion of the Steglitz Synod in Wolfgang Gerlach, *And the Witnesses Were Silent,* 94–99.

11. See my discussion of this in "The Role of the Churches: Compliance and Confrontation" (*Dimensions: A Journal of Holocaust Studies* 12, 2 [1998]: 27–31).

12. See Gerlach, *And the Witnesses Were Silent,* 13–16, 50.

13. Barnett, *For the Soul of the People,* 142.

14. I traced this history in more detail in an unpublished paper, "Christian and Jewish Refugee Efforts: The Ecumenical Context," delivered at the 1998 Scholars' Conference on the Holocaust and the Churches, Seattle, Washington.

15. Riegner said this in a speech delivered in 1983 at Hebrew Union College, Cincinnati.

16. Interview with Gerhardt Riegner, February 21, 2000, in Geneva, Switzerland.

17. For a more detailed discussion of this, see the entire issue, "The Churches and the Holocaust: A Reconsideration" (special issue of *Dimensions: A Journal of Holocaust Studies* 12, 2 [1998]).

18. Dietrich Bonhoeffer, *Ethics* (New York: Macmillan-Collier Books, 1986), 129.

19. Dietrich Bonhoeffer, "After Ten Years," in *Letters and Papers from Prison,* ed. Eberhard Bethge (New York: Macmillan-Collier Books, 1972), 16.

20. Darrell J. Fasching, *Narrative Theology after Auschwitz: From Alienation to Ethics* (Minneapolis: Fortress, 1992), 82–83.

Chapter 7: How Should We Then Teach American History? A Perspective of Constructive Nonviolence

1. I acknowledge the encouragement and help of the Nonviolent America Project of the Kansas Institute for Peace and Conflict Resolution at Bethel College (North Newton, Kans.) for my work on this issue. For a fuller development of the ideas and examples in this essay, see James C. Juhnke and Carol M. Hunter, *The Missing Peace: The Search for Nonviolent Alternatives in United States History* (Kitchener, Ontario, Canada: Pandora Press, 2001).

2. George Marsden, *The Outrageous Idea of Christian Scholarship* (New York: Oxford University Press, 1997), 98.

3. For a definition of the myth of redemptive violence, see Walter Wink, *Engaging the Powers: Discernment and Resistance in a World of Domination* (Minneapolis: Fortress, 1992), 13–31.

4. *Nonviolent America: History through the Eyes of Peace,* ed. Louise Hawkley and James C. Juhnke (North Newton, Kans.: Bethel College, 1993).

5. My approach to the task of a nonviolent historiography owes much to the ideas and personal encouragement of John Howard Yoder. See his section, "War Is Not the Way to Save a Culture," in *The Original Revolution: Essays on Christian Pacifism* (Scottdale, Pa.: Herald Press, 1971), 174–77; and Yoder, "The Burden and the Discipline of Evangelical Revisionism," in Hawkley and Juhnke, eds., *Nonviolent America,* 21–37.

6. Clyde Holler, "Lakota Religion and Tragedy: The Theology of *Black Elk Speaks*" (*Journal of the American Academy of Religion* 52 [March 1984]: 19–45).

7. Kenneth Boulding lecture at Bethel College, 1982.

8. *Virtual History: Alternatives and Counterfactuals,* ed. Niall Ferguson (New York: Basic Books, 1999), 88.

9. For example, see brief counterfactual scenarios by scholars of military history in "What If? The Greatest Might Have Beens of Military History," *Quarterly Journal of Military History* (February 1998): 65–80.

10. Alexander DeConde, *The Quasi-War: The Politics and Diplomacy of the Undeclared War with France 1797–1801* (New York: Charles Scribner's Sons, 1966).

11. Clifford L. Egan, "Thomas Jefferson's Greatest Mistake: The Decision for Peace in 1807," in *Proceedings of the Citadel Conference on War and Diplomacy* (Charleston: Citadel Development Foundation, 1979), 94–97.

12. Reginald C. Stuart, *The Half-way Pacifist Thomas Jefferson's View of War* (Toronto: University of Toronto Press, 1978).

13. Samuel Horst, *Mennonites in the Confederacy: A Study in Civil War Pacifism* (Scottdale, Pa.: Herald Press, 1967), 23–27.

14. S. L. A. Marshall, *Men Against Fire: The Problem of Battle Command in Future War* (Gloucester, Mass.: Peter Smith, 1978), 56–57. See also Gwynne Dyer, *War* (New York: Crown Publishers, 1985), 118–20.

15. Dave Grossman, *On Killing: The Psychological Cost of Learning to Kill in War and Society* (Boston: Little, Brown, 1995), 21–25.

16. See, for example, John Keegan, *The Face of Battle* (New York: Viking, 1995). On the Civil War, see the alternative perspectives of Gerald F. Linderman, *Embattled Courage: The Experience of Combat in the American Civil War* (New York: Free Press, 1987); and James M. McPherson, *For Cause and Comrades: Why Men Fought in the Civil War* (New York: Oxford University Press, 1997). None of these, however, adequately takes into account the reality of infantrymen refusing to kill.

17. Mary Hershberger, "Mobilizing Women, Anticipating Abolition: The Struggle against Indian Removal in the 1830s" (*Journal of American History* 86 [June 1999]: 15–40).

18. On the question of "success" and "failure" in the antislavery movement, see Carol Hunter, "Liberty for All: The Anti-Slavery Movement," in Juhnke and Hunter, eds., *The Missing Peace,* 100–2.

19. Charles DeBenedetti, *The Peace Reform in American History* (Bloomington: Indiana University Press, 1980). Lawrence S. Wittner, *The Struggle Against the Bomb: One World or None, A History of the Nuclear Disarmament Movement Through 1953* (Stanford, Calif.: Stanford University Press, 1993) and *The Struggle Against the Bomb: One World or None, A History of the Nuclear Disarmament Movement, 1954–1970* (Stanford, Calif.: Stanford University Press, 1998). See also Matthew Evangelista, *Unarmed Forces: The Transnational Movement to End the Cold War* (Ithaca, N.Y.: Cornell University Press, 1999).

20. Gordon Kaufman, *Relativism, Knowledge, and Faith* (Chicago: University of Chicago Press, 1960).

21. See, for example, Joyce Appleby, Lynn Hunt, and Margaret Jacob, *Telling the Truth About History* (New York: Norton, 1994).

Chapter 8: Christian Discourse and the Humility of Peace

1. A copy of Annan's address is available at the United Nations Web site, http://www.un.org/News/Press/docs/2001/sgsm8071.doc.htm.

2. Although Martin's argument can be sharply criticized, such criticisms do not gainsay the basic argument about complexity. See James Turner Johnson's "Onward Christian Soldiers?" review of David Martin, *Does Christianity Cause War?* (*First Things* 88 [December 1998]: 45–48).

3. Robert H. Bates, *Prosperity and Violence: The Political Economy of Development* (New York: Norton, 2001).

4. See T. Richard Snyder, *The Protestant Ethic and the Spirit of Punishment* (Grand Rapids: Eerdmans, 2001), 29.

5. Ibid., 31.

6. The concept of violence, itself, is sufficiently elastic that it covers a variety of actions and impulses, from physical harm to identity construction. Glucklich notes that violence "is a semiotic event" in contrast to pain, which "is a subjective sensation that is not easily observed or represented." So, I insist, claims about violence are always interpretive, involving rhetorical processes that affect meaning. See Ariel Glucklich, *Sacred Pain: Hurting the Body for the Sake of the Soul* (Oxford: Oxford University Press, 2001), 133.

7. By discourse, I mean both the style and content of symbol use. Thus, to develop a counterdiscourse of peace is to craft a message by reflecting on the resources available within both the paradigmatic and syntagmatic axes of meanings.

8. For a superb exposition of Christian nonviolence, see Richard Hays, *The Moral Vision of the New Testament* (San Francisco: HarperCollins, 1996), 317–46.

9. N. T. Wright argues convincingly that Jesus' fundamental plea to Israel was to abandon nationalistic fervor, with its attendant militant attitude toward Rome, and to accept "his way of peace." See *Jesus and the Victory of God* (Minneapolis: Fortress, 1996), 596 et passim.

10. All Scripture quotations are taken from *The Holy Bible: English Standard Version* (Wheaton, Ill.: Crossway, 2001).

11. See Kenneth Burke, "The Rhetoric of Hitler's Battle," in *The Philosophy of Literary Form: Studies in Symbolic Action,* 3d ed. (Berkeley: University of California Press, 1973), 218.

12. Ibid., 230.

13. Ibid., 280–81.

14. See Kenneth Burke, *Attitudes Toward History,* 3d ed. (Berkeley: University of California Press, 1984; orig. 1937), 171.

15. For further explication, see René Girard, *I See Satan Fall Like Lightning,* trans. James G. Williams. (Maryknoll, N.Y.: Orbis, 2001).

16. See Girard, *Things Hidden since the Foundation of the World,* trans. Michael Metteer (bk. 1) and Stephen Bann (bks. 2 and 3) (London: Athlone Press, 1987), 180.

17. For a panoramic view of how contagion, victimage, and scapegoating remain a pervasive part of contemporary social life, see Gil Bailie, *Violence Unveiled: Humanity at the Crossroads* (New York: Crossroad, 1995).

18. See Girard, *I See Satan Fall Like Lightning,* 189–90.

19. See Girard, *Things Hidden,* 182.

20. To be sure, the submission to God involves, at some level, a sort of sacrifice of those warring desires. Yet, as Milbank makes clear, this is not at all the kind of sacrifice that Girard and Burke identify. The personal sacrifice of spiritual growth within Christianity is a movement toward Being and, thus, toward receiving oneself back again, free from covetousness and the enslaving passions of violent contagion. See John Milbank, "Stories of Sacrifice" (*Modern Theology* 12 [January 1996]: 52). Also see William T. Cavanaugh *Torture and Eucharist: Theology, Politics, and the Body of Christ* (Malden, Mass.: Blackwell, 1998), esp. 233f. Cavanaugh relies on Augustine (*City of God* 19.23) to claim: "A true sacrifice does not subtract something from us, but unites us to God in holy fellowship by reference to our eternal end."

21. Wolfgang Huber, *The Unrelenting Assault on Human Dignity,* trans. Ruth C. L. Critsch (Minneapolis: Fortress, 1996).

22. Discouraging news about the persecution of Christians comes to us from India, Indonesia, Sudan, and Nigeria, for example. John Hanford, currently U.S. Ambassador-at-Large for International Religious Freedom, has stated, "On a worldwide basis, Christians are the most persecuted major religion in terms of direct punishment for practicing religious activities—public worship, evangelism, charity." See Stan Guthrie, *Missions in the Third Millennium: 21 Key Trends for the 21st Century* (Carlisle, U.K.: Paternoster, 2000), 182.

23. Walter Wink, *Engaging the Powers: Discernment and Resistance in a World of Domination* (Minneapolis: Fortress, 1992).

24. See Oliver O'Donovan, *The Desire of the Nations: Rediscovering the Roots of Political Theology* (Cambridge, U.K.: Cambridge University Press, 1996), 32.

25. Ibid., 150–51.

26. See Miroslav Volf, *Exclusion and Embrace: A Theological Exploration of Identity, Otherness, and Reconciliation* (Nashville: Abingdon, 1996), 302.

27. Ibid., 297.

28. Ibid., 272.

29. I certainly cannot be exhaustive in describing all possible symbolic options for the church when faced with violence. Some argue that violence may be one of those options, albeit a last resort that can be justified only in very dire times. For a theological and political discussion on the possibility of an oppressed church using violence against an illegitimate government, see the fascinating collection of essays in *Theology and Violence: The South African Debate,* ed. Charles Villa-Vicencio (Grand Rapids: Eerdmans, 1988).

30. See Cavanaugh, *Torture,* 232.

31. An exact correlation between practices and principles is neither helpful nor wise as one seeks a Christian discourse of peace. I draw the correlation here simply to illustrate how the principles are heuristic for generating additional scriptural insights into discursive practice. Of course, much more remains to be said about practice, and much more needs to be said about James, than I offer here.

32. See Volf, *Exclusion,* 29.

Chapter 9: Jesus and Just Peacemaking Theory

1. *Just Peacemaking: Transforming Initiatives for Justice and Peace* (Louisville: Westminster/John Knox Press, 1992).

2. See Stassen, "Ten Practices for Peacemaking in Kosovo" (*Sojourners* [July 1999]: 18–21). Other articles and information on just peacemaking theory can be found at www.fuller.edu/sot/faculty/stassen.

3. Ibid., 18–21.

4. As Walter Wink does in *Engaging the Powers: Discernment and Resistance in a World of Domination* (Philadelphia: Fortress, 1992), 215ff. and 224. For further explanation and bibliography, see Glen Stassen and David Gushee, *Kingdom Ethics: Following Jesus in Contemporary Context* (Downers Grove, Ill.: InterVarsity, 2003).

5. All Scripture quotations are taken from the Revised Standard Version.

6. See the old, but excellent, book by Norman Gottwald, *All the Kingdoms of the Earth: Israelite Prophecy and International Relations in the Ancient Near East* (New York: Harper & Row, 1964), on the peacemaking practices proclaimed by the prophets of Israel.

7. N. T. Wright, *Jesus and the Victory of God* (Minneapolis: Fortress, 1996), 23.

8. See Yoder, *Body Politics: Five Practices of the Christian Community Before the Watching World Body Politics* (Scottdale, Pa.: Herald Press, 2001).

9. My claim is not that conflict resolution is a wooden, detail-by-detail application of Jesus' teaching in our time. That is not how we are to follow Jesus' practices in a different historical period, and it is not, for example, how Paul followed them in 1 Corinthians 7:11. Rather we are to seek to understand as fully as possible the way Jesus' practice functioned in his social context and how the analogous practice functions in our social context, always paying attention to how it witnesses to Jesus and gives glory to God (Matt. 5:13–17). John Howard Yoder spells out the method in his *Body Politics* and in the final pages of his essay "Sacrament as Social Practice," in *The Royal Priesthood: Essays Ecclesiological and Ecumenical,* ed. Michael G. Cartwright (Grand Rapids: Eerdmans: 1994). I will follow this *via analogia* in the subsequent practices as well.

10. See Glen Stassen, "The Fourteen Triads of the Sermon on the Mount," forthcoming in the *Journal of Biblical Literature.*

11. Walter Wink, "Neither Passivity Nor Violence: Jesus' Third Way," in *The Love of Enemy and Non-retaliation in the New Testament,* ed. Willard Swartley (Louisville: Westminster John Knox, 1992), 114f. N. T. Wright, *Jesus and the Victory of God,* 290–91.

12. Clarence Jordan, *The Substance of Faith and Other Cotton Patch Sermons,* ed. Dallas Lee (New York: Association Press, 1972), 69.

13. The outline of this argument is in chs. 2 and 3 of *Just Peacemaking: Transforming Initiatives,* and in several articles mentioned in the website above, n. 2.

14. See Stassen, *Just Peacemaking: Transforming Initiatives,* ch. 3, for a fuller explanation.

15. Yoder, *The Politics of Jesus: Vicit Agnus Noster* (Grand Rapids: Eerdmans, 1972; 2d ed., 1993), ch. 5.

16. John Dominic Crossan, *The Historical Jesus* (San Francisco: Harper Collins, 1991), 135f.

17. Donald Shriver, *An Ethic for Enemies: Forgiveness in Politics* (New York: Oxford University Press, 1995), 36.

18. Ibid., 38–44.

19. Christopher D. Marshall, *Beyond Retribution: A New Testament Vision for Justice, Crime, and Punishment* (Grand Rapids: Eerdmans, 2001).

20. Desmond Tutu, *No Future Without Forgiveness* (Garden City, N.Y.: Doubleday, 1999).

21. Dietrich Bonhoeffer, *Ethics* (New York: Simon & Schuster Touchstone Edition, 1995), 110–16.

22. *Exclusion and Embrace: A Theological Exploration of Identity, Otherness, and Reconciliation* (Nashville: Abingdon, 1996). L. Gregory Jones (*Embodying Forgiveness: A Theological Analysis* [Grand Rapids: Eerdmans, 1995]) also develops the theme. And see its application to nations that make the transition from dictatorship or oppression to democracy and human rights, and that then need to act on amnesty, punishment, or truth and reconciliation, for their past rulers who so viciously oppressed them, in Walter Wink, *When the Powers Fall* (Minneapolis: Fortress, 1998).

23. Wright, *Jesus and the Victory of God,* 335.

24. Ibid., 61.

25. David Garland, *Mark: The NIV Application Commentary* (Grand Rapids: Zondervan: 1996), 433–39.

26. Wright, *Jesus and the Victory of God,* 11, 164f. Representative pages where Wright shows the biblical witness to Jesus' acting in the tradition of the prophets are 93, 97, and 116, but the evidence is amassed throughout the book. He discusses Jesus' announcement of the kingdom of God at 20f., 40, 50, 72, 101f.

27. See Stassen, *Just Peacemaking,* 71ff.

28. See Stassen and Gushee, *Kingdom Ethics,* ch. 17.

29. For example, see Michelle Tooley, *Voices of the Voiceless: Women, Justice, and Human Rights in Guatemala* (Scottdale, Pa.: Herald, 1997).

30. Russett's essay appears in *Just Peacemaking: Ten Practices for Abolishing War,* ed. Glen Stassen (Cleveland: Pilgrim), 93–108.

31. "Faster Just and Sustainable Economic Development," in Stassen, ed., *Just Peacemaking,* 109–32.

32. Wright, *Jesus and the Victory of God,* 191f.

33. Ibid., 246.

34. Paul Schroeder, "Work with Emerging Cooperative Forces in the International System," in *Just Peacemaking: Ten Practices That Abolish War,* Glen Stassen, ed. (Cleveland: Pilgrim, 1998), 138–39.

35. Russett, "Promote Democracy, Human Rights, and Religious Liberty ," in *Just Peacemaking,* 102. Russett refers to research results in Harry Bliss and Bruce Russett, "Democratic Trading Partners: The Liberal Connection," paper presented at the annual meeting of the Peace Science Society (International), Houston, Tex., October 1996; John Oneal, Frances Oneal, Zeev Maoz, and Bruce Russett, "The Liberal Peace: Interdependence, Democracy, and International Conflict, 1950–1986" (*Journal of Peace Research* 33, 1 [February 1996]: 11–28); Oneal and Russett, "The Classical Liberals Were Right: Democracy, Interdependence, and Conflict, 1950–86" (*International Studies Quarterly* 41, 2 [June 1997]: 267–93).

36. Russett, "Promote Democracy, Human Rights, and Religious Liberty," 103.

37. Bruce Russett and John Oneal, "The Third Leg of the Kantian Tripod for Peace: International Organizations Also Matter," paper presented at the annual meeting of the International Studies Association, Toronto, Ontario, Canada, March 1997.

38. Michael Joseph Smith, "Strengthen the United Nations and International Efforts for Cooperation and Human Rights," in *Just Peacemaking,* 146, 152.

39. See David Little, "The World's Fight" (*Christian Century* [February 27, 2002]: 22–25); and Alan Geyer, "America Goes It Alone" (*Christian Century* [June 5, 2002]: 11–12).

40. Sonni Efron, "America's Got an Image Problem, Panel Warns," *Los Angeles Times* (July 31, 2002), A9.

41. Wright, *Jesus and the Victory of God,* 275–78.

Chapter 10: Violence and the Atonement

1. José Miguez Bonino, *Christians and Marxists: The Mutual Challenge to Revolution* (Grand Rapids: Eerdmans, 1976), 58.

2. John Calvin, *Institutes of the Christian Religion,* trans. Ford Lewis Battles, ed. John T. McNeill, Library of Christian Classics (Philadelphia: Westminster, 1960), iv, xx, 12.

3. St. Augustine, *Letters,* trans. Sister Wilfred Parsons (New York: Fathers of the Church, 1953), Letter 3:138.

4. Joanne Carlson Brown, "Divine Child Abuse" (*Daughters of Sarah* 18, 3 [Summer 1992]: 28).

5. Report of the Committee to Study Physical, Emotional, and Sexual Abuse, *The Agenda for Synod 1992 of the Christian Reformed Church in North America* (Grand Rapids: CRC Publications, 1992), 313–58.

6. John H. Yoder, "A Consistent Alternative Within the Just War Family" (*Faith and Philosophy* 2, 2 [April 1985]: 112).

7. *The Heidelberg Catechism,* Questions and Answers 12–18, in Philip Schaff, ed., *The Creeds of Christendom, with a History and Critical Notes* (Grand Rapids: Baker, 1996), 3:311–313.

8. Brown, "Divine Child Abuse," 27.

9. Margo Houts, "Atonement and Abuse: An Alternative View" (*Daughters of Sarah* 18, 3 [Summer 1992]: 30–31).

10. Jan Rohls, *Reformed Confessions: Theology from Zurich to Barmen,* trans. John Hoffmeyer, Columbia Series in Reformed Theology (Louisville: Westminster John Knox, 1998), 95–96.

11. *Heidelberg Catechism,* Question and Answer 37, 319.

12. *Heidelberg Catechism,* Question and Answer 44, 321.

13. John Howard Yoder, *The Politics of Jesus* (Grand Rapids: Eerdmans, 1972), 97.

14. I discuss Yoder's views on these matters in considerable detail in my *Politics and the Biblical Drama* (Grand Rapids: Eerdmans, 1976), 98–116.

15. Oscar Cullmann, "Immortality of the Soul or Resurrection of the Dead: The Witness of the New Testament," reprinted in *Immortality,* ed. Terence Penelhum (Belmont, Calif.: Wadsworth, 1973), 60–63.

16. René Girard, *Violence and the Sacred,* trans. Patrick Gregory (Baltimore: Johns Hopkins University Press, 1977), 258–69.

17. John R. W. Stott, *The Cross of Christ* (Downers Grove, Ill.: InterVarsity Press, 1986), 150–51, 159–60.

18. James MacGregor Burns, *Leadership* (New York: Harper & Row, 1978), 20.

Chapter 11: Explaining Christian Nonviolence: Notes for a Conversation with John Milbank

1. See, for example, Robert Jenson's wonderful "Introduction: Much Ado About Nothingness," in *Sin, Death, and the Devil*, ed. Carl Braaten and Robert Jenson (Grand Rapids: Eerdmans, 2000), 1–6.

2. John Howard Yoder, *Nevertheless: Varieties of Religious Pacifism* (Scottdale, Pa.: Herald Press, 1992), 12.

3. Ibid., 133–38.

4. Ibid., 134.

5. Copies of Yoder's book, which were his lectures in his course on Christian attitudes to war and peace at Goshen Biblical Seminary, can be obtained from Cokesbury Book Store at the Divinity School, Duke University.

6. Yoder notes that the assumption that there is a state "as such" is an intellectual construct that "we can't help using for later purposes" even if it is not there for the early Christians. *Christian Attitudes to War, Peace, and Revolution*, 26. Yoder does not explain why we cannot refrain from asking about the "state as such" for "later purposes." In *The Christian Witness to the State* (Newton, Kans.: Faith and Life Press, 1964), Yoder rightly, I think, refuses to provide any account of the state as such. He understands such accounts cannot help but be ideological legitimations that too easily result in making the state more than it needs to be. As he puts it, "the Christian witness does not provide any foundations for government, either practically or philosophically, but . . . the Christian rather accepts the powers that be and speaks to them in a corrective way. It is when we speak to those in power and to the dominant majority groups in the population that we plead the case of the minorities and the absent; this does not mean that if we were speaking to the minority groups themselves we should be uncritical or flattering" (41).

7. Yoder, *Christian Attitudes to War, Peace, and Revolution*, 26. I have no idea why Yoder chose the example of Christians seeking to protect their graves, but he could not have found a better example in light of later scholarship. I am thinking, for instance, of Peter Brown's account of the importance of graves for Christians in his *The Cult of the Saints: Its Rise and Function in Latin Christianity* (Chicago: University of Chicago Press, 1981), as well as Robert Wilkens's *The Christians as the Romans Saw Them* (New Haven, Conn.: Yale University Press, 1984). Wilkens provides a wonderful account of Pliny's attempt to understand Christians as a burial society.

8. Yoder, *Christian Attitudes to War, Peace, and Revolution*, 31.

9. Ibid., 45–46.

10. Ibid., 428.

11. John Milbank, *Theology and Social Theory: Beyond Secular Reason* (Oxford, U.K.: Basil Blackwell, 1990), 5–6.

12. Milbank begins to develop his trinitarian reflections in *Theology and Social Theory* (422–30), but his most complete account is in his essay "The Second Difference," which is now to be found in his *The Word Made Strange: Theology, Language, Culture* (Oxford, U.K.: Blackwell, 1997), 171–93.

13. Milbank, *Theology and Social Theory*, 390.

14. Since *Theology and Social Theory*, Milbank has increasingly turned in a neo-Platonic direction. As a result I am not clear if he still believes that all Christian theology can do is to "out-narrate" other alternatives. In his more recent work there is at least a hint he thinks he now has at his disposal ontological moves that can in principle defeat all other alternatives. I take it that is why he wishes to distance himself from all "pragmatic" justifications of Christian convictions. See, for example, his "Intensities" (*Modern Theology* 15, 4 [October 1999]: 445–97).

15. Milbank, *Theology and Social Theory*, 396.

16. Ibid., 403.

17. Ibid., 407. Milbank even suggests that Augustine thought that a "Christian emperor will make the empire recede into the Church." Such a view may seem quite foreign to Yoder's account of Christian nonviolence, but I believe that Yoder would not in principle rule out the possibility of such a rule. See in particular Yoder's "The Christian Case for Democracy," in *The Priestly Kingdom: Social Ethics as Gospel* (Notre Dame, Ind.: University of Notre Dame Press, 1984), 151–71. Yoder observes that what we call government cannot be identified only by the sword. Accordingly, there are many "styles of involvement, of which 'the sword' should not be the dominant paradigm," 165.

18. Milbank, *Theology and Social Theory*, 418.

19. Augustine, according to Garry Wills, was actually very patient with the Donatists. See for example Garry Wills, *St. Augustine* (New York: Penguin, 1999), 105–26.

20. Milbank, *Theology and Social Theory*, 420.

21. Ibid., 422.

22. I respond to Milbank's criticism in my "Epilogue" to Paul Ramsey's *Speak Up for Just War or Pacifism* (University Park, Pa.: Pennsylvania State University Press, 1988), 176–77.

23. Milbank, *Theology and Social Theory*, 419. Milbank's reference is to Rowan Williams's article, "Politics and the Soul: A Reading of *The City of God*" (*Milltown Studies* 19/20 [1987]: 55–92. I also admire Rowan Williams's article and used it in the first chapter of my *After Christendom?* (Nashville: Abingdon Press, 1999). I cannot, however, find in Williams's article Milbank's suggestion that war must be "fundamentally unjust" if a Christian can engage in it. Rather Williams says war cannot be fought on behalf of the City of God. As he puts it, "So we arrive at the paradox that the only reliable political leader, the only ruler who can be guaranteed to safeguard authentically political values (order, equity, and the nurture of souls in these things) is the man who is, at the end of the day, indifferent to their survival in the relative shape of the existing order, because he knows them to be safeguarded at the level of God's eternal and immutable providence, vindicated in the eternal *civitas dei*" (67).

24. For my reflections on these matters, see my "Can a Pacifist Think about War?" in my book *Dispatches from the Front: Theological Engagements with the Secular* (Durham, N.C.: Duke University Press, 1994), 116–35.

25. James Childress has pointed out that there is a substantial difference between those who think just war is an attempt to develop a theory of exception to the general Christian prohibition against violence and those who assume that the aim of just war is to achieve justice. The latter position does not presume that we live in a world of peace to which war is some kind of interruption, but rather that we live in a world in which war can be and must be disciplined for just means and ends. These two positions require quite different accounts of how the various just war "criteria" are derived as well as justified. James Childress, "Nonviolent Resistance: Trust and Risk-Taking Twenty-five Years Later" (*Journal of Religious Ethics* 25, 2 [Fall, 1997]: 213–20).

26. There is, after all, no one thing called punishment. Excommunication and the ban are interesting examples of a community pronouncing judgment that is meant to help people understand that they are not being punished further but rather are being offered a way to return to the community. How would they know they have estranged themselves and need to be reunited unless they are told that is the state they are in whether they know it or not? Of course, excommunication and the ban may be wrongly used, but that does not invalidate them as forms of "punishment" by nonviolent communities.

27. Milbank, *Theology and Social Theory*, 418.

28. Thomas Aquinas, *Summa Theologica*, II–II, 29, trans. Fathers of the English Dominican Province (Westminster, Md.: Christian Classics, 1981).

29. Stanley Hauerwas, *Christian Existence Today: Essays on Church, World, and Living in Between* (Grand Rapids: Brazos Press, 2001), 89–97. This book was originally published by Labyrinth Press of Durham, N.C., in 1988.

30. Aristotle, *Nicomachean Ethics,* trans. Martin Ostwald (Indianapolis: Bobbs-Merrill, 1962), 1155a, 1–5. I am on record expressing agreement with Milbank's arguments against MacIntyre's account of the virtues. I think, however, his case would have been stronger if Milbank had shown how MacIntyre's account requires not only charity but peace. See Stanley Hauerwas and Charles Pinches, *Christians among the Virtues: Theological Conversations with Ancient and Modern Ethics* (Notre Dame, Ind.: University of Notre Dame Press, 1997), 55–69.

31. Hauerwas, *Christian Existence Today*, 253–66.

Chapter 12: Violence: Double Passivity

1. Editors' note: An earlier version of this essay was prepared for the Christianity and Violence conference at Wheaton College (Wheaton, Ill.), March 2000. This current version is the expanded essay published in John Milbank, *Being Reconciled: Ontology and Pardon* (London: Routledge, 2003).

2. See ch. 1 in Milbank, *Being Reconciled*.

3. See my discussion of Jean-Yves Lacoste on this point in ch. 7 of Milbank, *Being Reconciled.*

4. Alain Badiou, *Ethics: An Essay on the Understanding of Evil* (New York: Verso, 2001).

5. See John Milbank, *Theology and Social Theory: Beyond Secular Reason* (Oxford, U.K.: Blackwell, 1991), 380–438.

6. See Michel Foucault, *Discipline and Punish: The Birth of the Prison,* trans. Alan Sheridan (London: Penguin, 1986); and Talal Asad, *Genealogy of the Secular* (Baltimore, Md.: Johns Hopkins University Press, 2002), ch. 2, "On Agency and Pain."

7. See *The Sublime: A Reader in British Eighteenth-Century Aesthetic Theory,* ed. A. Ashfield and P. de Bolla (Cambridge, U.K.: Cambridge University Press, 1996), 30–40, 131–40, 180–95.

8. Plato, *Republic* 439e–444a; Augustine, *Confessions* 2.2.

9. See John Milbank, *The Word Made Strange* (Oxford, U.K.: Blackwell, 1997), ch. 8, "The Force of Identity."

10. See Catherine Pickstock, *After Writing: On the Liturgical Consummation of Philosophy* (Oxford, U.K.: Blackwell, 1998), 47–100.

11. Talal Asad, *Genealogies of Religion: Discipline and Reasons of Power in Christianity and Islam* (Baltimore: Johns Hopkins University Press, 1993), 55–79.

12. I am indebted to discussions with Catherine Pickstock at this point.

13. See John Milbank, "Stories of Sacrifice" (*Modern Theology* 12, 1 [January 1996]: 27–55).

14. J. G. Ballard, *Super-Cannes* (New York: Picador, 2001).

15. See the discussions of the protagonists in Alan Wall's novel *The School of Night* (London: Vintage, 2001); and ch. 8 in Milbank, *Being Reconciled.* And see also John Milbank, "Poetry Is Not Fiction," in *The Mercurial Wood: Sites, Tales, Qualities* (Salzburg, Austria: Salzburg University Press, 1997), xii–iv.

16. This can be related to Kierkegaard's treatment of Socratic irony.

17. Plato, *Republic* 376c–412a.

18. Franz Baemann Steiner, "Orientpolitik, Value, and Civilization" in *Selected Writings,* ed. Jeremy Adler and Richard Pardon (New York: Bergbahn, 1999). I am indebted to long-standing discussions with Michael Mack about all this.

19. See Bernard Williams, *Shame and Necessity* (Berkeley: University of California Press, 1993), passim.

20. Thomas Aquinas, *Summa Theologica* II–II, Q 22a1; Q 24aa1–12; Q 26aab–11.

21. See ch. 9 in Milbank, *Being Reconciled.*

22. Charles Péguy, *The Mystery of the Charity of Joan of Arc,* trans. Jeffrey Wainwright (Manchester, U.K.: Carcenet, 1986).

23. For all its evidently rabid bias, Charles Maturin's *Melmoth the Wanderer* (Oxford: Oxford University Press, 1995) still proffers a subtly penetrating critique of monasticism.

24. With regard to erotic love, see Guillaume de Loris and Jean de Meun, *The Romance of the Rose,* trans. Frances Hogan (Oxford: Oxford University Press, 1994), ch. 11, "The Sermon of Genius" lines 19409–20638, 300–318. For example, 19461: "But if a man strives with all his might to preserve Nature, keeps himself from base thoughts and toils and struggles faithfully to be a true lover, let him go to paradise crowned with flowers"; 19569: "When they are first created, God has the same love for all, and gives rational souls to men as well as to women; therefore I believe that he wants every soul, not just one, to follow the best path and to come as quickly as possible to himself. So if he wants some people to live chaste, the better to follow him, why would he not want others to do so? What reason would deter him? In that case it would seem as though he did not care if generation ceased" [this essentially follows through the logic of an Augustinian as opposed to Greek patristic position on sex and procreation]; 19855: "Concentrate on leading a good life; let every man embrace his sweetheart and every lady her lover with kissing, feasting and pleasure. If you love one another loyally, you ought never to be reproached for it. And when you have played enough in the way that I have recommended, remember to make a good confession so as to do good and renounce evil, and call upon the heavenly God, whom Nature acknowledges as her master. It is he who will come to your aid in the end, when Atropos buries you. He is the salvation of body and soul, the fair mirror of my lady, who would never know anything were it not for this fair mirror. He directs and governs her, and my lady knows no other law. He taught her all she knows when he took her for his chamberlain."

Later in this chapter, the blighting of the Golden Age and the arrival of work and sterility is ascribed, after Virgil, to the jealousy of the Olympian gods. The Christian God, by contrast, elevates humanity to paradise, and knows no jealousy of human beatitude, nor of corporeal pleasures (since of course his infinite spiritual nature is not a lack of anything). The White Lamb (Christ) has conserved always the fold of the earthly paradise, and this still awaits us (20213) even with its flowers that "are neither too closed nor too open" (19901).

With regard to chivalric warfare, see A. T. Hatto, "An Introduction to a Second Reading," in Wolfram von Eschenbach, *Parzival* (London: Penguin, 1980), 412–39: "Before during and after Wolfram's time there is historical evidence of a deep desire in lay circles to be more closely associated with clerical institutions in piety somewhat short of the taking of monastic vows"; "the function of the Great Society . . . is to inculcate an image of self-discipline in young men and women in joint service to God—coupled with and despite high living" (417). This Grail milieu was a "second paradise," though it might involve "fights to the death" as well as tournaments and dancing. Hatto stresses that Parzival's almost exclusively outward activity, the activity which wins him the Grail when at last he pursues it in the right spirit, is that of knightly combat. He goes on to say that "The chivalric orders had from the outset enshrined lofty Christian principles in their statutes, which, however, were often more neglected than observed. It was Wolfram's aim through a sympathetic discussion of knighthood as reflected in the early life of Parzival to raise this *latent potential* in the general chivalric order. In order to do so Wolfram had to shield the knighthood from the wounding arrogance of the ascetic clergy, who took the uncharitable view that as men of blood knights were damned. Apart from his positive teaching, mainly through the mouth of Parzival, Wolfram furthered his aim by the simple device of having no other clergy in his story than those required for the formalities of baptism, marriage and celebration of the mass, leaving confession and discussion of such burning issues as homicide, rebellion against God and religious despair to his laymen" (414).

25. I am entirely indebted here to Alison Milbank.

Chapter 13: Christian Peace: A Conversation between Stanley Hauerwas and John Milbank

1. John Milbank, *Theology and Social Theory: Beyond Secular Reason* (Cambridge, Mass.: Blackwell, 1991), 396.

2. Ibid., 398.

Afterword

1. *Understanding Islam: An Introduction to the Muslim World,* 2d ed. (New York: New American Library, 1990), ix.

2. *Decline and Fall of the Roman Empire,* vol. 2, ed. J. B. Bury (New York: Modern Library, 1995), ch. 51, 1843–44.

3. *Fear and Trembling, Repetition,* trans. Howard V. Hong and Edna H. Hong (Princeton: Princeton University Press, 1983), 54, 68.

4. *The Curse of Cain: The Violent Legacy of Monotheism* (Chicago: University of Chicago Press, 1997).

5. Schwartz assumes throughout *The Curse of Cain* that God's decision to accept Abel's sacrifice and reject Cain's is an arbitrary one. She does not seem to have noticed a feature of the narrative that is quite striking to anyone who knows the habitual reticences of Hebrew narration: that Abel is specifically credited with setting the best he has before God ("the firstlings of his flock, their fat portions"), while Cain is merely said to have brought "an offering" (Gen. 4:3–4). There is also the possibility, in light of the law to come, that God had called specifically for blood sacrifice. But in either case, the assumption of divine capriciousness seems unjustified by the text.

6. "Christopher Hitchens: You Ask the Questions," *Independent* (March 6, 2002): http://news.independent.co.uk/people/profiles/story.jsp?story=271283.

7. *People of the Book: Christian Identity and Literary Culture* (Grand Rapids: Eerdmans, 1996), 97–103.

8. "Two Spiritualities of Violence" (*National Catholic Reporter* [October 26, 2001]: http://www.natcath.com/NCR_Online/archives/102601/102601m.htm). I will make but one comment here: one would not learn from Radford Ruether that Spanish Christian culture was "not without ambivalence" toward the

Inquisition or the execution of Native Americans—not for her the complex discriminations of the essay by Luis N. Rivera-Pagán in this collection.

9. "What I Believe," in *Two Cheers for Democracy* (New York: Harcourt, 1951), 71–77.

10. http://www.press.uchicago.edu/Misc/Chicago/741990.html.

11. "Religion's Misguided Missiles" (*The Guardian* [September 15, 2001]: http://www.guardian.co.uk/wtccrash/story/0,1300,552388,00.html).

12. I have not been able to discover the source of this quotation, or indeed whether these were Voltaire's precise words.

13. Eco, *Kant and the Platypus: Essays on Language and Cognition,* trans. Alastair McEwan (New York: Harcourt, 2000), 49–50.

14. Eldredge, *Reinventing Darwin: The Great Debate at the High Table of Evolutionary Theory* (New York: John Wiley, 1995); Gould, "Darwinian Fundamentalism" (*New York Review of Books* [June 12, 1997]: http://www.nybooks.com/articles/1151). Thanks in part to the work of Gould and Eldredge, Dawkins is often taken to believe that natural selection is the *sole* agent of genetic change, but this he has repeatedly and rather heatedly denied. Not only does Dawkins not hold this position himself, he believes that no one does: see his treatment of the "Caricature" Darwinian in *The Blind Watchmaker,* 2d ed. (New York: Norton, 1996), 308–11.

15. In his book *River Out of Eden: A Darwinian View of Life* (New York: Basic Books, 1995), Dawkins suggests that one key aspect of religious belief—the nearly universal tendency to attribute purpose to events—is "a natural one in an animal that lives surrounded by machines, works of art, tools and other designed artifacts"; on the other hand, he admits that our technologically primitive ancestors seem to have had the same tendency (96). For one of Gould's most concise articulations of this same principle—both men have been repeatedly eloquent on this subject—see his essay "The Streak of Streaks," in *Bully for Brontosaurus: Reflections in Natural History* (New York: Norton, 1991), 467–68.

16. See, e.g., Pascal Boyer, *Religion Explained: The Evolutionary Origin of Religious Thought* (New York: Basic Books, 2001).

17. *River Out of Eden,* 96.

18. *Keywords: A Vocabulary of Culture and Society,* 2d ed. (New York: Oxford University Press, 1983), 329–31.

19. *Discipline and Punish: The Birth of the Prison,* trans. Alan Sheridan (New York: Pantheon, 1977).

20. "Co-Optation," in *The New Historicism,* ed. H. Aram Veeser (New York: Routledge, 1989), 172.

21. "Almost Pragmatism: The Jurisprudence of Richard Posner, Richard Rorty, and Ronald Dworkin," in *There's No Such Thing As Free Speech, and It's a Good Thing, Too* (New York: Oxford University Press, 1994), 204–5.

22. "Force," in *Doing What Comes Naturally: Change, Rhetoric, and the Practice of Theory in Literary and Legal Studies* (Durham, N.C.: Duke University Press, 1989), 504–5. Fish's attack on the supposed neutrality and noncoercive character of procedure and principle has continued in his more recent collection, *The Trouble with Principle* (Cambridge: Harvard University Press, 1999) and in his brilliant essay "Mutual Respect as a Device of Exclusion," in *Deliberative Politics: Essays on Democracy and Disagreement,* ed. Stephen Macedo (New York: Oxford University Press, 1999), 88–102.